Radical Innovators

Radical Innovation

Radical Innovators

*The Blessings of Adversity in Science
and the Arts, 1500–2000*

Anton Blok

polity

First published in Dutch as *De vernieuwers*, © Anton Blok, 2013

This English edition © Polity Press, 2017
This publication has been made possible with financial support from the
Dutch Foundation for Literature

N ederlands
letterenfonds
dutch foundation
for literature

Polity Press
65 Bridge Street
Cambridge CB2 1UR, UK

Polity Press
350 Main Street
Malden, MA 02148, USA

ISBN-13: 978-1-5095-0551-7
ISBN-13: 978-1-5095-0552-4 (pb)

A catalogue record for this book is available from the British Library.

Library of Congress Cataloging-in-Publication Data

Names: Blok, Anton.
Title: Radical innovators : the blessings of adversity in science and the arts,
    1500-2000 / Anton Blok.
Other titles: Vernieuwers. English
Description: English edition. | Cambridge : Polity, 2016. | Includes
    bibliographical references and indexes.
Identifiers: LCCN 2016016765 (print) | LCCN 2016025562 (ebook) | ISBN
    9781509505517 (hardcover : alk. paper) | ISBN 1509505512 (hardcover : alk.
    paper) | ISBN 9781509505524 (pbk. : alk. paper) | ISBN 1509505520 (pbk. :
    alk. paper) | ISBN 9781509505548 (mobi) | ISBN 9781509505555 (epub)
Subjects: LCSH: Science--History. | Art--History. | Anthropology.
Classification: LCC Q125 .B582713 2016 (print) | LCC Q125 (ebook) | DDC
    509/.03--dc23
LC record available at https://lccn.loc.gov/2016016765

Typeset in 10.5 on 12pt Sabon by Servis Filmsetting Ltd, Stockport, Cheshire
Printed and bound in the UK by Clays Ltd, St. Ives PLC

For further information on Polity, visit our website: politybooks.com

CONTENTS

PREFACE
AND ACKNOWLEDGMENTS

This book investigates how people from different backgrounds and in different circumstances could accomplish a breakthrough in science or the arts. What did these pioneers, along with their differences, have in common? Which forces were operating in the development of a new point of view?

Insofar as these questions have been raised before, scholars have searched for an answer in the area of talent, intelligence, and other inborn gifts. Subsequent longitudinal research, however, has shown that highly intelligent students are not always also highly creative.[1] More recent research emphasizes the early acquisition of skills with feedback from a mentor: informal teaching, including self-study, is more likely to encourage radical innovation than formal education.[2] Due to the lack of systematic comparative research, little is known even now about the circumstances and drives that moved these people, often at an early age, to excel in a specific field of science or the arts and produce trailblazing achievements. The present book explores a collective biography of about one hundred pioneers in the sciences and the arts working in Europe and North America between about 1500 and 2000. The strength of a collective biography, writes Tilly, is not in supplying alternative explanations, but in specifying what is to be explained.[3]

To anticipate the outcome of this research, nearly all the pioneers were confronted with early adversity resulting in social exclusion. Adversity could take different forms, including illegitimate birth, parental loss, parental conflict, the father's bankruptcy, chronic illness, minority status, poverty, physical deficiencies, detention, and exile. In histories of science and the arts, some of these conditions or "factors" have been explored to explain radical innovation, but mostly in the form of one-factor analysis, including chronic illness, parental loss, and birth order. What *all* the different forms of adversity turn out to have in common – justifying the use of one common denominator – is social exclusion, which implies the strategic position of the outsider. This comes down to Butterfield's recommendation of "handling the same bundle of data as before, but placing them in a new system of relations with one another by giving them a different framework."[4] Bringing together a host of phenomena, usually seen as separated from one another, under one common denominator, as attempted in this book, constitutes a synthesis which Kuhn has called a "discovery."[5] Having little to lose, outsiders are more likely to notice and take chances to find a niche – including protection and support from relatives, friends, teachers, mentors, or patrons. As outsiders, they also have more space and freedom to experiment in their field – and are therefore more likely to notice anomalous, unanticipated, and strategic data in their field.[6]

The research for this book has taken about ten years. An early interest in biographies (at high school in the 1950s) could be turned into a systematic inquiry of a substantial collective biography. Second, I had to familiarize myself with the state of the art: the discussion among historians and psychologists on groundbreaking work of the great pioneers in science and the arts active between about 1500 and 2000. For a better understanding of the roots of radical innovation in these fields, the present book argues for a more comparative sociological and anthropological approach focused on the social position of pioneers: their place in sets of social relationships, whether institutional, conjunctural, or both.[7]

In writing this book, I have incurred numerous debts to friends and colleagues. An early single bibliographical reference had far-reaching consequences for the argument of this project. In a brief exchange, visiting classicist Karin Bassi referred me to Syme's statement on the position of Thucydides: "exile may be the making of an historian. That is patent for Herodotus and Polybius. If a man be not compelled to leave his own country, some other calamity – a disappointment or a grievance – may be beneficial, permitting him to look at things with detachment, if not in estrangement."[8] This observation dovetailed with the overall detachment and aloofness that mark the habitus of the radical innovators outlined in the collective biography.

I am also indebted to Peter Burke, who carefully read the Dutch version of the book shortly after its publication in the fall of 2013. His letter provided several corrections of names and places as well as pointing out the absence of some outstanding examples of radical innovators who had been affected by early adversity, including Leonardo da Vinci (illegitimate birth, homosexual), Michelangelo (parental conflict, homosexual), and itinerant Thorstein Veblen (émigré, minority status, poverty). The book certainly shows "omissions" but this is perhaps inherent, even in a substantial collective biography that covers a long period of time. The foremost intention was to search for recurrent patterns in the collective biography and to make sense of them: explaining that following adversity and social exclusion, radical innovators tended to be outsiders – having less to lose, they could take more risks than their established colleagues, who tended to stick to mainstream views and practices.

Omissions may provide test cases. I hesitated to include the great Dutch painter Johannes Vermeer (1632–75), a contemporary of Spinoza: little is known about Vermeer's youth. Research over more than a century produced more questions than answers, as Montias notes in his painstaking biography of Vermeer and his milieu in which he is careful "to identify conjectures and not let them be confused with solid facts."[9] All we know from documented facts about his youth are his baptism in October 1632 in Delft, as the son of a Protestant innkeeper and art dealer, and his conversion to Roman Catholicism to marry a girl from a rich and distinguished Roman Catholic family in April 1653 in nearby Schipluy. This step also made him a member of a minority discriminated against in Delft's predominantly Protestant population.[10]

The same year Vermeer entered St. Luke's Guild as a master painter. The local guild became the center of his public life. Vermeer kept a low profile. He lived with his wife (who gave him no fewer than fifteen children) in the big house of his wealthy mother-in-law, where he also had his studio. She took a genuine liking to him and from the beginning financially and materially supported her daughter's family. Biographer Montias notes that Vermeer's absence from Delft's notarial archives "makes it seem as if he wished to withdraw from civil society, perhaps because he was engrossed in his work or because he had joined a religious minority subject to prejudice and discrimination."[11] These circumstances help explain his modest production of masterworks, with rarely more than two paintings on average a year. Vermeer had one major patron and collector and never accepted commissions.[12]

Acknowledgments

In writing this book, I have incurred numerous debts to friends and colleagues. Apart from those already mentioned above, Karen Bassi and Peter Burke, I am most grateful for suggestions and comments to Chris de Beet, Chris Connery, Arturo Giraldes, Donna Goldstein, Johan Heilbron, Longina Jakubowska, Job Lisman, Nienke Muurling, Mai Spijkers, Thijl Sunier, and Bonno Thoden van Velzen. Some friends have taken the trouble to read earlier versions of the entire manuscript. For a critical last-minute reading I would like to thank Henk Driessen: in a book of this scope a reference to the life and work of Van Gennep could not be missed. Rod Aya has been my sparring partner from the very beginning of this project. As before on similar occasions, I have learned a great deal from his comments and I am also grateful for his editorial help. I am especially beholden to Huub de Jonge. Over the years, he has been my most constant source of stimulus and illumination, providing comments on the manuscript in its various stages and suggesting numerous editorial improvements. Finally I owe a special debt to Ann Bone, copy-editor at Polity Press, who greatly improved the original manuscript down to the smallest details.

Soest, The Netherlands
May 31, 2016

For granted that individuals may have historical effect, they have to be in a position to do so, as Raymond Aron reminds us, and "position" means a place in a set of relationships, whether institutional, conjunctural, or both. We have to overcome certain received ideas of an unbridgeable opposition between cultural order and individual agency . . .

Marshall Sahlins, *Apologies to Thucydides*

— 1 —

THE MARGINS AS A PLACE
OF INNOVATION

Many men who are very clever – much cleverer than the discoverers –
never originate anything.

Charles Darwin, in a letter to his son, 1871[1]

Recent research into the history of science shows that radical
innovation did not come from people who were more talented, intelligent, or knowledgeable than ordinary people. Nor did radical innovators mostly come from privileged backgrounds. What distinguished
them from ordinary people was an early and overpowering interest in
a specific branch of the arts or science and seizing windows of opportunity. Their dedication was both lasting and passionate; it took them
from self-study to an extended period of apprenticeship in relative
isolation, often with a mentor providing feedback. Rather than talent
or skill, daily practice and chance encounters were decisive.[2]

This book provides a detailed empirical and theoretical account
of this viewpoint, spelled out on the basis of a collective biography
of about one hundred radical innovators, virtually all of them active
in Europe and North America in the past five hundred years. This
so-called prosopographic approach is comparative and analyses the
background, location, and setting of innovators. According to sociologist and historian Charles Tilly,

> the strength of collective biography is not in supplying alternative
> explanations, but in specifying what is to be explained. Historians who
> have specified what is to be explained via collective biography often
> find themselves turning to explanations stressing the immediate setting
> and organization of everyday life, or relying on something vaguely
> called "culture." That moves them back toward anthropology.[3]

1

What did radical innovators have in common that enabled them to distinguish themselves from ordinary mortals? Why Charles Darwin? Why Sigmund Freud? Why Albert Einstein? Why Jane Goodall? To say, as generations of historians of science and cognitive psychologists have done, that they had more talent or were more creative is not wrong but tautological and begs the question. To say that most of them were young or new to the field in which they made new discoveries is only taking one step in a promising direction, leaving open the background of their drive and failing to explain late production.[4]

The history of science is more about science than about scientists. As the history of ideas it remained a disembodied affair. Biography as a genre is still primarily descriptive and is only rarely comparative and analytical. Therefore it fails to suggest or establish compelling links between the life and the work of its subjects. If the author of a recent biography of Galileo is correct when he says that "biography is not seen as a respectable genre by professional historians,"[5] this may be largely attributed to the predominance of the monographic – and not infrequently monomaniac – treatment of isolated cases at the expense of comparative research. Another critical historian of science concludes that it is "difficult for authors of a case study not to become prisoners of their subject. The stronger the lens used by the observer, the greater the possible discovery, and the greater also the danger of becoming so involved in one's case that one forgets to distance oneself from it. At that point no generalization is possible."[6]

The situation is no different in the history of art and literature. Both focus primarily on art and literature themselves, leaving the life and work of their practitioners to biographers, who usually restrict themselves to one particular person and his or her work. Here, too, life and work remain separated, making any attempt at explanation strongly ad hoc in character. One misses a comparative perspective focusing on context: the social position of innovators, their place in networks of relationships from their earliest youth onward – an approach that can identify similarities and differences in the lives of innovators and also pays attention to "negative" cases: people who might have been innovative but who refrained from taking a further decisive step.

This book attempts to explore these uncharted territories by systematically comparing the lives of about one hundred scientists and artists whose work both has been innovative and has had an enduring impact. The criterion for selection is a canon of *reconceptualization* or radical innovation.[7] For scientists this comes down to the presentation of a new and more comprehensive perspective. In the early seventeenth century, for example, William Harvey's discovery of the blood circulation system was based on an analogy: the heart functioning as a (single) pump at the center. Harvey's system replaced the multiple systems posited by Galen. This was not the only discovery based on an analogy. Darwin's discovery of natural selection as the driving force of the evolution of species, relegating the theory of creation to the realm of myth (and proving the contemporary belief in the inheritance of acquired properties wrong), was an achievement of similar proportions and also founded on several analogies.[8] Nicolaus Copernicus's heliocentric model of the world replaced the prevailing geocentric model of Ptolemy based on countless loose observations. Using Johannes Kepler's discovery of the elliptical orbits of planets, Isaac Newton completed the Copernican revolution with his discovery of the universal law of gravitation. Most likely as a tribute to the work of his predecessors Kepler and Newton, whom he admired, Einstein observed that "No fairer destiny could be allotted to any physical theory, than that it should of itself point out the way to the introduction of a more comprehensive theory, in which it lives on as a limiting case."[9]

To find out what radical innovators had in common and to arrive at a new perspective, I also explored a number of scientists who could have been innovative, but stuck to received wisdom. These "negative" cases enable us to sort out independent variables that help account for radical innovation.[10] Which circumstances enabled the young Einstein to formulate the special theory of relativity while Hendrik Lorentz and Henri Poincaré – much older scholars – only came very close? All three scientists possessed an *esprit préparé*, to use Louis Pasteur's famous phrase about the role of chance in scientific discovery.[11] What stopped two of them, with hindsight, from taking that single step? How and why could Newton complete the Copernican revolution with his discovery of the law of universal gravitation, while fellow scientists Robert Hooke and Christiaan Huygens did not? What enabled Baruch Spinoza to emerge as the radical pioneer of the Enlightenment, rather than his contemporary Gottfried Wilhelm Leibniz? Darwin and Alfred Russel Wallace, though from different backgrounds – the opposite sides of Victorian England – simultaneously discovered the struggle for existence and natural selection as the driving forces of evolution. What did they have in common and where did they differ from their colleagues? The same questions apply to breakthroughs in modern art: why Ludwig van Beethoven, Henrik Ibsen, Paul Cézanne, Vincent van Gogh, Arthur Rimbaud, Constantin Brâncuşi, and Franz Kafka, and not one of their teachers or fellow artists?

3

To answer these questions this book focuses on the blessings of adversity in the lives of about a hundred artists and scientists in Europe and North America between approximately 1500 and 2000. Their work not only brought about fundamental innovations, but also had a lasting impact. It still appeals to us today – often also because of the surprising simplicity and elegance of their findings and discoveries.[12] Their vision changed the way we see the world and ourselves. Some of them have become historical figures. Others – like Darwin with *The Origin of Species* (1859), Freud with *The Interpretation of Dreams* (1900), and Max Weber with his study of the Protestant ethic and the spirit of capitalism (1905) – are still our contemporaries. We have made ourselves familiar with great works of art. They have become part of our mental world, part of how we see, feel, and think about life. We can identify with Antigone, Hamlet, and Rembrandt's Bathsheba, and with many other unforgettable female characters in literature, including Tolstoy's Anna Karenina, Ibsen's Hedda Gabler, Strindberg's Miss Julie, Schnitzler's Fräulein Else, and Tennessee Williams's Blanche DuBois. All these examples show the relative autonomy of artists and their art with respect to the societies from which they came. According to Norbert Elias, the question about the relative autonomy of the artist has yet to be answered, but "its complexity should not relieve us from the obligation to further explore the relationship between creator and society."[13]

What all these achievements have in common, both in the arts and science, is originality and the effect of an enduring esthetic sensibility. People speak of the "intrinsic beauty" of the double helix structure of the DNA molecule, the discovery of which pointed the way to the transmission of genetic materials ("information") and opened the era of molecular biology. According to one of the discoverers, the structure was "too pretty not to be true."[14] Kepler's discovery of the elliptic orbits of planets has been called a prime example of elegance in science and the beauty of simplicity.[15] The same qualities have been ascribed to Einstein's special relativity theory, and he later illustrated that in a presentation in 1933: "It is true that the theoretical physicist who has no sense of mathematical elegance, beauty, and simplicity is lost in some essential way."[16] Darwin's theory of natural selection as the principle of evolution also unmistakably shows, along with the additional principle of divergence, the elegance and simplicity of a scientific discovery. The description applies to Newton's discovery of the universal force of gravitation, which keeps planets and moons in their orbits. Inspired by Huygens, Newton benchmarked the concept of "centripetal forces." The core theme of his *Principia Mathematica* was the quantitative elaboration of this new concept. Perhaps we should realize that the scientific researcher and the artist face similar tasks. Both are in search of unity, structure, and coherence in a plethora of isolated data and information.[17]

Anticipating the main conclusions of this study, I mention the independent variables – the antecedents in the lives of radical innovators that should explain the dependent variable of radical innovation. They try to answer the question of why these people rather than others were able to bring about radical innovation in science and the arts. Here we are dealing not just with one factor or variable which applies in all cases, but with a set of necessary conditions in varying combinations which occur in the antecedents of each radical innovator.[18] In a single stroke they can be brought together under the common denominator of *adversity*. Recall that problems are often solved – and new discoveries made – not by providing more information but by rearranging what is [already] known.[19]

Based on a substantial collective biography, the present research indicates that radical innovation has come from people who had to deal with far-reaching forms of adversity, mostly at an early age, including illegitimate birth, early loss of parents, abuse by parents or other members of the family, conflict with parents, bankruptcy (of the father), social degradation of the family, poverty, minority status, peripheral origin (coming from peripheral areas), illness, physical deficiency, demotion, exile, and incarceration. All these forms of adversity, often in combination, resulted in social exclusion and alienation from mainstream life. Prevailing practices and views were no longer taken for granted; they were questioned. Social exclusion and alienation created the space and freedom for the development of new insights – the spur to radical innovation in science or the arts, which could not take place without seeing and seizing chances – windows of opportunity. Looking back on these lives, a pattern of adversity and exclusion unfolds in the scenario of radical innovation. Such an outcome can only be traced and understood with the benefit of hindsight. We may agree with historian Carlo Ginzburg, who is skeptical "about the teleological approach that sees a sort of straight line going from the childhood of an individual to his or her maturity . . . Constraints don't work in a definite direction . . . . You can become an atheist because you are the son of a priest, but you can also become a saint. The outcome is predicable only retrospectively."[20]

Desiderius Erasmus (1466/9–1536) *was* the son of a priest and subject to humiliation and discrimination as a child because of his illegitimacy, a double anomaly. He claimed to have suffered from it his whole life. Moreover, he was strikingly small of stature, a deficiency his friend Hans Holbein disguised in his famous portraits of Erasmus.[21] Apart from some loyal friends and kindred spirits in England, Italy, Switzerland, Germany, and the southern Netherlands, Erasmus did not want to belong to any group, and this was eventually held against him by both Roman Catholics and Protestants. The religious tensions escalated to such an extent that in 1529 Erasmus was forced to leave his beloved Basel after the city had chosen the side of the Reformists. Erasmus settled elsewhere, at Freiburg, "to safeguard his independence."[22]

During his adult life Erasmus traveled widely through Europe but never revisited his native land. Apart from his years at the Latin school of the Brothers of Common Life, in Deventer, and later in 's-Hertogenbosch, Erasmus did not have good memories of that time. It was not just because of his illegitimate birth and the death of both his parents in a plague while he was still a child; he also hated the monastic schools to which his guardians sent him. Later he felt the same about the study of theology, for which his patron, the Bishop of Cambrai, provided a scholarship. Erasmus did not finish these studies. Huizinga summarized his trials with an understatement: "circumstances had not made it easy for him to find his way."[23] Yet all these disappointments would later form the breeding ground for his most famous book, The Praise of Folly (1511): his best and lasting work, Huizinga stated, "for only when humor illuminated that mind, did it become truly profound. In The Praise of Folly Erasmus produced something that no one else could have given the world."[24]

As this book seeks to point out, adversity resulting in exclusion is not only the basis for social dislocation but also for the development of radicalism, the formation of a rebellious mind and the development of a new perspective. A person is not only hardened by adversity; in relative isolation they can also be inspired by it and go on to achieve beyond expectations. Anthropologist Claude Lévi-Strauss (1908–2009), belonging to the Jewish minority in France in the 1920s, spoke for many when he remarked in an interview, as his biographer observed, "Being part of a traditionally persecuted group brought a heightened awareness and a sense that he had to overachieve in order to compete fairly."[25]

Of course not all outsiders have opened new horizons in science or the arts. We are talking about necessary, not sufficient, conditions. The researcher should avoid making the logical error and confuse the necessary with the cause, or "affirming the consequent." As Taleb explains: "That all millionaires were persistent, hardworking people does not make persistent hard workers become millionaires."[26] Most outsiders have disappeared in anonymity. The unfavorable connotations of the word "outsider" reflect a common unfortunate fate. But some outsiders have challenged vested interests and views, and tried their luck. As outsiders they had little to lose and could therefore take more risks. To survive, they took risks in their search for a niche of meaningful activities that required solitude; hence their choice of a field in science or the arts and their first steps on this road in the form of self-study. Some of them were fortunate enough to get a chance and alert enough to note and take advantage of such windows of opportunity – offered by parents, other kin, friends, teachers, mentors, mediators, patrons, or sponsors. These serendipitous encounters turned out to be decisive. By means of self-study, and encouragement, material support, and feedback from a mentor, they developed a growing interest in a specific subject. Early in their apprenticeship this interest took on an enduring character; it became a passion to which all other activities were subordinated. Their work became a calling – a dedication dominating everything. The word "passion" is used here in its double meaning, well rendered in the German *Leidenschaft*, about which Hegel noted, "Es ist nichts Grosses ohne Leidenschaft vollbracht worden, noch kann es ohne Solche vollbracht werden [Nothing great has been achieved without passion, nor can it be achieved without it]."[27] This circumstance also explains the striking similarities in their lifestyle and habitus, which have often been wrongly given the unfortunate designation of "personality," with that considered the explanation of their innovativeness. No less misleading is the question about the "motivation" of innovators. Where love, zeal, dedication, and passion set the tone, the use of the term "motivation" is out of place.

Discussing parts of the first versions of this book with friends and colleagues, I was often asked why so few women appear in the collective biography. Prejudice was suspected. As is generally known, but less well explained, most radical innovators in science and the arts have been men – in spite of the considerable emancipation of women in the twentieth century. In his historical overview, *Human Accomplishment: The Pursuit of Excellence in the Arts and Sciences* (2003), Charles Murray explains why women across the board form a minority in the pursuit of excellence in science and the arts:

When we discuss accomplishments ... we are commonly talking about perfectionist, monomaniacal devotion to a calling. That calls

7

for a much more ruthless tradeoff than the ones ordinarily required by a job and children. We should not be surprised or dismayed to find that motherhood tempers the all-consuming obsession that great accomplishment in the arts and sciences often requires.[28]

As Murray explains,

> Motherhood affects women's achievement through several mechanisms. The central importance of motherhood means that many women do not want to jeopardize the opportunity to become a mother. Single-minded devotion to a profession involves such a risk. Recall that the mean age at which peak accomplishments occur, following years of preparation, has been about 40. The years crucial to realizing great achievements have been precisely those years during which women are sexually most attractive, best able to find mates, and best able to bear children.[29]

Western societies long remained a predominantly masculine social order, with laws made by men and with magistrates who judged the behavior of women from a masculine viewpoint. This was observed in a draft by the Norwegian playwright Henrik Ibsen (1828–1906) for his pioneering stage play *A Doll's House* (1879).[30] To have their books published (around the middle of the nineteenth century), the unmarried Brontë sisters had to use male pseudonyms.[31] At the time, literature was (still) considered a male profession and not a suitable one for women.[32] The interests of the young Freud (1856–1939) were self-evidently put before those of his sisters: "When, intent on his schoolbooks, he complained about the noise that Anna's piano lessons were making, the piano vanished never to return."[33] This incident took place in about 1870 in Vienna. For many more years, "a room of one's own" remained an unfulfilled desire, even for women in the homes of the western intelligentsia. In *La domination masculine* (1998), anthropologist Pierre Bourdieu argued that male dominance is so firmly entrenched in our unconsciousness that we do not notice it anymore, that it is so much in accordance with our expectations that we have difficulty raising it for discussion.[34] This point of view sharpened one of Bourdieu's key concepts: "symbolic violence."

The women mentioned in this book confirm the results of the observations of both Murray and Bourdieu: women were a tiny minority among the pioneers in science and the arts. Most of them were unmarried, or single at the time of their breakthrough; still others were married and worked together with their partner and had no children. They include Jane Austen (1775–1817); Emily Brontë (1818–48); Marie Anne Paulze (1758–1836) – wife of Lavoisier;

Marie Sophie von Brühl (1779–1837) – wife of Clausewitz; Marianne Weber (1870–1954) – wife of Max Weber; Virginia Woolf (1882–1941); Hannah Arendt (1903–75); Germaine Tillion (1907–2008); Simone de Beauvoir (1908–86), who with *The Second Sex* (1949) heralded a "reconceptualization" of women; and Jane Goodall (1934–) – twice married, but after her innovations in primatology.

A third variant includes the Polish émigrée Marie Curie (born Skłodowksa, 1867–1934), winner of two Nobel prizes (physics in 1903; chemistry in 1911). In 1895 she married her former teacher Pierre Curie, with whom she shared the Nobel prize for physics; from this marriage she had two daughters, born in 1897 and 1904. They were taken care of by a foster-mother and later educated by her father-in-law, a widowed medical doctor, who lodged with them; later these tasks were taken on by a governess.[35] Paulze, Von Brühl, and Marianne Weber not only substantially contributed to the work of their respective partners, Antoine Lavoisier, Carl von Clausewitz, and Max Weber, but also went on to complete their work after their death and take care of its posthumous publication. In this way, they ensured their international reputation as radical innovators. Alma Reville, the wife of Alfred Hitchcock (1899–1980), also closely cooperated with her partner from the very beginning: every film under his name was a collective product.[36]

The men in this biographical research show a similar pattern. Most of them were single, including Erasmus, Copernicus, Galileo, Thomas Hobbes, René Descartes, Spinoza, Newton, Leibniz, David Hume, Adam Smith, Alexander von Humboldt, Gregor Mendel, Elias, and Grigori Perelman – or unmarried before their breakthrough, like Herman Boerhaave, Alfred Wegener, John Maynard Keynes, James Watson, and W. D. Hamilton,[37] while a handful of married ones, including Darwin, Einstein, and Freud, can be considered functionally single because their wife took care of the household and the education of the children. This was also the case in the families of Kepler and Johann Sebastian Bach, who each married twice and had large families. Bach's second wife was a young soprano and helped him substantially with his work, including copying his scores. Freud's wife was a typical *Hausfrau* and the family revolved around Freud, who summarized his lifestyle in a single sentence when he remarked, "I cannot imagine life without work as really comfortable."[38] Darwin's son Leonard, one of his eight children, said his father was "never comfortable except at work. He hated idleness and talked about holidays as a punishment for the pleasure he had in his work." To his friends he expressed himself in similar words.[39]

9

The unmarried state is not only the most visible aspect of a lifestyle of seclusion among radical innovators. With the dominating devotion to work it is also the most revealing element because of its implicit rejection and undermining of fundamental social institutions: marriage, family, and community. In his stage play *An Enemy of the People* (1882) Ibsen shows that the community is not the noble and reliable social institution most people usually take it for. As Friedrich Nietzsche recognized in his statement, "Jede Gemeinschaft macht, irgendwie, irgendwo, irgendwann – 'gemein' [Every community makes – somehow, somewhere, sometime – *mean*]."[40]

No less relevant for the argument of this book are marriages that remained childless – and therefore, strictly speaking, did not form a "family" – as exemplified in the cases of Harvey, Lavoisier, Clausewitz, Michael Faraday, Alexis de Tocqueville, James Maxwell, Weber, Keynes, Giuseppe Tomasi di Lampedusa, and Samuel Beckett. In some of these cases, the wife substantially contributed to the work of her husband and also edited his posthumous publications, as already noted in the cases of Lavoisier, Clausewitz, and Weber. Clausewitz's only book, the standard work *On War*, appeared after his untimely death, completed and edited by his wife, Marie Countess von Brühl. After Weber's death, his wife Marianne Weber completed and edited the major part of his work and only then did it become widely known. Their marriage, as in the cases of Lavoisier and Clausewitz, was an intellectual comradeship, which also held good for Hannah Arendt, Simone de Beauvoir, and Jane Goodall, whose partners shared their interests.

What is revealing for the argument of this book is the "negative" case of Mileva Marić, Einstein's first wife. She was four years older than him and had been his sparring partner in discussions on physics since they studied together at the Polytechnic Institute in Zurich during the last years of the nineteenth century. She was his "brilliant inspirer and guardian angel," as he wrote to her and as he also told her father in Serbia during a visit to her paternal home in Novi Sad. In a letter of March 27, 1901 he phrased her part in his work as follows: "I'll be so happy and proud when we are together and bring our work on relative motion to a successful conclusion."[41] Yet Mileva lost her interest in science when she became pregnant and had children. Her place as interlocutor/discussant and sounding board was taken over by Maurice Solovine and Conrad Habicht, with whom Einstein formed the informal discussion group "Akademie Olympia." After they had left Bern in 1904, Einstein's friend Michele Besso became his colleague at the Patent Office and had a decisive part in Einstein's embarking on the relativity theory in 1905.[42]

Mileva was not the only brilliant woman who, after helping her partner along the path to breakthrough and fame, had to settle for less once she became pregnant and had children. About the same time – in the early 1900s – a similar fate befell sculptress Clara Westhoff shortly after she married Rainer Maria Rilke, whom she had introduced to Auguste Rodin, her teacher, in Paris. Soon after she had given birth to a daughter, Rilke left her. Although they stayed in touch, eventually Clara had to take care of herself and her daughter, and for her entire life she remained "Frau Rilke," in the shadow of the poet. Meanwhile, he created a furore, mostly traveling from one castle in Europe to another, working at the invitation of mostly wealthy, aristocratic, and predominantly female protectors.[43] Rilke was undoubtedly the most itinerant of the innovative artists of his time.[44] "Il faut travailler, rien que travailler. Et il faut avoir patience [You have to work, only work. And you have to have patience]" was Rodin's favorite maxim, which Rilke approvingly wrote down when he was the sculptor's biographer in the early 1900s – observation and hard work replaced waiting for inspiration.[45] In the fall of 1907, Rilke wrote to his wife in the artists' colony at Worpswede near Bremen about his almost daily visits to Cézanne's retrospective at the Salon d'Automne in Paris, a year after the painter's death. Much later, the letters culminated in his *Briefe über Cézanne*.[46] Both Rodin and Cézanne had a decisive influence on Rilke. They made him put in the hard work to get to the bottom of things, his poem "The Panther" being an early and famous example.

All the scientists and artists who figure in this book subordinated nearly everything to their work. The unmarried Newton (1642–1727), known as "the reclusive Cambridge don," was "never at rest," according to Richard Westfall, who also gave this title to his biography (1980). Radical innovators in science and the arts not only demonstrated a basic incompatibility between marriage and work. Some of them also clarified this personal dilemma in letters and diaries.[47] In the summer of 1838, Darwin, still single, made pencil notes on the back of a letter setting out in parallel the pros and cons of marriage (notes which his granddaughter Nora Barlow saved and included at the end of a later edition of Darwin's autobiography).[48] He opted for marriage, but neglected to mention in his autobiography that his father was only willing to continue supporting him financially if he got married. Darwin complied with the request and decided to ask his cousin Emma, a daughter of his mother's brother, whom

11

he had known since childhood. They were not in love, but did like each other. Their union was considered a marriage of convenience, far from uncommon among the gentry, not least because it kept property within their class.[49] Darwin's marriage resulted in no fewer than ten children, of whom eight survived childhood.

The priority (among scientists) of being unmarried and not being part of a family is implied in the remarks made by the historian of science W. I. B. Beveridge about examples of "unparalleled" excitement after a new discovery or breakthrough: "The scientist seldom gets a large monetary reward for his labours . . . But the greatest reward is the thrill of discovery. As many scientists attest, it is one of the greatest joys that life has to offer."[50] In his autobiographical account, Watson, twenty-five years old and unmarried, describes his excitement after their discovery of the double helix structure of the DNA molecule, the copying mechanism responsible for the transmission of genetic material from one generation to the next: "my morale skyrocketed . . . Even more exciting, this type of double helix suggested a replication scheme much more satisfactory than my briefly considered like-with-like pairing."[51] An account of Einstein's discovery of special relativity in 1905, which he had worked on in his free time for more than seven years, tells us:

> The discovery was without doubt Einstein's most intensive experience. The five weeks he needed to work out his find and make it ready for the press were a happy time with sensations of the highest joy. He was speechless. To his colleague Sauter at the Patent Office, where he worked full-time six days a week, he repeatedly said only: "My joy is indescribable."[52]

As indicated in the epigraph for this book, the approach followed here assumes that, to have historical effect, a person must be in a position to do so, arising from their place in sets of social relationships – institutional, conjunctural, or both. The history of science, however, deals more with science than its practitioners. Their *work* has a central place and is spelled out in great detail. Their *life* hardly gets any attention at all. It is assigned to the genre of the biography, in which a chronological, descriptive account is favored over a comparative, analytical approach. Chapter titles of important textbooks carry the big names in science, describe the work of these pioneers, and place it in the framework of intellectual history, but tell us little or nothing at all about their life. As the history of ideas, the history of science has long remained a disembodied science. In a concise biography of Darwin, one of the authors draws attention to this trend or practice, which is certainly not absent in the genre of biography: "In the first half of the twentieth century people studied Darwin primarily as a thinker who had 'forerunners' and whose ideas were 'revolutionary' or were 'in the air.' His life was considered as an episode of intellectual history."[53]

The standard work of I. Bernard Cohen, *Revolution in Science* (1985), running to more than 700 pages, is a striking example of this common practice. The chapters are named after the revolutionary scientists, including the usual suspects, Copernicus, Kepler, Galileo, Descartes, and Newton, without a single word about their life and therefore nothing either about the relationship between the life and the work.[54] Yet the author does have a strong opinion on the subject. One of his so-called revolutions in science concerns a change in the scientific enterprise at the end of the nineteenth century: from scientists who worked more or less independently, with limited scientific means, to a structure in which research was organized in teams, initiated and controlled by scientific societies and institutions, universities, research institutes, and committees. According to Cohen, this development made "single performances" in science out of date.[55] As will be shown, this allegation should be seriously doubted.

Cohen's point of view ignores at least ten cases of recognized great twentieth-century breakthroughs from pioneers who carried out their research independently and with limited means and without close relationships with mentors at universities or research institutes. We are talking about scholars of the magnitude of Freud, Weber, and Einstein. As mentioned above, they changed the directions in three different areas of research at the beginning of the twentieth century. Some years later, meteorologist Wegener (1880–1930) single-handedly, and operating similarly on the margins of the academic world, formulated his theory on the origins of continents and oceans (later called continental drift). The first version appeared in 1915 and drew little attention. In the late 1920s, a revised English version of Wegener's theory was finally dismissed by an international conference of geologists because of lack of evidence. It was only half a century later, following research on ocean floors, that Wegener's theory found support and brought about a revolution in the earth sciences.[56] Wittgenstein (1889–1951) preferred to work in isolated locations in a self-imposed exile and twice effected a reversal in the philosophy of language: first with the *Tractatus* (1922), which was also called a work of art, and later with his similarly aphoristic *Philosophical Investigations* (1953) in which he propagated a more anthropological approach with his notion of language games.[57] One

13

of his friends in Cambridge, Keynes (1883–1946), who had not formally studied economics but had informally followed lectures in this field and had much practical knowledge at his disposal, wrote *The Economic Consequences of the Peace* (1919) and *A General Theory of Employment, Interest, and Money* (1936) and became the most influential economist of the century, called "the father of macroeconomics."[58] In 1953, at the Cavendish Laboratory in Cambridge, Watson and Francis Crick discovered the double-helix structure of the DNA molecule in a race with colleagues at King's College in London and the American chemist Linus Pauling, who had come close to the solution but had to drop out for personal reasons. Their discovery of the "secret of life" would bring about a revolution in microbiology and result in three Noble prizes. It was one of the great discoveries of twentieth-century science and has had great effects on our lives in many ways.[59]

Without any academic education, but as protégée of paleontologist and anthropologist Louis Leakey, who supervised her at a distance from his museum in Nairobi and provided feedback, Jane Goodall studied the behavior of chimpanzees in the wilds of Gombe (Tanzania) in the early 1960s. From her long-term fieldwork with participant observation – a new departure in her discipline – she established that these primates had more in common with humans (fabrication and use of tools, eating of meat, social skills) than was generally assumed. Her breakthrough in the study of primates earned her the title of "the woman who redefined man."[60]

Evolutionary biologist and geneticist Hamilton (1936–2000) investigated social altruism among insects, and the question of how to fit altruism into Darwin's theory of natural selection (the struggle for existence) as the mechanism of evolution. Hamilton was a graduate student at the London School of Economics without the usual supervision of a tutor because of the unpopular subject (genetics and behavior). In 1963 he published two pioneer articles in which he coined the key concept of "inclusive fitness" (later called "group selection") and put his finger on the genetic mechanism which – as a correcting completion of Darwin's discovery of natural selection – helps explain altruism and self-sacrifice between close relatives.[61] Hamilton's theory is still contested, though his work has become widely known and accepted since the publication of sociobiologist Richard Dawkins's *The Selfish Gene* (1976).

In 2002 the Russian mathematician Perelman (1966–) found the proof for "Poincaré's Conjecture." This achievement in geometric topology is considered the mathematical breakthrough of the century.[62] For this discovery Perelman was nominated for the Fields Medal and the Millennial Prize. After both were offered to him, he refused to accept these honorary distinctions because he had to share them with two other mathematicians who had functioned as peer reviewers of his work. Following these events, Perelman canceled his membership of the international Mathematical Society and would also have stopped practicing mathematics.[63] Perelman, unmarried and very much on his own, had worked in quietness and solitude at the Steklov Mathematical Institute in St. Petersburg, and as a postdoc in the 1990s he attended lectures at various American universities, where he had also given lectures himself. At the end of 2002, after seven years of research, he put the proof for Poincare's Conjecture online, and in April 2003 he gave presentations by invitation at Stony Brook and the Massachusetts Institute of Technology, where he mentioned to a colleague in the corridors that it would perhaps take more than two years to understand his proof.[64]

Out of the ten twentieth-century scientists mustered above, only Watson (1928–) and Crick (1918–2004) formed a team. They worked at the Cavendish Laboratory at Cambridge University (from September 1951 through March 1953).[65] To what extent does their teamwork respond to the prevailing picture indicated in Cohen's *Revolutions in Science*?

The unmarried American James Watson, twenty-three, a protégé of S. E. Luria, gained a doctorate in microbiology and a postdoctoral scholarship to Europe, searching for a subject in genetics with which he could make his mark. In 1951, as a crystallographer, he joined the older and married Crick, who had not yet finished his PhD and had not made much progress either in the research for which he had been appointed at the Cavendish Laboratory. During their research on the structure of the DNA molecule they were sporadically and informally in touch with two colleagues at King's College, University of London. That team included the unmarried Rosalind Franklin, recently appointed as crystallographer, joining the older Maurice Wilkins, who had likewise made little progress with the same research into the structure of the DNA molecule.

In his essay on serendipity Robert Merton indicates that this specific case of "collaboration" within and between two teams can be considered as a textbook example of the unplanned nature of short-term scientific research; its zigzag course and the role of serendipity are rarely reported and spelled out by the specialist journals and periodicals, particularly where the work of pioneers is concerned.[66] Merton points to the decisive role of the haphazard presence of experts at the laboratory and the limited knowledge possessed by both Watson and Crick before they started their jobs, as Watson repeatedly acknowledges in his autobiographical account. Following up Merton's report, critical historian of science Weisberg made a painstaking reconstruction of the activities of Watson and Crick and their brief discussions with various colleagues at the Cavendish Laboratory.[67] Weisberg describes the history, the dramatic research itself, and how the results were reached in spite of the tensions within one team and between the two teams, as well as wrong decisions made by the directors of both labs who were expected to supervise the research of the teams. It was especially the young, ambitious, and not very scrupulous Watson, whom colleagues at the laboratory ironically called "Honest Jim," who took the initiative. He operated in extremely self-willed ways, close to the edge of what is acceptable, to obtain research data from the colleagues in London, as he frankly writes in his autobiographical account of the research, *The Double Helix* (1968). The discovery of the double helix structure of DNA in March 1953, published the next month in *Nature* (with an appendix by the colleagues in London), did not meet any resistance. The "biggest scientific discovery of the twentieth century," for which three people were awarded the Nobel Prize for medicine in 1962 (the fourth, Rosalind Franklin, had died in the meantime), linked up with Pauling's preliminary work. It took Pauling only five minutes to be convinced and he directly congratulated the discoverers. It was a matter of knowledge acquired in part by informal consultations, effort, time, and serendipity which determined who in the race would scoop up the honors.

As is well known, Freud (1856–1939) did all his work at home in the Berggasse in Vienna, where he also received his patients. Partly due to the anti-Semitic climate in the city, his professorship at the university came late and remained marginal, restricted to a single weekly lecture – a nominal professorship for a general audience. Freud was exclusively interested in the title, which he could use to reinforce the authority of his psychoanalytic movement.[68]

Max Weber (1864–1920) followed a reverse road. His master-work, *The Protestant Ethic and the Spirit of Capitalism* (1904–5), originated in a self-chosen exile, after he had resigned as a professor from the university because of a chronic disease. He, in the company of his wife, Marianne, searched for healing in the solitude of spas and travels through Europe in the years around 1900. Their marriage remained childless. During a stay in Rome, Weber gained new insights on attitudes toward work in Protestant Germany. Weber was not the first person to discover the North in the South, but he was certainly the first scholar to build on this confrontation to write an epoch-making book, which after more than a century still gives inspiration and cause for discussion. His biographer Radkau raises the question, "What would Weber have been if he had not fallen ill?" He arrives at insights that touch the heart of the present book: Weber's illness (adversity) led to his departure from the university and his travels, to social exclusion, alienation, and doubts about conventional beliefs and practices.

> The Weber of 1903 had lost that foundation, and this sharpened his mind for the question of what constituted the essence of science when it was stripped of its bureaucratic corset . . . From an early age Weber cultivated a sense of himself as an insider and held parvenus in contempt – a contempt that still rose in him later in life. *He now experienced what it was like to be an outsider. Anyone who knows both situations is aware of how different the world looks from each. Many insights are best gained from an external viewpoint.* For his part, Weber was best able to ground a new self-awareness on the "existentialist" conviction that *intensive experience of marginal situations was the way to deeper knowledge.*[69]

Radkau's formulation "who knows both situations . . ." recalls one of the few autobiographical notes by Thucydides (460–395 BC) in his book on the Peloponnesian War: "It was also my fate to be an exile from my country for twenty years after my command at Amphipolis; and being present with both parties, and more especially with the Peloponnesians by reason of my exile, I had leisure to observe affairs more closely [i.e. from both sides]."[70] With foresight, Thucydides considered his book "not as an essay which is to win the applause of the moment, but as a possession for all time."[71] The impact of Thucydides' work extended to that of Machiavelli and Hobbes and, with their writings, into the twentieth century. It was then that sociology and anthropology increasingly became part of political history, as exemplified in the work of pioneers, including Max Weber, Johan Huizinga, Marc Bloch, Norbert Elias, Fernand Braudel, and Charles Tilly, who anticipated and gave form to the tradition of the journal *Annales* with studies of long-term historical processes.

After his illness and return to Heidelberg, Weber could fall back on his intellectual resources – especially those of his wife and some colleagues and friends – and profit from his lasting distance from the university, a situation which he, like Darwin, could enjoy because of the availability of family capital, including that of his wife. Because of his illness, Weber found himself in an exile of sorts, a seclusion in which he could thrive and regain his health – reflect and recover, supported and assisted by his wife, who was a prominent scholar in her own right. Six years after Weber's death in 1920, she completed his biography and later also edited his voluminous posthumous work. Her feedback, altruism, noble-mindedness, and erudition would help make Weber one of the most influential social scientists of the twentieth century.

In 1900 Einstein (1879–1955) obtained a certificate from the Polytechnic Institute in Zurich, which enabled him to teach math and physics in secondary schools (which he did for a while). From 1902 onward, through the mediation of the father of his close friend and colleague, the mathematician Marcel Grossmann, Einstein worked as a junior civil servant at the Swiss Patent Office in Bern. More than once he had failed to obtain a position as assistant/graduate student at a university. His former professors also blocked his applications elsewhere. Yet these adverse outcomes turned out to be unanticipated blessings. In many respects, the patent office was a perfect place for him, a "secular monastery," as Einstein called it. His daily duties mostly involved inspecting electrotechnical innovations (patents) in the domain of the synchronization of measuring time, which seamlessly linked up with the theoretical work he was doing in his free time and discussing with his intellectual friends. They became his "guardian angels," all of them recruited from chance encounters, including the meeting with his future wife Milena Marić, who was four years older and a student at the same school in the same class.[72] As Einstein himself realized, and later proposed as a generalization, his position at the patent office also kept him away from the influence and constraints of the established order and the pressure of current specialisms in his field. In this way he had more freedom and latitude than the much older and more established Lorentz and Poincaré, who had come closer to the theory of relativity than they themselves realized – but who were not in a position that encouraged them to take risks and take that last and decisive step.[73]

The adversity of being repeatedly rejected for a position as a graduate student at a university turned into the blessings of the Swiss patent office – six days a week from nine to five, of which Einstein only needed two or three hours daily for his work of processing requests for patents. The remaining hours of the workday he spent on his own scientific work at this "secular monastery," where he could nurture his most beautiful ideas and where he had landed by chance after the road to academic institutions was blocked. This serendipitous setting and the encounters that had brought Einstein to this place would provide the space for the seven most creative years of his life. Self-study and feedback from his friends kept him informed about the state of the art in his field, as attested by his numerous publications (mostly reviews) in *Annalen der Physik* before his four revolutionary papers in 1905 appeared in the same journal – "after which physics would no longer be what it had been before."[74]

Einstein's first thoughts on the relativity of time and space date from his last school year in Aarau before he started his studies in physics and math at the Polytechnic in nearby Zurich in 1895. To reach this high achievement he required a learning period of about ten years – which corresponds exactly to Ericsson's scenario for reaching "perfect performance" in music, sports, and the arts, and "eminence" in science, where he expected a learning period of about ten years of "deliberate practice" amounting to about eighty hours a week. This comes down to sustained hard work in relative solitude with feedback from a mentor.[75]

Like pioneers mentioned earlier, meteorologist and polar explorer Alfred Wegener also worked on the margins of the academic world. At an early age, and together with his slightly older brother Kurt, he had participated in ballooning competitions and had broken records. Later he learned a great deal from two polar expeditions in Greenland (1906–8, 1912–13). Meanwhile he developed a lasting interest in "continental displacements." After two printed presentations on the subject in 1912, he published in 1915 a full account in his book on the origin of continents and oceans that was based on his theory of "continental drift." Wegener argued that numerous identical fossils and rock formations were found on both sides of the Atlantic Ocean, most notably along the coasts of Brazil and Africa, and rejected the current theory of geologists and geophysicists about a land bridge between the two continents, said to have existed in the distant past. Wegener also argued that the slow, immense, lateral movements of clouds, glaciers, ice fields, and icebergs provided inspiring analogies: a "cognitive source," models and metaphors for large masses moving invisibly over the surface of the earth – analogies for units of large land masses breaking off in pieces and flowing away to constitute the present continents of America and Africa.[76]

Wegener received support and encouragement from his brother Kurt, a physicist and likewise a meteorologist. He also obtained advice and feedback from his former professor of climatology, Wladimir Köppen, who had in the meantime become his father-in-law. Wegener aspired to a synthesis of all earth sciences. But that project and his related theory of continental drift met strong resistance on the part of geologists and geophysicists, both in his own country, Germany, and elsewhere. Though he did not lack supporters, his innovation was rejected because of "lack of evidence" (a common reaction and knockdown argument against any new viewpoint), as well as on ad hoc grounds. Geologists and geophysicists felt threatened and considered Wegener an outsider and therefore not an expert in their field. One of his opponents, during a conference of the American Geological Society in 1926, revealingly concluded on the basis of eighteen objections: "If we have to believe Wegener's hypothesis then we have to forget everything we have learned in the last seventy years and start all over again."[77] One of Wegener's biographers commented, "The appeal of vested interests is directly visible. Without any doubt professional and personal interests played a great role in the rejection of Wegener's theory."[78]

The amiable Wegener acknowledged that he could not indicate the mechanism of continental drift. But neither Copernicus nor Kepler could do so for their discoveries of planetary movements around the sun. The so-called Copernican Revolution could only be accomplished after Newton's complementary work on universal gravitation.[79] Wegener died in November 1930 during his third polar expedition in Greenland. He did not live long enough to see his theory of continental drift confirmed by the results of geophysical research of ocean floors in the 1960s, which was given the name "plate tectonics."[80] With the theory of plate tectonics, which indeed explains numerous geological phenomena (earthquakes, volcanoes), Wegener was recognized as the first discoverer of "floating continents" and rehabilitated.[81] Even more important, like a latter-day Copernicus and Kepler, he envisaged a synthesis, in this case a synthesis between the earth sciences. As one historian of science summarized Wegener's merits:

> He was a farseer, a tireless worker in many fields, for whom disciplinary boundaries were irritating conventions standing in the way of a comprehensive vision of the whole. Like Kepler, his reputation will always be second to that of the future Newton of earth science. Wegener, working in astronomy, geology, paleontology, meteorology, and geophysics, was one of the first of the modern *earth* scientists, and saw not only the fundamental problem to be solved but also the range of the evidence that must be amassed for its solution. This comprehensive vision, which he practiced rather than preached, is perhaps his most enduring contribution.[82]

The case of Wegener was by no means exceptional. The young Einstein, Goodall, and Hamilton experienced similar rejections of their early pioneering work – or simply silences on the part of the established scientists in their respective fields. As young outsiders they lacked academic credentials. Einstein and Hamilton were considered "unknown graduate students" and, as such, their work was at first dismissed or ignored. After his breakthrough in 1905, Einstein worked at the patent office for another four years before he was appointed as professor at a university.[83]

At the presentation of the results of her research at the international conference "On Primates" in April 1962 in London organized by the Zoological Society of London, Jane Goodall (1934–) was reproached for being trained only as a secretary. That she was a woman and also attractive and blond conflicted with the dominant stereotype of an academically trained researcher. The resistance came in particular from the older and established Solly Zuckerman, president of the Zoological Society and chairman of the conference. He objected in a disparaging manner to Goodall's research method, her long-time fieldwork in the form of participant observation among chimpanzees. Therefore he doubted her evidence on the eating of meat and the absence of harems among the chimpanzees she had studied in Gombe, Tanzania.[84]

The active principle in these four cases – Einstein, Wegener, Hamilton, and Goodall – and also in several similar ones comes down to a reaction to unwelcome and unpleasant facts. In a dialogue in a Dutch novel between two young geologists at work in northern Norway, one of them refers to his elderly professor and captures the essence of the issue: "For a period of fifty years, nobody has contradicted him. What interest does he have, in the evening of his career, in supporting another point of view? Why would he abandon his own life's work?"[85]

Keynes, the most influential economist of the twentieth century and rightly called the "father of macroeconomics," never formally studied economics at a university. He was a friend of Wittgenstein at Cambridge, where both were teaching, with interruptions, but kept some distance from the university. Keynes developed his views on macroeconomics and state intervention for the most part outside the beaten paths of academic areas. He learned a great deal from his practical work for the British government and participated in the peace talks after the First World War. His views were contained in his study of the economic consequences of the humiliating peace treaty of 1919; initially they were considered anti-establishment but later generally confirmed and accepted. The same held true for his *General*

Theory of Employment, Interest, and Money (1936), in which he warned against unbridled capitalism. This book served as a theoretical justification for government intervention to deal with the recession. Demand rather than supply provided the key for the control of the general level of economic activity, and Keynes pleaded for an active government policy to stimulate demand in times of unemployment through investment in infrastructure and public works. Generally considered the basis of modern macroeconomics, the book only made Keynes famous by the end of his life – a confirmation of his status as an outsider. After a decline in interest in the second part of the twentieth century, his vision was again embraced following the advent of the global financial crisis of 2007–8 – and the "return of the master" was posthumously celebrated.[86]

Keynes's life as an outsider to academia started in the family where he grew up, with a younger brother and sister and with tolerant, hospitable, and generous parents. His father taught economics at the University of Cambridge and remained a friend and advisor to his son, whom he also outlived. As a student Keynes was often ill and missed school. This condition entailed seclusion and had the advantage, as Skidelsky has emphasized, of creating the occasion for observing, reading, and reflecting, and for doubt about current thought: all necessary conditions for the development of new insights. Keynes studied philosophy and mathematics and as a graduate student informally followed lectures in economics. It is not clear if he ever completed his studies. If he did not, according to Skidelsky, this emphasized his status as an outsider even more – together with his membership of a number of famous informal societies in Cambridge, his work for the government, and his broad cultural concerns, including his avowed homosexuality.[87] According to Skidelsky, there is nothing paradoxical in these conjunctions. On the contrary, Keynes perfectly fits the general pattern outlined in our collective biography of scientists and artists who have developed a new approach in their field: "a change in the perception and evaluation of familiar data," as Kuhn summarizes his key concept of "reconceptualization" in his *Structure of Scientific Revolutions*; "That awareness of anomaly opens a period in which conceptual categories are adjusted until the initially anomalous has become the anticipated. At this point the discovery has been completed . . . [T]hat process . . . is involved in the emergence of all fundamental scientific novelties."[88] Keynes was not unlike most pioneers in science and the arts who disliked formal education and preferred to follow their own interests. Note that Keynes's height (1.90 meters), his slender physique, and his charm distinguished him from other people and may have contributed to his authority.

Wittgenstein, born in Vienna to a wealthy and cultured upper-class family with four older brothers and three older sisters, also figures as an outsider to the academic world, to which he took a certain dislike.[89] Even as a student he led an itinerant life. He followed lectures with Gottlob Frege in Berlin, studied engineering in Manchester for a while, and after consultation with Frege he turned to Bertrand Russell in Cambridge to study and discuss philosophy. After the outbreak of the First World War he voluntarily reported as an Austrian citizen to go to the front. Afterwards he chose to stay in remote locations, including a self-built wooden house on a Norwegian fjord, where he also received friends to talk about his work. Later, toward the end of his life, he lived by himself in an isolated farmhouse near Galway on the west coast of Ireland. He claimed only to be able to work in exile. His first book, *Tractatus Logico-Philosophicus* (1922), was largely written in the trenches of the eastern front, when he was formally still a student. Later, as a prisoner of war in Italy, Wittgenstein stayed in touch by letter with Russell about this work. Partly because of its unusual aphoristic form, the manuscript was rejected by several publishers and only appeared in print thanks to a complimentary foreword by the established Russell, who had also mediated between author and publisher. Wittgenstein's later (posthumously published) work originated from seminars with handpicked students in Cambridge, where he raised questions and dictated notes. The selection of the students took place on the principle that his lectures were not intended for tourists.

Decisive for the writing of the posthumously published *Philosophical Investigations* (1967) were the conversations Wittgenstein had in Cambridge around 1930 with the Italian economist and political refugee Piero Sraffa, a protégé of Keynes. Sraffa taught economics at Cambridge and Wittgenstein met him through the mediation of Keynes. Sraffa had read the *Tractatus* and could, with the help of simple examples and questions, convince Wittgenstein to see things from a different perspective. One of these examples concerned a Neapolitan gesture of brushing his chin with his fingertips, asking "What is the logical form of *that*?" Wittgenstein told his friends that the discussions with Sraffa made him feel like a tree from which all the dead branches had been cut. As biographer Monk puts it, "The metaphor is carefully chosen: cutting dead branches away allows new, more vigorous ones to grow (whereas [Frank] Ramsey's objections [against the *Tractatus*] left the dead wood in place, forcing the tree to distort itself around it)."[90] The talks with Sraffa led Wittgenstein to a more anthropological approach in which language is no longer (as in the *Tractatus*) dealt with in isolation from the circumstances in which it is used. In *Philosophical Investigations* Wittgenstein emphasized the "stream of life" from which linguistic utterings derive their meaning: "language games" that cannot be described without referring to the activities and the way of life of the people who are engaged in a language game: the meaning of a word lies in its use.[91]

Among the pioneers in science should be mentioned the Dutch historian Johan Huizinga (1872–1945), known as the country's "most famous historian who never studied history at university." This designation implies an oblique reference to his position as an outsider. Huizinga was born in Groningen, the most northern city in the Netherlands. He was the second son of a physiology professor at the local university. He lost his mother when he was two years old. His father remarried two years later and Huizinga, with an older brother and his sisters, grew up in a harmonious family. From the beginning as a student at the University of Groningen, he was mainly interested in language and culture – together with other cultures, which he approached by way of language and literature. Huizinga studied Dutch, Indo-Germanic, and Sanskrit. At an early stage, his father called his attention to the work of anthropologists. Edward B. Tylor's *Primitive Culture* (1871) made a particular impression. For his dissertation he followed the suggestion of his Sanskrit professor and chose the figure of the court jester Vidusa, in the Old Indian theater. A better understanding of Huizinga's later work can be gained through the role of his patron, mentor, and fatherly friend P. J. Blok, professor of history in Groningen and later in Leyden. He saw in Huizinga the future historian of culture and carefully headed him in that direction, nominating him for appointments at the university, first in Groningen (1895) and later at Leyden (1915). A visit to an exhibition of the fifteenth-century paintings of the brothers Van Eyck in Bruges in 1902 suggested the idea of making a study of the forms of life in Burgundy in the Middle Ages, in particular the lifestyle and ideals of the Burgundian nobility and clergy – not a chronological report, but a profile of a culture in decline: "The late Middle Ages not as an announcement of what is to come, but as a departure from what passes away."[92]

With *The Waning of the Middle Ages: A Study of the Forms of Life, Thought, and Art in France and the Netherlands in the Fourteenth and Fifteenth Centuries* (1919), Huizinga prompted a great deal of resistance from Dutch and German medievalists, who considered charters as their most important source. Nonetheless, Huizinga laid the foundations for a new science of cultural history, anticipating the work of the *Annales* school of Bloch and Lucien Febvre, as well as the rapprochement between historians and anthropologists that developed later in the twentieth century in Europe and the United States. The so-called history of mentalities refers back to the pioneer work of Huizinga. What captivated him were "forms of life," the configuration of an entire cultural complex at a defined period of time; hence his affinity with the work of Bronisław Malinowski, with whom he also became friends.

Huizinga married in 1902 and also had children. His wife died in 1914 and Huizinga long remained single, only to remarry in 1937. It was not by chance that during this long period of relative solitude he produced his most important work, including *The Waning of the Middle Ages* already mentioned, a biography of *Erasmus* (1924), and the original and brilliant *Homo Ludens: A Study of the Play-Element in Culture* (1938).[93]

All these examples of single, driven, and somewhat withdrawn scholars and artists, who as outsiders renewed their field, form the opening of the present book. They show that the historian of science I. Bernard Cohen was wrong in arguing that by the end of the nineteenth century innovative research organized in teams and coordinated from the top down had replaced research carried out by single pioneers. Cohen is oblivious to the enduring importance of self-study and other forms of informal training, including feedback from mentors and discussions with friends and other kindred spirits, for a better understanding of revolution in science. Has ever a new perspective or insight of any importance been discovered other than by a single person?[94] In the early 1950s, Watson formed a team with Crick at the Cavendish Laboratory in Cambridge, providing each other with informal feedback. They were supposed to collaborate with a similar team of two colleagues at King's College London. It was the ambitious, determined, single-minded and unscrupulous Watson who found the solution toward which he had worked with Crick for a year and a half, including the time during which their boss had taken them off the DNA project following a disappointing preliminary report. As pointed out above, the discovery of the "secret of life" took place in spite of teamwork organized from the top, but mainly because of serendipitous, last-minute encounters at the Cavendish Laboratory.[95]

Biographies form the second branch of the history of science and the arts. They provide a monographic report, mostly a chronological description of the life and work of a single pioneer. Containing a rich source of essential data, they have been indispensable for the research of the present book. Yet a monographic report can also become a straitjacket if the collection of data is not guided by an idea, theory, or interpretation of the facts (or specific facts) and highlights of plausible connections between life and work. Often lacking a comparative-analytical perspective, the biographical genre has maintained a predominantly narrative character, leaving little room for analysis and the development of an argument that indicates which factors in a biography have been decisive in the making of a radical innovator. A single example may suffice to show how easily one may be caught by a number of common pitfalls.

In the epilogue to his detailed description of the life and work of astronomers Copernicus, Tycho Brahe, Kepler, and Galileo in *The Sleepwalkers: A History of Man's Changing Vision of the Universe* (1964), Koestler raises the question of what characteristic features these pioneers had in common that are responsible for the important mutations in the history of thought. Anyone who expects that the author will revert to his biographical materials will be disappointed. Generalizing, he points to the following aspects:

> their skepticism, often carried out to the point of iconoclasm, in their attitude towards traditional ideas, axioms, and dogmas, towards every-thing that is taken for granted; on the other hand, an open-mindedness that verges on naïve credulity towards new concepts which seem to hold out some promise to their instinctive gropings. Out of this combination results that crucial capacity of perceiving a familiar object, situation, problem, or collection of data, in a sudden new light or new context: of seeing a branch not as part of a tree, but as a potential weapon or tool; of associating the fall of an apple not with its ripeness, but with the motion of the moon. The discoverer perceives relational patterns or functional analogies where nobody saw them before, as a poet perceives the image of a camel in a drifting cloud. This act of wrenching away an object from its habitual associative context and seeing it in a new context is an essential part of the creative process. It is an act both of destruction and of creation.[96]

Nobody will strongly disagree with this summary of the creative process in science. The text is largely derived from a passage in the opening of Butterfield's *The Origins of Modern Science, 1300–1800*, a handbook on the history of ideas, to which Koestler refers in a foot-note. But the summary does not answer the question about the specific circumstances that played a decisive role in the lives of Copernicus, Kepler, Galileo, and Newton, and enabled them to develop a new point of view. Even less do we hear about what distinguishes them from ordinary people, among whom there are many to be found who are also skeptical, open-minded, and benefit from imagination, but who have not stood out in either science or the arts. What exactly made Copernicus, Kepler, Galileo, and Newton tick? Koestler made a serious but common mistake in taking necessary conditions for sufficient conditions. Moreover, he indulges in psychological and biological determinism: an explanation in terms of "skepticism," "open-mindedness," "capacity," and "instinct" that gets bogged down in circular reasoning and throws up the same question, only in different words – a description disguised as an answer to the question of what made these "geniuses" so special. Koestler thus ignores what he described in his book in some detail and where we find the specific circumstances of adversity and serendipitous encounters which inspired Copernicus, Kepler, Galileo, and Newton to carry out their groundbreaking work.

Looking back at their lives, we find in these circumstances a general pattern of early adversity and social exclusion – as well as a string of serendipitous encounters. In their position as outsiders, estranged from current thought and making use of their unanticipated freedom, they could raise critical questions about everything the established regarded as self-evident. Having ended up on the margins of society, they were in a different place. With little to lose, they were in a position to take risks and seize scarce chances – windows of opportunity that could provide them with a niche for study and protection. Their position as outsiders resembled the position of an anthropologist investigating a foreign culture. The anthropologist's own culture functions as a sounding board, a mirror for understanding the unfamiliar culture – and vice versa. Independently of each other, two prominent anthropologists, looking back at their work, have caught this epistemological point in a single sentence: "It takes another culture to know another culture";[97] "We live between two worlds and feel somewhat detached from both, but each gains meaning through its contrast with the other."[98]

Koestler mentions various details of the life of Nicolaus Copernicus that are relevant for the argument of the present book. He lost both parents when he was ten and came under the protection of his uncle, his mother's brother, who later became Bishop of Ermland in northwest Poland and offered him the chance to study at university, first in Kraków, later in Bologna and Padua. The benefactor also provided him with a stipend as member of a chapter in his bishopric. At a time when nepotism was not yet a doubtful practice but a moral obligation, Copernicus made good use of these chances. His brother Andreas, four years his senior, was offered the same opportunities but, during his studies in Italy, he chose a more adventurous life, became chronically ill, and died under unknown circumstances. Koestler mentions all these particulars but loses their interconnections and the patterns that show up from a systematic comparison with the circumstances in which Kepler, Galileo, Newton, and other pioneers grew up. Of course, all of them were skeptical and open-minded, almost by definition, but these characteristics are part of the question, not of the answer, which can be found in their place in sets of social relationships.

It is also tempting to speak here of "personality": Copernicus was shy, Tycho Brahe was arrogant, Galileo was moody, and Kepler was a hypochondriac. Along with a fundamental objection (reductionism) mentioned in an earlier note, this emphasizes differences, also existing in wealth and class, as between the well-to-do aristocrat Tycho Brahe and the poor outcast Kepler. Similar differences also existed between the rich and favorably positioned Darwin and his counterpart, Wallace, whose father suffered bankruptcy, forcing the thirteen-year-old Wallace to leave school and look for a job (as a surveyor in his older brother's firm). Only later did he develop a passion for collecting exotic specimens, which he had to sell to make a living: first he spent four years in Brazil and shortly afterwards six years in the Dutch East Indies – eventually forestalling Darwin with his famous Ternate paper.[99]

To answer the question of how and why both developed into groundbreaking pioneers, we have to ask what they, along with their undeniable differences, had in common. The differences in background, class, wealth, and education between Darwin and Wallace could hardly have been greater. They came from opposite sides of Victorian society and culture.[100] Precisely these differences make their similarities more visible and hence suggest an answer to the question: why Darwin and why Wallace – and not one of their colleagues? Presumably independently from each other, both discovered natural selection as the mechanism of evolution. With this "materialistic" result they changed the image that people had of themselves and of the world in which they lived.

In the history of science I know of only one example of a comparative and analytical study based on a collective biography of sorts and a sustained argument trying to show the connection between social position and radical innovation: Frank Sulloway's *Born to Rebel: Birth Order, Family Dynamics, and Creative Lives*. In the next two chapters we will see to what extent Sulloway's work has contributed to a better understanding of the conditions under which scientists became groundbreaking pioneers in their distinctive fields.

—— 2 ——

SIBLING RIVALRY

Firstborns are the police. Laterborns are the outlaws.

From a Darwinian point of view, the evolutionary costs of risk taking are low whenever the prospects of survival or reproduction are also low.

Frank Sulloway, *Born to Rebel* (1996: 438, 112)

In *Born to Rebel*, Sulloway argues that pioneers of radical scientific innovation are formed by the dynamics of the family, especially by rivalry between siblings. Birth order is decisive for their place in the family. Laterborns have a greater chance than firstborns of bringing about a revolution in science. The reception of innovation shows a similar pattern: support comes from laterborns rather than from firstborns. The mechanism is rivalry between siblings, who compete to obtain attention and investments from their parents. In this competition, firstborns have an advantage because they are older, bigger, and stronger. They also know more and identify with the parents and are usually on their side. Therefore firstborns have the choice of the most readily available niches in the family. Moreover, they share the authority of the parents and are well placed to maintain and shore up the status quo. In addition, they are the next after the grandparents to be considered for the role of stand-in parents for their younger siblings – a circumstance that confirms and reinforces their position of power.

To obtain attention and investments from parents and to survive, laterborns search for unoccupied niches inside or outside the family. This requires not only openness and curiosity, but also risk taking. If they have the fortune to succeed in their search and find a niche, this divergence also lessens competition with their older siblings. In the working of this Darwinian principle of divergence, Sulloway also

29

finds the most important reason why children from the same family differ so much from one another. Mostly without realizing it, siblings go out of their way to be different. They differ more from one another than from children from other families. For laterborns, Sulloway holds, deviating from the norm (divergence) is in their Darwinian interest, because this "strategy" increases the chance of surviving in an unequal competition with an older brother. Moreover, finding an unoccupied place decreases the competition and makes the relationship easier to endure. This development during childhood would explain why laterborns rather than firstborns belong to the pioneers and pacemakers of radical innovation.[1]

Sulloway indicates the limiting conditions of his thesis. To bring about the effect of birth order, children have to grow up together between the ages of seven and sixteen.[2] Moreover, age differences are important: the lesser the age differences, the more rivalry. The number of children in the family also influences the effect of birth order: larger families are less prone to sibling rivalry. Finally, conflicts with parents on the part of firstborns can turn them into functional laterborns. The point in Sulloway's Darwinian theory is family dynamics and, in particular, rivalry between children to get attention and investment from their parents. In this competition, firstborns incline to preservation of the status quo, while laterborns, motivated to discover new ways and to survive in an available niche, tend to resist the status quo and resist prevailing views, taking a critical stand and subjecting them to examination.

With his focus on conflict between the children in the family, Sulloway goes against the theories of Marx and Freud, whose work also put conflict at the center of attention, but who looked for an explanation in the relationships between classes and generations, respectively.[3] Sulloway draws on another celebrated thinker who put conflict at the core of his work and to whom Marx and Freud also remained tributary: Darwin. Take the heading of a paragraph in the third chapter of *The Origin of Species*. It contains the core of a book of more than 500 pages: "Struggle for life most severe between individuals and varieties of the same species."[4] The explanation follows directly:

> But the struggle almost invariably will be most severe between the individuals of the same species, for they frequent the same districts, require the same food, and are exposed to the same dangers. In the case of varieties of the same species, the struggle will generally be almost equally severe, and we sometimes see the contest soon decided . . .[5]

After this we return to the human family, in which the struggle between brothers has been recorded and discussed since ancient times, starting with the killing of Abel by his brother, Cain, and the conflict between Jacob and Esau.[6]

At first sight, Sulloway's book is a relief, as is also evident from the jubilant expressions of support and recommendations by various leading scholars with which *Born to Rebel* opens, and the long, positive review by Jared Diamond in the *New York Review of Books* in November 1996, shortly after the book appeared. *Born to Rebel* is based on comparative biographical research into radical innovators and comprises a distinct argument: to demonstrate a specific relationship between the life and the work of pioneers over the last 500 years, with radicalism and the position of children growing up in the family being decisive. But does Sulloway show he is right and can he convince the reader? What is the value of the evidence for his bold theory?

On closer inspection, *Born to Rebel* principally addresses the *reception* of radical innovation in science. Much less is heard about the pioneers themselves – the life and work of the makers of revolutionary innovations. For his assertion and conclusion that laterborns are over-represented, Sulloway bases himself on reception history derived from statistical databanks of several thousand respondents, the sources not being revealed. As he explains in an appendix, his correlations are different from causal relationships, but the prior direction and tone of the book weaken this proviso.[7] The book is concerned with statistically tracing and indicating "predictors," "main effects," and "consequences" of birth order and then principally in the reception of radical innovation. His treatment of the pioneers themselves remains underexposed, sketchy, secondary, impressionistic, and illustrative throughout the whole book – it has been described as an "abortive collective biography."[8] This priority is evident in the entire design of the book and is everywhere visible: *Born to Rebel* is chiefly a reception history of "controversial" scientific revolutions.[9] This priority is also obvious in some incidental but nonetheless significant additions, such as: "Even when the initiators of the new theories turn out to be firstborns – as was the case with Newton, Lavoisier, Einstein, and Freud – the supporters are still predominantly laterborn. Among radical scientific innovators, firstborns are the exception, just as they are among scientists who welcome radical innovations."[10] In a comment on the use of his sources, Sulloway reveals his real priority: "I have not collected data on the development of electromagnetic theory by Faraday, Maxwell, Hertz, and others (which received 273 page references). I was unable to find a sufficiently detailed account of the reception of these ideas to justify a formal statistical survey."[11] That both James Maxwell and Heinrich Hertz were firstborn remains unmentioned in this explanation. Sulloway's statement that firstborns are the exception among pioneers in science belies his own count ("sample") based on an official canon: no fewer than eighteen of the thirty-one cases were firstborns.[12]

Because Sulloway does not specify the sources and composition of his statistical accounts about the positive reception of radical innovation, the results of the most important part of his research are difficult to judge and equally hard to replicate. This flaw has also been recorded in earlier receptions of his book: Modell points to "the omission of conventional information about sample size."[13] Townsend concludes his review of these shortcomings with the remark: "combining selection bias with undisclosed data allows Sulloway to create dramatic results."[14]

I restrict my assessment of *Born to Rebel* to the initiators in science, the pioneers themselves. Sulloway argues that they are predominantly laterborns and that laterborn status is the key variable: "Among radical scientific innovators, firstborns are the exception."[15] Yet the pioneers of scientific radical innovation (sometimes with portraits, etc.) figure more as illustrations for his theory than as proper case studies of a collective biography. For some of them only their birth order is mentioned. The position of Nicolaus Copernicus figures only in a casual remark, more as an illustration of his theory, that "Copernicus himself was the youngest of four children."[16] Nowhere does Sulloway mention factual information about rivalry with his brother, Andreas, four years his senior. What has to be demonstrated (sibling rivalry) is simply assumed. Neither do we hear if all his cases meet the second condition Sulloway considers important to produce the birth order effect: growing up with siblings in the age span between seven and sixteen years old. It often happens in Sulloway's book that what has to be demonstrated is taken as proof. Nonetheless, his exceptions deserve further research and critical attention, as does his theoretical scheme indicating the position of laterborns as the key variable: the primary antecedent of radical innovation.[17]

— 3 —

HEURISTIC EXCEPTIONS

There was one quality of mind which seemed to be of special and extreme advantage in leading him to make discoveries. It was the power of never letting exceptions pass unnoticed.
Francis Darwin, "Reminiscences of My Father"[1]

This chapter explores the way Sulloway deals with his exceptions and what we can learn from it. We bear in mind Darwin's research strategy mentioned by his son Francis (who worked with him for years) in his "Reminiscences of My Father": "There was one quality of mind which seemed to be of special and extreme advantage in leading him to make discoveries. It was the power of never letting exceptions pass unnoticed."[2] This approach comes down to the practice of not adapting exceptions to the working model or theory but doing the reverse: adjusting the model to the exceptions.[3] The question is to what extent Sulloway (for whom Darwin was both hero and example) respected this principle in dealing with the exceptions we come across in his *Born to Rebel* about the connection between the life and work of pioneer scientists who are regarded in the annals of science as part of an official canon of radical innovators.[4]

Sulloway mentions a total of thirty-one pioneers, of whom eighteen turned out to be firstborns. They do not form a clearly defined sample, nor are they neatly arranged in any figure or table. It is left to the reader to sort them out: to trace the pioneers and collect the relevant biographical information (the independent variables), which Sulloway provides in anecdotal fashion to explain radical innovation (the dependent variable).[5] The seventeen firstborns include Galileo, Kepler, Harvey, Newton, Leibniz, James Hutton, Lavoisier, Charles Lyell, Mendel, Maxwell, Freud, Einstein, Niels Bohr, Max

Born, Pauling, Watson, and Crick. Three of them, Hutton, Mendel, and Bohr, had older sisters and were treated as eldest sons and therefore count as functional firstborns. Sulloway, however, codes them as laterborns.[6] The thirteen laterborns in Sulloway's book are Copernicus, Francis Bacon, Hobbes, Descartes, Huygens, Thomas Malthus, Alexander von Humboldt, Faraday, Darwin, Wallace, Planck, Wegener, and Hamilton. None of them can be considered a functional firstborn. How does Sulloway deal with seventeen exceptions after turning three of them (elder sons Hutton, Mendel, and Bohr) into laterborns?

Except for Darwin, whose life and work get a great deal of attention throughout his book, Sulloway does not delve deep into the biographies of his pioneers. Only in some cases (Galileo, Kepler, Newton) does the reader get sketches of the interconnections between the life and work of radical scientists amidst biographical information about random examples, including kings, politicians, and friends and colleagues of radical scientists, intended to illustrate Sulloway's thesis of birth order effects.[7] Sibling rivalry, suggested as the driving force of radical innovation, is assumed rather than spelled out in particular cases. Sulloway compensates for the lack of evidence about sibling strife among pioneers by providing various random cases of sibling rivalry among kings and other non-pioneers. Instances of friendship and cooperation (rather than conflict) with an older brother (Humboldt, Faraday, Darwin, Wallace, and Wegener) are systematically ignored. Nor does Sulloway spell out whether the pioneers in his sample all grew up with brothers or sisters between their seventh and sixteenth years: another important condition he sets to be able to speak of any birth order effect.[8] What has to be demonstrated or proved is accepted as given. As mentioned above, elder sons, including Hutton, Mendel, and Bohr, who each had older sisters, are automatically and wrongly coded as laterborns.[9]

Mendel (1822–82), a laterborn but elder son, was raised as a firstborn and marked out to succeed his father on the family farm near Heizendorf, a hamlet in Silesia, a German-speaking region of Moravia in former Sudetenland. Mendel had an older and a younger sister.[10] His role of elder son was definitely scripted for him. An enthusiastic gymnasium pupil, Mendel would not hear of any work on the farm and was set to pursue his studies. The looming conflict was neatly settled. The husband of Mendel's older sister bought the farm and the youngest sister supported her brother financially from her inheritance. Mendel made grateful use of these opportunities.[11] He would later reciprocate and pay for the education of his three nephews.[12] This is only one of several cases mentioned in this book in which a mother's brother appears as the protector of his sister's children. The subject still requires further comparative investigation.[13]

For further education, penniless Mendel was helped out by his tutor at the Philosophical Institute, who suggested he should join the monks at the monastery of St. Thomas at Brünn, which was known for its scientific reputation and housed one of the most famous scientific societies in the country. The monastery itself "felt more like a college dormitory than a house of God. St. Thomas was run according to the Augustinian credo *per scientiam ad sapientiam*: from knowledge to wisdom."[14] With a new first name, Gregor, Mendel came under the protection of Abbot Cyril Napp, a friend of Mendel's tutor, who had recommended him for this position. After Mendel's additional studies in botany and mathematics at the University of Vienna, Napp provided him with facilities for his research experiments on crossbreeding varieties of pea plants, which would take up eight years (1856–63). In that time, he discovered the mechanism of species stability: hereditary traits do not blend or get otherwise lost but remain, as either dominant or recessive. Mendel's "laws of inheritance" proved the independence of hereditary traits. The outcome of his experiments laid the foundation of what was much later to be called "genetics," and filled a major gap in Darwin's theory of natural selection.[15]

Mendel first presented his results in two local lectures in 1866, which appeared in print the following year, comprising just forty-four pages. He sent offprints to various scientists (including to Darwin), but the only reaction he got was from Karl von Nägeli, an established botanist at the University of Munich, who waited almost two months before writing to Mendel. Where Mendel emphasized stability, Nägeli insisted on variation. Where Nägeli believed in a blending of traits, Mendel's evidence could be interpreted as a disproof of blending. Nägeli "no doubt saw that if Mendel was right, then he, Nägeli, had to be wrong . . . In Mendel's system the traits that seem to disappear . . . show themselves in the next generation not to have blended at all. If Mendel's data got out, what would become of Nägeli's considerable reputation?"[16] For several years, Nägeli kept Mendel on hold, telling him to collect more evidence, until the monk was promoted to the position of abbot of St. Thomas and had to give up his research and correspondence with Nägeli. Recalling the previous cases of Einstein, Wegener, Hamilton, and Goodall, another case demonstrates how and why radical innovation initially evokes silence, indifference, and strong resistance. Vested personal and professional interests may prevail. Yet, as Kuhn argues, this resistance may also be functional: "By ensuring that the paradigm will not be too easily surrendered, resistance guarantees that scientists will not be lightly distracted and that the anomalies that lead to paradigm change will penetrate existing knowledge to the core."[17]

Mendel's single-handed pioneering was ignored and the monk died unrewarded. It would take well over three decades before a handful of his offprints were traced and rediscovered – not without other fights over priority. In the end, Mendel was posthumously hailed as the creator of a new discipline, as "the father of genetics."[18] His biographer Robin Marantz Henig observes: "maybe he would be pleased to find that the science named in his honor, Mendelian genetics, is at the heart of a revolution not only in biological thought but in thought itself."[19]

Birth order does not seem to have played a significant role in Mendel's case. His pioneering work had entirely different antecedents: early exclusion from his classmates at the village school (puzzled by his early intellectual interests), alienation from farm work (which he hated) and the local farming community, and resistance against his parents because of the pressure to take over from them at the farm. These circumstances of relative isolation favored his early scientific passion, as did the support of his sisters and the protection of mentors, including various teachers and the abbot of St. Thomas. The monastery, where scientific research was the main priority, proved a blessing for Mendel, who could make use of all its facilities for his painstaking research on the hybridization of pea plants. Mendel's discovery of the "laws of heredity" was the work of one man, very much like that of his predecessors Kepler, Galileo, Newton, and Darwin, as well as that of later pioneers, including Weber, Einstein, Wegener, Keynes, Wittgenstein, Goodall, Hamilton, and Perelman. But Mendel was unfortunate. No contemporary scientific colleague noticed his fundamental achievement and could champion him. The only colleague who did recognize his breakthrough remained silent. Nägeli simply kept Mendel busy, urging him to collect "more evidence": the cliché response to any new idea or theory in science.

In contrast with his treatment of elder son Mendel as a laterborn (rather than a functional firstborn), elsewhere in his book Sulloway discusses leadership in political revolutions by elder sons he marks as functional firstborns. In his sketch of the composition of the twelve architects of the Reign of Terror (1793–4) during the French Revolution, there are seven firstborns and presumably five elder sons, that is, functional firstborns.[20] The activities of the notable firstborns Robespierre and Louis de Saint-Just increasingly resembled the terror and arbitrariness of the *ancien régime* of king and nobility against which the revolution had at first been directed: the "twelve who ruled" were "almost all autocratic, jealous, and short-tempered – typical firstborn traits."[21] Assessing the effects of independent variables, Sulloway applies a double standard. This manipulation of independent variables is repeated in his judgment and treatment of the operations of the revolutionary leaders in Cuba in 1959. Laterborn Fidel Castro and firstborn Ché Guevara *both* had a leading part in this political revolution.[22] In his critical review of Sulloway's book, Townsend notes, "These two men engaged in the same activities over the same period but were of different birth orders. How does Sulloway explain this? No problem. Since Castro was a later-born, Sulloway ignores his authoritarian actions and focuses on his rebellious behavior, but since Guevara was a first-born, Sulloway flip-flops and focuses on Ché's authoritarian actions."[23]

By clinging to birth order as the key and primary factor in radical scientific innovation and letting other circumstances, including family dynamics, "interact" with birth order, Sulloway was obliged to wriggle, including tying himself in knots to accommodate numerous exceptions to his model.[24] In this way, his exceptions take on the look of artifacts – artificially constructed facts and proofs. This chapter tries to demonstrate that Sulloway repeatedly missed chances to test the model and where necessary adjust it by taking a step toward a more inclusive theoretical scheme into which exceptions could fit and be accommodated – and thus cease to be "exceptions." Firstborns Kepler (1571–1630) and Newton, asserts Sulloway, came from "atypical" families.[25] Kepler was born in the town of Weil not far from Stuttgart in what was then the Duchy of Württemberg. The ties with his parents were disrupted. There were twelve children, of whom the last three died young. As a mercenary, his father was often away from home, twice in one year in the company of his wife, while the seven-year-old Kepler was placed with his grandparents in another town. Having served as a Protestant mercenary in Spanish armies fighting his coreligionists in the Low Countries, the father did not return to his family. His fate remained unknown.

Kepler excelled at the Latin school, though he got into trouble with his classmates. Eventually he obtained a grant at the recommendation of the Duke of Württemberg to study theology at the University of Tübingen – to replenish the Duke's Protestant staff. One of his teachers was the mathematician Michael Maestlin, a prudent Copernican, who encouraged Kepler's enthusiasm for mathematics and astronomy. After completing his studies in theology, and through the mediation of Maestlin, Kepler obtained his first job as a teacher of mathematics and astronomy at the gymnasium in Protestant Graz. On the basis of his *Mysterium Cosmographicum* (1596), an invitation followed from the rich Danish aristocrat and astronomer Tycho Brahe (1546–1601), again after mediation by Maestlin, to become his assistant at the Imperial Astronomical Observatory in the castle of Benatek just outside Prague, later relocated to the city itself. Tycho's accurate astronomical measurements (without a telescope until 1610) enabled Kepler to describe the movements of planets in terms of elliptical orbits around the sun.[26]

This summary of the career of a poor and myopic stargazer shows a scenario with at least seven windows of opportunity, chances which Kepler was alert to and seized: excelling at the Latin school; being recommended by the local ruler for a university grant; becoming Maestlin's protégé; being appointed in Graz on Maestlin's recommendation; publishing *Mysterium Cosmographicum*; being invited by Tycho Brahe, through Maestlin, to be his assistant; becoming Tycho's successor after his death and making further use of his observations. After these experiences, years of sustained hard and dedicated work followed, alongside obligations to two successive families, each with lots of children. In the end Kepler obtained his reward: the discovery of the elliptic forms of the planetary orbits around the sun. With interruptions, Kepler had worked eighteen years on this achievement, laying the foundation for modern astronomy.[27] Instead of prematurely classifying the family in which Kepler grew up as "atypical," Sulloway could have tried to answer the question raised by Kepler's biographer Koestler: "His eye-deficiency seems the most perfidious trick that fate could inflict on a stargazer; but how is one to decide whether an inborn affliction will paralyse or galvanize?"[28]

To understand Kepler's achievement we should focus on family adversity: its poverty and neglect on the margins of society – a brilliant pauper from the periphery. For the young but alert Kepler, apparently without opportunities, there was one main alternative: the niche of school and university with the balm of science. Second, he recognized and seized a series of unique chances provided by his patrons and developed through hard work, passion and perseverance. Looking back on Kepler's career, his biographer Koestler notes it was the life of someone who had "that mysterious knack of finding original outlets for inner pressure; of transforming his torments into creative achievement."[29]

The life and work of Newton show a similar scenario, with analogous beginnings in adversity. Like Kepler and numerous other radical innovators, Newton also came from the provinces – from Woolsthorpe, a rural community in Lincolnshire. His family was well-to-do, but Newton was born three months after his father's death. When he was three years old, his mother married a clergyman from the same area. She placed her son at her parents' farm and moved to the vicarage with her new husband. After seven years she became a widow again and, with three children from her second marriage, she settled at her parents' farm. A year later, Newton left the family to continue his education in nearby Grantham, where he lodged with a local pharmacist. Thus, Newton did not grow up with his siblings, the condition predicated by Sulloway for the effect of sibling rivalry and radicalism, but ignored in this case. It was not birth order but parental abandonment that was Newton's adversity. He was born without a father and later bullied at school. After three years his mother remarried and excluded him from her new family. Nothing is known about the care on his grandparents' farm. Newton never talked about it.[30] Biographer Westfall mentions that Newton "formed no bond with any of his numerous relations that can be traced in his later life. The lonely boyhood was the first chapter in a long career of isolation."[31]

For Newton to finish school and go to Cambridge, three people from his environment had to talk to his mother. She had to be persuaded that this was more suitable for her son than work on the family farm, which she had marked out for him even before he had finished school. Newton's teacher was so impressed by his achievements that he was ready to take him into his house without charge for the last school year. Newton's mother's brother, a clergyman who had studied in Cambridge, also supported this plan. Finally, there was the strong support of the brother-in-law of the pharmacist, named Humphrey Babington, who was a clergyman in a neighboring village and also a fellow of Trinity College, who would later figure as Newton's patron.[32] His mother's grant was not enough for him to manage at the Cambridge college. As a result, Newton had to work as a sizar – a college domestic – until, recommended by Babington, he was considered for a scholarship and later also for a fellowship.[33]

In both cases – Kepler and Newton – birth order was irrelevant or "spurious." In the families in which they grew up the father was lacking, while the mother neglected or outright abandoned them, or left them to the care of others. As will be shown, these families, which Sulloway calls "atypical," were far from exceptional among prospective radical innovators. Many families in which radical innovators grew up were "atypical." This may help explain why they did not become "typical" mainstream citizens themselves, but outsiders and radical innovators. The brilliant mathematician and physicist Robert Hooke (1635–1703), colleague and later sworn enemy of Newton, whom he unjustly suspected of plagiarism, lost his father, a clergyman, when he was thirteen, when his father hanged himself at home. Other contemporaries and colleagues of Newton, including Huygens (1629–95) and Leibniz (1646–1716), likewise lost a parent when they were still children. This also applied to Boyle (1627–91), who also belonged to the circle around the Royal Society; his mother died when he was still a young child. Descartes (1596–1650) lost his mother when he was not yet one year old; he grew up with his maternal grandmother and was not included with his siblings in his father's new family.[34] All six radical scholars remained single, like their famous contemporary and colleague Spinoza (1632–77), who lost his mother before he was six and later became friends with his neighbor and colleague Christiaan Huygens, who likewise had lost his mother early.

The so-called "exceptions" and "atypical" families in which Kepler and Newton were born were by no means exceptional or atypical – in fact, they were more the rule than the exception among the families in which later pioneers were born and grew up. They thus call into question Sulloway's theoretical scheme. Many radical innovators, including his hero Darwin, missed parental attachment, not only because of early loss of their mother, but also from the following failure of substitute care. As Sulloway concludes in his sketch of Darwin's youth: "What was remarkably absent in Darwin's childhood was a feeling of secure attachment to anyone."[35] Sulloway states an important fact of adversity (parental loss) but fails to recognize its impact and ignores the close ties Darwin maintained from early on with his older brother Erasmus – a basic fact that contradicts the key role of sibling rivalry in Sulloway's theory of radical innovation.[36] As the present book tries to demonstrate, it is not birth order but social exclusion following adversity that is the main force, the mechanism driving radical innovation. Solitude opened the road to science and the arts – activities that do not require the presence of other people. The disposition to seclusion, a somewhat withdrawn lifestyle, "precious solitude," as Einstein called it, would become the main characteristic of the habitus of many radical innovators.

Charles Darwin's brother Erasmus, four years older, was certainly not his rival. On the contrary, he was the only person in the family (apart from the older sisters who acted as surrogate parents) who took care of his younger brother, taking him out on trips, encouraging his interest in biology and chemistry, and giving him support at the local school. Later on, too, at the colleges in Edinburgh and Cambridge, Erasmus was a great friend and companion. After Darwin returned from his trip with the *Beagle* in the fall of 1836, Erasmus introduced his brother to his London circle of intellectuals and lent him a copy of Malthus's *Essay on Population*. Darwin read it in September 1838 and it gave him his breakthrough idea of "natural selection" – the mechanism of evolution.[37]

Sulloway recognizes that, along with sibling rivalry, cooperation between brothers does also happen. He mentions in this connection Hamilton's theory of social altruism and cooperation (including self-sacrifice) between genetically close relatives, in particular between brothers who share 50 percent of their genes. Sulloway considers Hamilton's rule of inclusive fitness (later called "kin selection") to be the most important step in the theory of evolution since Darwin and Mendel. Yet he omits to mention the generous Erasmus, the unmarried brother of Darwin (who himself had a large family), as a striking example of the working of Hamilton's rule of social altruism.[38] This is one of the most important objections against the execution of *Born to Rebel*: what does not match the model is left out or made to fit and omitted from testing. Although Sulloway admits that altruism between siblings can be "considerable," he easily passes it off. He argues, for example, that children without brothers or sisters can also experience sibling rivalry in their resistance to the weaning process: "by resisting the mother's efforts at weaning, which in turn affects her likelihood of conceiving a rival for parental investment ..."[39] More important, Sulloway's statement about weaning is contrary to his most important condition for birth order effect: growing up together with siblings between the ages of seven and sixteen.[40]

The early loss of parents does not fit well into Sulloway's theory, which is after all based on rivalry between siblings who compete to obtain parental attention and investment. When there are no parents and no siblings to compete with, the birth order theory finds itself in trouble.[41] The early loss of parents, Sulloway argues, is one of the factors that "interact" with birth order and social class. This may be so, and Sulloway gives several interesting and acceptable examples of this "interaction." But when he is off guard, as in two footnotes, two generalizations about a main feature of pioneers – in which birth order turns out to be irrelevant – elude him.

41

The first statement says: "The most open individuals are laterborns who lost a parent early."[42] At this crucial point, Sulloway overlooks his prime example, Darwin, and instead continues to insist on Darwin's status as a laterborn as the main (independent) variable to explain radical innovation. Meanwhile he once more stays silent on the lifelong friendship and cooperation between Charles and his brother Erasmus, who (as noted above) took care of him after the early death of their mother. Moreover, the authoritarian character of Darwin's father, Robert Waring Darwin, does not fit Sulloway's picture of the typical laterborn. In his whole behavior toward his children, and also toward those of his sister and his Wedgwood brother-in-law when they were visiting, Darwin's father manifested the typical personality features of Sulloway's firstborn: authoritarian, intimidating, suspicious, jealous, impatient, easily offended, and short-tempered – just as the man was described by his next of kin, especially the children.[43] Undoubtedly, youngest son Charles suffered most under the continuous criticism from his father. In his autobiography Darwin mentions one of his father's humiliating outbursts in the presence of other relatives when he was studying at Cambridge: "You care for nothing but shooting, dogs, and rat-catching, and you will be a disgrace to yourself and all your family."[44] His scolding only stopped after Darwin's return from the trip on the *Beagle* (1831–6), when it became clear that the son had made a reputation in science. What remained, however, writes biographer Bowlby, was a deep insecurity about his achievements: "Unflagging industry and a horror of idleness were to dominate his life."[45]

The second generalization, directly following the first one, runs like this: "Firstborns having the same experience [i.e., early loss of parents] become close-minded."[46] Were eight of the ten firstborn radical innovators who lost a parent early then close-minded? They are Kepler, Newton, Leibniz, Hutton, Lavoisier, Maxwell, Born, and Pauling. The text linked to this note includes the following statement: "Birth order influences openness to innovation, but social class and parental loss do not (at least directly)."[47] This contradiction is followed by another contradiction. Sulloway mentions the shy Max Born, son of an upper-class family, who at the age of four was hit by the loss of his mother and suffered, together with his younger sister, a severe regime of foster parents. He was later awarded the Nobel prize in physics and was one of the early champions of Einstein's relativity theory. Sulloway comments, "Born's support would have been more difficult to understand had he not lost a parent when he was young."[48] What here goes for Born, apparently does not go for the seven other firstborns who lost a parent early.

Sulloway devotes ten pages to the subject of "parental loss." Six of them deal with Darwin and his family. They concern the failing care of his father and two older sisters, who denied him, at only eight years old, any form of mourning and any reference to his deceased mother; they also used to follow him in an annoying fashion and sometimes humiliated him – hence his famous "doggedness," as Darwin notes in his *Autobiography*.[49] Yet Sulloway does not recognize the working of the independent variable "early loss of parents," and neither does he link this experience to Darwin's revolution in biology.[50] For Sulloway, who argued initially that "the most open individuals are laterborns who had lost a parent early," Darwin's achievement comes entirely on account of his birth order. Darwin was a laterborn, the fifth of six children. Sulloway does not breathe a word about sibling rivalry and also ignores the cooperation and close friendship between the Darwin brothers. In a book of more than 500 pages dealing with birth order effects, and with Darwin as the main test case, these omissions are puzzling and amount to ignoring unwelcome evidence. Manipulating the evidence and juggling with variables, Sulloway demonstrates a form of poor scholarship that goes beyond his tunnel vision.

Sulloway dwells briefly on the friendship and cooperation between the brothers Wilhelm (1767–1835) and Alexander von Humboldt (1769–1859), who lost their father when they were still young and grew up with a cold and distant mother. Although different in character and habitus – Alexander adventurous and keen on traveling, and linguist Wilhelm, two years his senior, more stay-at-home – they spent their youth in "inseparable comradeship" under the leadership of a beloved mentor, who acted *in loco parentis* until they had completed their studies at university in Berlin. The loss of their father (when Wilhelm was ten and Alexander eight) clearly had no adverse consequences for their relationship or for their lifestyles. Even after finishing their studies, the brothers remained close.[51] But Sulloway doesn't find that this lasting friendship and cooperation between the brothers Von Humboldt, like that between Alfred and Kurt Wegener, and the example of Charles and Erasmus Darwin just mentioned, is any reason to revise his theory about sibling rivalry as the single driving force of radical innovation. The parents of these three pioneers were well-to-do. Nevertheless Sulloway argues that the "strategy" of cooperation between brothers tends to occur especially in families in the lower social classes, where extensive parental investment is not to be expected.[52] This can sometimes be the case, as we noted in the cases of Faraday, Mendel, and Wallace, but it also appears with Humboldt, Darwin, and Wegener. To these three cases can be added that of Max Born (1882–1970). He was born in Breslau (now Wrocław) as the son of an anatomy professor at the university in that town; his mother came from a family of industrialists. She died young and the four-year-old Born and his sister, two years younger, came under the severe regime of foster parents, which, writes Sulloway, led to a "twinning" effect: close ties developed between the two.[53]

Contradicting himself, Sulloway argues that early loss of parents in the lower social classes has an opposite effect. There is polarization between older and younger children because the former take over authority from the parents: "The earlier the loss, the more polarization between siblings in the lower classes."[54] He does not provide examples, but his own sample of radical scientists includes several cases that contradict him: Faraday, Wallace, and Pauling show cooperation between siblings after parental loss. The evidence for sibling rivalry as the driving force of radical innovation fails to materialize in Sulloway's book, while indications for cooperation between brothers accumulate – irrespective of class and income of the parents.

Early loss of parents afflicted about half of the thirty-one radical innovators in Sulloway's abortive collective biography: Kepler, Newton, Copernicus (who lost both parents when he was ten), Bacon, Hobbes (whose father left the family after a serious physical fight with a clergyman colleague, whom he thought he had killed), Descartes (who lost his mother when he was not yet one and was taken care of by his maternal grandmother, but had to accept an absent father, who moved elsewhere with his older children), Leibniz (who was six when his already aged father died – in his third marriage – and was educated by his mother), Hutton, Lavoisier, Humboldt, Faraday, Maxwell, Born, and Pauling. Care did not fail in all these cases, yet most of them, as far as we know, were affected by solitude, which helped them to develop an early interest in science – in spite of their place in the birth order.

Nevertheless, the status of laterborn should be noted as one of the forms of adversity that may entail social exclusion and indicate the road to radical innovation – a necessary condition alongside other analogous conditions that can help to produce the same effect of adversity and exclusion. The recognition of a new pattern in research materials, bringing a number of loose observations and facts under a common, more inclusive denominator, has been described by Kuhn as a process of "conceptual assimilation," or "reconceptualization and possibly the formation of a new 'paradigm.'"[55] The step from a geocentric to a heliocentric presentation of the world was a most striking example of a paradigmatic shift. Similar examples include Darwin's evolution theory based on natural selection, Harvey's discovery of the systemic character of blood circulation, in which the heart functions as a pump, Kepler's ellipses, and Newton's formulation of the laws of gravitation.

Darwin developed his key concept of "natural selection" with the help of a double analogy: one between geographical variation and variation in time, and one between geological and biological gradualness, where he drew on the work of his mentor and friend Lyell. Darwin also compared natural selection with selection in domesticated animals. Next he was inspired by Malthus's insight about population growth, that, in the end, it would outnumber any increase in the means of subsistence and would result in a struggle for life in which only the strongest (i.e., the best fitted) would survive. Adam Smith offered help, too, with his analogous concept and doctrine of "laisser-faire economics" and the working of the "invisible hand." Discussing the individual agent in the world of laisser-faire, Smith argues: "He generally, indeed, neither intends to promote the public interest, nor knows how much he is promoting it . . . he intends only his own gain, and he is in this, as in many other cases, led by an invisible hand to promote an end which was no part of his intention."[56]

In this connection, there are descriptions of the esthetic aspects of revolutionary theories and the great excitement experienced by pioneers about their discoveries. In *Elegance of Science: The Beauty of Simplicity* (2010), Glynn discusses various examples, including Kepler's discovery of the orbits of planets in the form of ellipses when he, at one stroke, created order in a mass of observations of celestial bodies.[57] This characterization strongly appealed to Einstein. As mentioned above, on various occasions he declared that a similar synthesis is the highest ideal in the practice of science and inspires the greatest possible joy.

Returning to the problem of firstborn pioneers, we dwell a moment on Sulloway's treatment of firstborn Galileo (1567–1642) as an exception and test case. To begin with, he mentions two reasons why a family dynamics model can make "mistaken predictions": because of erroneous data in biographical sources and because of insufficient biographical information.[58]

> One particularly glaring error by a family dynamics model involves Galileo. As the first of four children, Galileo's predicted probability of supporting radical causes is only 30 percent. Yet he was an energetic opponent of scholastic truth based on authority . . . of the 3,111 predictions made by a family dynamics model, Galileo represents the greatest mistake.[59]

However, Sulloway believes he has found a plausible explanation for Galileo's radicalism in Drake's biography, where Galileo's relationship with his father is spelled out. The father was both a professional musician and a known expert in music theory. He made his son familiar with both fields. Galileo also learned from his father that he should not accept from other people what he could investigate himself, preferably with the use of experiments. Drake suggests that Galileo became a radical because he was the son of a radical.[60] Yet the question remains of how a conservative firstborn can become a revolutionary both through parental conflict and through conforming to a parent, as was rightly argued in a critical review of Born to Rebel.[61] To save what can still be saved in this particular case, Sulloway suggests yet another (ad hoc) possibility. Because of the great difference in age from the other children in the family – nine years – Galileo was after all an only child and these children, precisely because they do not have any brothers or sisters, "are freer to become radicals themselves."[62] Yet earlier Sulloway argued that, for the birth order effect to happen and children to develop sibling rivalry for attention and investment from their parents, they have to grow up with their siblings between the ages of seven and sixteen.[63] So we are back where we started.

Two recent biographies of Galileo mention independently from one another that already as a child Galileo had a difficult relationship with both parents. Described as "uncooperative as usual," "recalcitrant," "terrible," his mother "appears deeply hostile to her son . . . and keen to get him in trouble with the authorities."[64] Probably for that reason he liked the monastic school in Vallombrosa, not far from Florence, where, because of the silence and his love for study, he wanted to remain as a novice and also make his vows. His father had other plans and thwarted the intentions of the fourteen-year-old by sending him to another school. Galileo's father did not want his son to become a monk (and poor), but a physician (and rich). The adolescent Galileo put up strong resistance. Eventually, he did not study medicine, but mathematics, with which the father later reluctantly agreed.[65]

For an explanation of Galileo's radicalism we have, ironically, to turn to the model Sulloway himself presented: rebellion of a firstborn against his parents following disagreement about career choice. Galileo will then become an example of a firstborn who, because of parent–offspring conflict, becomes a functional laterborn. As we will see, there are more examples among the pioneers in science and the arts of rebellious firstborns (and also of laterborns) because of disagreement with their parents about their choice of a career.

46

Sulloway gives more examples of "parent–offspring conflict" among firstborn pioneers and automatically assumes that laterborns systematically rebel against their parents. Hence his expression "functional" or "honorary" laterborns for firstborns who revolt against their parents.[66] Yet, like the early loss of parents, conflict with parents does not fit well into Sulloway's theory of birth order. The variable "conflict with parents" also doesn't square with this birth order theory, which after all starts from structural rivalry between siblings for attention and investment from their parents – and not from conflicts between the generations, as Sulloway emphatically argues in his criticism of Freud.[67] This may explain why Sulloway neglects the importance of the difficult relationships Galileo had with both parents as the main cause of his radicalism.

No less problematic is Sulloway's treatment of other radical firstborns. Their birth order is mentioned, but their radicalism is mostly played down in an ad hoc way and "explained" ("discounted" would be a better expression) as "creative puzzle-solving in science," or a "technical" revolution, like Watson and Crick's discovery of the structure of DNA that led to a revolution in molecular biology.[68] Sulloway imperturbably manipulates the dependent variable, radical innovation (which has to be explained): "Firstborns are much more likely to make scientific breakthroughs of a technical nature than they are to pioneer radical revolutions. Consistent with this trend, Watson and Crick are both firstborns, as was Linus Pauling, their closest rival in the race for the structure of DNA."[69] Sulloway's classification of technical revolutions also includes Harvey's discovery of blood circulation, Bacon and Descartes with their scientific method, Newton's discovery of celestial mechanics, Lavoisier's chemical revolution, Lyell's geological revolution (uniformitarianism), Freud's psychoanalytic approach, Wegener's theory of continental drift, and Einstein's special and general theory of relativity. In this way, Sulloway gets rid of no fewer than ten of his exceptions of firstborns who brought about a breakthrough in their respective fields: Harvey, Newton, Lavoisier, Lyell, Maxwell, Hertz, Freud, Pauling, Watson, and Crick.

Laterborns Bacon, Descartes, Huygens, Humboldt, Faraday, Planck, Wegener, and Hamilton hardly get further attention: for their pioneer work Sulloway confines himself to mentioning their birth order without referring to limiting conditions and other possible antecedents – briefly, a fundamental neglect of context. Here Sulloway has to pay for not having a full-fledged collective biography that allows analysis and comparison of case studies of radical innovators, spelling out differences and similarities. As noted before, Sulloway often falls into a *petitio principii*: what has to be demonstrated or proved is already (wrongly) accepted as proven. Sulloway does acknowledge that Maxwell and Hertz (also firstborns) have carried out pioneering work, in Faraday's slipstream, in the field of electromagnetic theory, but because of a lack of information about the reception of their work they do not get attention in his book.[70] With these statements, Sulloway clearly indicates his priorities: not with the pioneers but with the champions, the supporters of radical scientific innovations, and similarly not with the "technical" revolutions, but with the "ideological" revolutions in science. It is as if the work of all those dismissed firstborns was never controversial or raised resistance. Yet, in the second chapter of *Born to Rebel*, entitled "Birth Order and Scientific Revolutions," *all* twenty-eight classified revolutions and innovations are coded as "controversial."[71]

At the end of his chapter on exceptions, Sulloway presents so many provisos about his theory that he in fact withdraws it from testing and thus makes confirmation or rejection impossible. As he puts it, "Although my treatment of individual biographical instances, such as Kepler and Newton, may occasionally seem like post hoc attempts to salvage a theory about birth order, this approach is firmly grounded in the methods of science."[72] Sulloway does not specify which methods he has in mind. In a rhetorical turn he adds, "No single aspect of the family experience is an infallible predictor of human behavior, precisely because the causes of behavior are overdetermined. Multiple predictors therefore provide a far better guide to personality development than do single predictors."[73] At this point we are left with the question, who has ever seriously searched or looked for "infallible predictors" concerning human behavior? One may agree with the statement of cognitive psychologists, who have changed their mind about the long professed historiometry – large-scale one-factor analysis in their field – and are presently of the opinion that "predictability may have been a false god."[74] Moreover, Sulloway's "various combined predictors" all depend on the variable birth order with which they "interact."[75]

Instead of looking for "multiple predictors" in line with Sulloway's proposal, this book prefers comparative case studies with special attention to the position of prospective pioneers in sets of relationships – within the family and beyond. This comparative research shows how various forms of adversity have resulted in social exclusion as a necessary condition of radical innovation. Close attention to Sulloway's "exceptions" provided an heuristic effect and led to a reconceptualization of individual cases under the common denominator of adversity and exclusion as the general, necessary condition of radical innovation in science and the arts. All these widely different events (or "factors") – illegitimate birth, early parental loss, parent–offspring conflict, bankruptcy, poverty, chronic illness, physical deficiencies, minority status, peripheral origin, detention, and exile – are manifestations of one and the same mechanism: social exclusion following adversity.

This book thus recognizes an implication of Sulloway's theory: the position of laterborns may also, along with and analogous to comparable forms of adversity and exclusion, start radical innovation in science or the arts. In this way, the factor of birth order obtains a new aspect: laterborns may suffer adversity and experience social exclusion in the family. Hence laterborn status may appear as an independent variable – and necessary condition – along with those of parental loss, illegitimate birth, bankruptcy of parents, chronic illness, exile, etc.

To recall Einstein, the formation of a new point of view mostly turns around the recognition of the unity of a complex of known phenomena which in direct sensorial observation present themselves as totally separated things. Close inspection of Sulloway's exceptions led to the conceptualization of adversity and exclusion as the moving factor or mechanism of radical innovation in science and the arts. That is why they are, in this study, called "heuristic" exceptions. By chance they led to a new insight into the complex world of radical innovation in the history of science and the arts.

Radical innovation tends to come from outsiders, from people who, after suffering adversity and exclusion, stand with their back to the wall. They have little to lose and can therefore take more risks and notice and take advantage of windows of opportunity. As Sulloway concisely phrases it, "From a Darwinian point of view, the evolutionary costs of risk taking are low whenever the prospects of survival or reproduction are also low. Risk taking is a useful strategy in the quest to find an unoccupied niche, and it is an important component of openness to experience."[76] If you have little to lose, you can take more risks, but there is no certainty. Taleb reminds us, "Clearly risk taking is necessary for large success – but it is also necessary for failure."[77] Retrospectively, the success goes for all radical innovators; failure afflicts the majority – victims of *nature's broom*.

In spite of numerous shortcomings that have largely to do with the execution of *Born to Rebel*, it would be wrong to put the book away, as an early critic justly suggested.[78] One of my former teachers once remarked in an oblique reference, "sometimes one can learn more from a bad book – a book with serious shortcomings – than from a good book." Sometimes the writer can be wrong in an interesting way. Sometimes, too, the deficiencies of a book can serve as a "whetstone for the mind." Close study of Sulloway's unfortunate dealings with exceptions yielded heuristic results. Further research did more than indicate the limitations of the birth order model, it also drew attention to the analogies with the position of laterborns (as outsiders in the family), analogies which in their turn – as an important source of insight – opened the road to reconceptualization, whereby a considerable number of disconnected "factors" could be put together under a general denominator: adversity resulting in social exclusion – the double spur for the scenario of the way to pioneering achievements in science and the arts.

With his theory about birth order and family dynamics to explain radical innovation in science, Sulloway opened a rich vein. But instead of exploring this source further, he stopped and tried to fit the increasing number of exceptions into his original scheme, in which everything continued to turn on birth order. Although inspired by Darwin's work, and in particular by his principle of divergence and the related point of view that the costs of taking risks are low when the prospects and chance of survival are also low, Sulloway systematically avoided following Darwin's research strategy. Rather than accommodating his research model to his numerous exceptions, he chose the opposite: trying to get his staggering number of exceptions into his original birth order model.

Sulloway had an important point, but stared himself blind. As a consequence his model became a straitjacket. What moved him to prematurely close off a promising beginning? What kept him from taking the next step toward the design of a more inclusive model? This question also holds for the numerous supporters mentioned by name on the cover and the long list with which his book opens, who gave high but premature praise to the book and to the author for his achievement.[79] To answer these questions, one is reminded of what the American cognitive psychologist Robert Sternberg said on the blocking of new insights and how this works. "Often," writes Sternberg, "insightful solutions are blocked . . . because the problem-solver never allows himself or herself to explore whole regions of the potential solution space. People tend to buy high, pursuing only those potential problem solutions or ideas that are obvious or commonly chosen routes to problem solution."[80] Continues Sternberg, "Why do people limit themselves when working on a problem or project? As in financial investment, the key may be the risks, which are inherent to buying low ..."[81] Losing is indeed possible if one gambles with money or ideas. Yet those who do not take chances (risks) will get no reward. An echo of this point of view can be heard in Taleb's *Fooled by Randomness*: "as most successes are caused by very few 'windows of opportunity,' failing to grab one can be deadly for one's career. Take your luck!"[82]

Here the image of mainstream scientists emerges, the broad mass who drift with the stream and choose certainty, safety, and caution. They will certainly not run any risks. Their habitus and everything they stand for excludes the taking of risks. Because there is too much at stake, they "buy high" and practice *normal science*. Nevertheless, innovation and progress are both of fundamental importance for the scientific undertaking. But pathbreaking research cannot be planned. Innovation cannot take place without taking risks, educated guess-work, and trial and error – the formulation and testing of daring hypotheses. "Now, that the matter of no new truth," writes Peirce, "can come from induction or from deduction, we have seen. It can only come from abduction; and abduction is, after all, nothing but guessing."[83]

Comparative research and an eye for analogies turn out to be cogent sources of insight. Interdisciplinary research links up with this point of view. "Like in ordinary language, the language of science is tropological. And the most pervasive trope is the metaphor. We have found that models are metaphors which function like analogies and that non-propositional modes of thought are essential in scientific creativity."[84] This is to see the heart as a pump for the discovery of blood circulation, the orbits of planets considered as ellipses, to discover the universal law of gravitation from the fall of an apple and the tides from the movements of the moon, to note continental drift from slow lateral movements of huge masses like icebergs and glaciers, and to invent printing after observing the working of a wine press. For his discovery of natural selection as the mechanism of evolution, Darwin drew from no fewer than half a dozen analogies – from geology, the-ology, geography, economy, demography, and artificial selection.[85]

In the next two chapters we once more examine the background and antecedents of pioneers to further test earlier and provisional findings and consider additional cases. On the basis of a collective biography of groundbreaking scientists and artists, most of them living in Europe and North America during the past 500 years, we search for the hidden blessings of adversity and exclusion, keeping in mind Newton's adage, "no great discovery was ever made without a bold guess."[86] The question is who, under what circumstances, will

51

allow themselves to guess. A preliminary answer to that question says: those who have little to lose and can therefore take more chances – rather than the established, with their reputation vested in accepted truth. Decisive for both types is their place in sets of social relationships. As noted above, a majority of radical innovators came from the margins, from the peripheries of the family, of the community, and of society at large.

— 4 —

ADVERSITY

His eye-deficiency seems the most perfidious trick that fate could inflict on a stargazer, but how is one to decide whether an inborn affliction will paralyse or galvanize?
  Arthur Koestler on Kepler in *The Sleepwalkers* (1964: 239–40)

Most of the artists who survive the selection of history had a deficiency to overcome that inspired them to alter and expand the language of their art.
  Charles Rosen, "Prodigy without peer," *TLS* (2004: 3–4)

Property, class, talent, and education are seldom decisive for the development of new insights. A privileged position can inhibit creative achievement rather than encourage it. The evidence collated for this book shows that adversity and exclusion are crucial necessary conditions for radical innovation. Yet scholarly literature gives only incidental attention to adversity in the making of radical innovators. If it is noticed at all in one form or another, it is usually considered paradoxical – a hindrance to radical innovation. The concurrence of adversity and radical innovation, when noticed, mostly occasions surprise. Only analytical comparative research based on case studies can enhance understanding of their intimate interconnection.

Reviewing Jay Parini's biography of William Faulkner, J. M. Coetzee asks:

Who would have guessed that a boy of no great intellectual distinction from small-town Mississippi would become not only a famous writer, celebrated at home and abroad, but the *kind* of writer he in fact became: the most radical innovator in the annals of American fiction, a writer to whom the avant-garde of Europe and Latin America would go to school?[1]

53

William Faulkner (1897–1962) was a firstborn who often got into trouble with his shiftless father but was close to his mother, who encouraged his interest in literature. Save for a few interludes, he lived where he grew up: Oxford, Mississippi. He situated his novels and short stories there on the basis of what, from early youth, he saw, heard, and absorbed from his surroundings, and what he learned from great poets and writers. Faulkner not only failed at school and in military service, where he was initially rejected for being too short, but then on other fronts, too. His first stories and novels had no immediate success. Most local people considered him a loser, a good-for-nothing, a poseur – his nickname "the Count" later expanded to "Count No-Count" – a handyman, vagabond, and outcast who hung around, the scion of a famous lineage in decline and no match for a rich family's daughter, with whom he went to school and who shared his interest in literature. Her parents had her marry another suitor and she moved away. After getting divorced ten years later, she returned home with two children and married Faulkner.

It took years before his stories and novels were appreciated and widely known. This happened only after French translations of his novels appeared in the 1930s and 1940s – at the urging of a French literature professor at Princeton University – and they were enthusiastically received by Jean-Paul Sartre, Albert Camus, Simone de Beauvoir, and André Malraux, who made Faulkner known throughout Europe as an "important innovator." With ethnographic precision and from various narrative points of view, Faulkner shows how everyday local events interweave with great themes of history: the antebellum South, the aftermath of slavery, the decline of old landed families, and the rise of a new class of entrepreneurs. He sums up his work in an iconic aphorism: "The past is never dead. It's not even past."[2] The point is briefly and brilliantly rendered in the short story "A Rose for Emily" (1930) to which Bourdieu devotes one of his essays on the rules of art.[3]

Coetzee, himself an outsider, examines the first thirty years of Faulkner's life and also mines earlier biographies, yet misses all the telltale signs of a great writer in the making: he sees no more than "a would-be writer with an uncommon tenacity but without great gifts." But Faulkner's intellectual baggage, which Coetzee deems light, was actually substantial. He started writing early, and before the "matchless time" between 1929 and 1942 he not only read a great deal, but also published several novels. Asked in an interview how a person becomes a great writer, he answered: "Reading, reading, reading." Moreover, neither great "intellectual baggage" nor formal

54

education is a necessary condition for radical innovation. Both can equally block originality. Like other radical innovators, Faulkner built his achievements on informal instruction: self-education and feedback from mentors and friends. It proved crucial that he stayed a year in New Orleans under the tutelage of Sherwood Anderson before going to Europe for several months in 1925, after submitting his first novel, *Soldiers' Pay*, to a publisher.

Informal schooling was also decisive for that other great – some say the greatest – American writer, Herman Melville. In *Moby-Dick* Ishmael says, "if, at my death, my executors, or more properly my creditors, find any precious MSS. in my desk, then here I prospectively ascribe all the honor and the glory to whaling; for a whale-ship was my Yale College and my Harvard."[4]

Faulkner's blessings of adversity remain hidden for Coetzee, possibly because they are so obvious, especially so for a writer who is himself an outsider.[5] At the end of the review, Coetzee ponders Faulkner's chronic alcoholism, but fails again to note its connection with his position as an outsider – always more observer than participant and anything but sociable. Alcohol can put one beyond the pale of the moral community. Parini describes various events to which Faulkner was invited and (uneasy at the prospect of discomfort) showed up tipsy, and from which later in the evening (after more whiskey) he had to be led away.[6]

Recounting the life and work of Baruch Spinoza (1632–77) in *Radical Enlightenment*, Jonathan Israel is oblivious to the importance of adversity and exclusion in radical innovation. He is surprised that Spinoza's achievements as pioneer and backbone of the radical Enlightenment concur with his modest background, limited education, and outsider status. A Portuguese Jew, Spinoza belonged to a tolerated minority in seventeenth-century Amsterdam. His mother died when he was five, his father when he was twenty-one; in 1655 he was saddled with the bankruptcy of his late father's business and in 1656 excommunicated from the Jewish community for heresy. Israel implies that everything Spinoza achieved occurred in spite of – not because of – adversity and exclusion. He says:

> no one else during the century 1650–1750 remotely rivaled Spinoza's notoriety as the chief challenger of the fundamentals of revealed religion, received ideas, tradition, morality, and what was everywhere regarded, in absolute and non-absolute states alike, as divinely constituted political authority. . . . But is it likely, one may well object, or even conceivable, that any single seventeenth-century author, let alone an aloof, solitary figure raised among a despised religious minority who

lacked formal academic training and status, can have fundamentally and decisively shaped a tradition of radical thinking which eventually spanned the whole continent, exerted an immense influence over successive generations, and shook western civilization to its foundations? Can one thinker meaningfully be said to have forged a line of thought which furnished the philosophical matrix, including the idea of evolution, of the entire radical wing of the European Enlightenment, an ideological stance subscribed to by dozens of writers and thinkers right across the continent from Ireland to Russia and from Sweden to Iberia? The answer, arguably, is yes.[7]

Excepting the premature death of Spinoza's mother, Israel notes various relevant circumstances – his aloofness, solitude, minority status, bankruptcy of the family firm, excommunication from the Jewish community, and with it the loss of business connections – but does not recognize them as antecedents of radical innovation. Nor does he recognize the benefits of doing without formal education in the genesis of radical innovation. Spinoza's early self-education and informal apprenticeship with critical Cartesians in Amsterdam go unnoticed as building blocks of radicalization.

To explain Spinoza's radicalism, Israel first refers to fundamental changes in philosophic thought going back to Erasmus and Calvin, followed by Galileo and Descartes, who produced "the new rigorously mechanistic world-view, the indispensable conceptual apparatus – mathematical rationality as the sole and exclusive criterion of truth."[8] He then sketches the intellectual milieu in Amsterdam, especially Spinoza's friendship and meetings with the Cartesians he joined after 1650 and whose nestor (his Latin teacher Francis van den Enden) may have been his tutor. Already by 1660 Spinoza was a "mature and formidable philosopher deploying a complete new system, had disciples of his own, and could convince Oldenburg [the secretary of the Royal Society in London, who visited him in Rijnsburg] that he had outflanked Cartesianism."[9]

But reference to predecessors and Spinoza's mid seventeenth-century intellectual milieu (however important and interesting as necessary conditions) does not answer the question Israel raises: Why did Spinoza of all his learned contemporaries become a radical innovator? By ignoring or minimizing adversity and exclusion, Israel (like so many biographers) trips over his own question. Why Spinoza and not another learned contemporary like Leibniz or Spinoza's friend Huygens? The same reasons Israel cites for Spinoza apply to them too: predecessors, spirit of the age, intellectual climate are all necessary but not sufficient conditions, which Israel wrongly takes them for.

The irony of Israel's account is its mistaken assumption that Spinoza developed a radically novel point of view *in spite of* – not *because of* – his outsider status. He fails to notice the importance of self-education and the impact of informal apprenticeship with the Cartesians as an advantage over formal teaching at school and university, which can stifle rather than encourage originality. For these reasons, to the surprise of biographers and ordinary readers, some radical innovators at school were average or unremarkable students more interested in questions than in prearranged, drummed-in answers. Formal education, however important for citizenship and socialization in general, rarely captures the imagination of gifted students.

Spinoza had to cope with adversity and social exclusion early in life – especially the loss of his mother when he was five. He soon had a stepmother, his father's third wife, about whom little is known – as indeed little is known about Spinoza's early life except his excellent record at the Talmudic school in Amsterdam. His older brother died when Spinoza was seventeen, promoting him to oldest son and (with a younger brother) successor to his father's ailing business. And consider his status as a Portuguese Jew in Amsterdam. Israel uses the word "despised," but none of Spinoza's friends and acquaintances disparaged his ethnic background, though the aristocratic Huygens, who lived on his Hofwijck estate near The Hague and was Spinoza's neighbor for a time – occasionally visiting him to discuss their shared interests in astronomy and lens making – referred to him in letters to his brother as "that Jew." When he received the young Leibniz in Paris in 1672, however, he referred to Spinoza as "our Jew." He also had a high opinion of the *Tractatus Theologico-Politicus*.[10] These simple, almost careless, qualifications mark Spinoza's status as an outsider: "that" implies exclusion, "our" implies inclusion. Though he had friends and protectors, especially among the printers and publishers of his work, he preferred solitude and kept a low profile. Like Einstein, Kafka, Wittgenstein, and Perelman, Spinoza did not want to belong to any group, coterie, or community.[11] Hence his retiring lifestyle: first in Rijnsburg, then in Voorburg, and the last six years of his life in The Hague. In all three places, he rented rooms from friends and made his living by grinding and polishing lenses, which Huygens thought superior to his own.[12]

There was only one definite and formal exclusion: Spinoza's excommunication for heresy from the Jewish community in 1656 – the only community he ever belonged to and whose language (Portuguese) was the only one he spoke fluently. It occurred a year after the death of his father, who bequeathed a trading firm in trouble from the first Anglo-Dutch War (1652–4) when ships bearing cargo from the Mediterranean and Caribbean were seized. Israel describes all this in detail but confines analysis of its connection with Spinoza's revolutionary work to the remark that it hastened his decision to live in relative isolation and spend his time on philosophy.[13]

Spinoza's thought met with strong opposition from both religious and secular authorities. Much of his work appeared anonymously (B.D.S.), clandestinely, or posthumously. Printers, sellers, and buyers could be prosecuted. One of Spinoza's friends and followers, Adriaen Koerbagh, published two critical books, for which he was condemned to ten years in prison plus ten years of banishment – he died after a year in the Amsterdam Rasphuis.[14] In the *Ethics*, Spinoza writes that the notion of God as an autonomous judge who confers rewards and punishments is based on absurd anthropomorphism. He considered the basis of organized religion to be superstition, ignorance, and prejudice. In reality, he argues, God is simply infinite substance and as such identical to (the laws of) Nature.[15] Einstein was a great admirer of Spinoza. Asked if he believed in God, he replied, "I believe in the God of Spinoza."[16]

Despite three centuries of secularization, hostility to Spinoza has abated but not disappeared. In the Netherlands, long a clerical country where the division of society into separate religious "pillars" slowed secularization far into the twentieth century, Spinoza was rehabilitated only recently. Now a learned society, a scientific prize, and a study program carry his name; and a statue stands near where he grew up in Amsterdam. The wooden "Spinoza Cottage" in Rijnsburg outside Leiden where he lived in the early 1660s is in a dismal neighborhood and has just been renovated after years of neglect. In Israel he is anathema to many who cannot forget his *posto em cherem* in 1656.[17]

For very similar reasons, resistance continues against Darwin's *Origin of Species* even to this day for further undermining the foundations of traditional worldviews by giving a central place to a materialistic cosmology at the expense of Divine Providence. Darwin's biographers agree that the "materialistic" implications of his work caused him much trouble and may have contributed to his chronic illness. On the other hand, as Darwin acknowledged himself, his illness also made his work possible: it provided an excuse not to receive visitors, or made them leave early.

Israel's long essay on Spinoza suffers from the absence of a comparative perspective.[18] Without comparative case studies in the social and behavioral sciences, we are left in the dark about plausible connections. There is always the danger of getting stuck in ad hoc explanations. This is the Achilles tendon of the genre of the biography. Yet by chance we have at our disposal a comparative study in which Spinoza's life, work, and habitus are systematically compared with those of his contemporary Leibniz. In *The Courtier and the Heretic: Leibniz, Spinoza, and the Fate of God in the Modern World* (2006), biographer Stewart intuitively chooses to use a "negative" case in comparative research. Along with similarities, differences may help to identify critical factors to explain different outcomes.[19]

Looking at the similarities and differences between both scholars, Stewart develops a better understanding of the achievements of Spinoza linked with his position as an outsider: his "double exile" eventually made his radical step possible and liberated philosophy from theology.[20] This position of a double exile, according to Stewart, would become part of the driving force of Spinoza's philosophy. Because of this strategic position on the extreme margins of society Spinoza could clearly see that the old God was dying and that his theocratic rule was falling apart.[21] An offer of the chair of philosophy at the University of Heidelberg reached Spinoza in February 1673. This happened about six months after his protector Johan de Witt, together with his brother, was lynched by an Orange crowd in The Hague. After a month Spinoza politely turned the offer down for the sake of maintaining his peacefully retired existence in Holland. He concluded the letter to the Elector with the words, "my reluctance is not due to the hope of some better fortune, but to my love of peace, which I believe I can enjoy in some measure if I refrain from lecturing in public."[22]

Leibniz, on the contrary, remained in both his life and habitus, as in his work, loyal to the pillars of the *ancien régime*: church, king, and nobility. Hence he remained dependent on their patronage and protection, ruling out any chance of radical innovation. He was and remained the prototype of an insider and champion of the status quo – the "court intellectual par excellence," as Nadler puts it.[23] Not surprisingly, Leibniz always dismissed the work of Spinoza, the philosopher whom he probably secretly admired and perhaps also wanted to be.[24]

There is no lack of biographers who ignore the role of adversity and social exclusion in the making of radical innovators. Even those who notice both adversity and social exclusion may still be puzzled and see in them a contradiction or paradox. Paleontologist Stephen Jay Gould, an admirer of Darwin's work, in his review of the first volume of Janet Browne's biography, traces her picture of Darwin's youth at school and sketches him as a quiet, friendly, awkward, introvert figure who was inconspicuous – if his classmates could even remember him. Writes Gould: "Darwin did develop a passion for natural history, expressed most keenly in his collection of insects – but many children, then and now, are devoted to a similar hobby of a passing nature in a life that moves elsewhere."[25] No one, he considers, could have predicted *The Origin of Species* from a childhood insect collection. Darwin was an indifferent student in each stage of his formal education.

These characterizations confuse several things. First, Darwin's collection was not of a passing nature. It was the first step in a long life of systematically and passionately collecting natural specimens, eventually providing the evidence for his discovery of natural selection as the mechanism of the evolution of species. As both Gould and Browne could know, Darwin's "hobby" resulted directly from the early death of his mother when he was eight years old and when he was told by his father and his two older sisters never to mention her name. Earlier, biographer Bowlby convincingly demonstrated, on the basis of comparative research, how collecting insects linked up with Darwin's solitude and estrangement both at home and at school as a result of the death of his mother and the failing care of his surrogate parents.[26] Second, of course nobody could have predicted Darwin's *magnum opus* from a collection of insects, if only because history is contingent. But we do know that passionate collecting often follows the loss of a dear one, which in turn can, as in Darwin's case, lead to scientific interests.[27] Even when we cannot predict how a life will develop, we can try to read history backwards and find out under what circumstances and in what context a life might take this or that turn. As historian Carlo Ginzburg pointed out, "You can become an atheist because you are the son of a priest, but you can also become a saint. The outcome is predictable only retrospectively."[28]

Along with a depressive [and] authoritarian father, Darwin experienced the well-meant but annoying supervision of two older sisters, arming himself against it with a "doggedness" that suited him later on as a useful quality in his scientific work.[29] While he was a student at Cambridge, Darwin developed a passion for hunting, which biographer Browne correctly describes as obsessive, but she fails to detect in it a continuation of his collecting craze "by other means." She merely classifies these activities as a normal children's hobby and a customary leisure pursuit of the gentry, which of course they also were. For Darwin, however, hunting clearly had a very different function and meaning, which, according to the comments of his hunter colleagues, was apparently out of the ordinary. They asked him why he brought special ledgers to carefully record every partridge, pheasant, and hare he shot. Darwin answered that unless he carefully registered his booty, hunting had no meaning for him.[30] Darwin's (older) brother Erasmus did not collect insects and neither did he have any interest in hunting. Browne does not make much of Darwin's loss of his mother, because "the death of one of the parents at that time was not an unusual happening." She believes, therefore, that in our judgment we should not press our norms on those of the society at that time.[31] Together with Browne's previous general statements and judgments regarding Darwin as a child and adolescent, this remark also represents a categorical statement without any further illustration or empirical evidence, and ignores a long discussion among historians on the subject of changing attitudes toward death, starting with the well-known and pioneering work of Philippe Ariès, *The Hour of Our Death*, in 1977.[32]

These slips are remarkable for a biographer who claims and aspires to improve the genre (and is recognized for doing so) by paying more attention to the social context in which scholars like Darwin grew up.[33] Yet she does not record Bowlby's comparative description and analysis of the consequences of Darwin's early loss of his mother. Browne mentions his study in her bibliography, but does not refer to his work in the text. Darwin's scanty interest in formal education at school and university and his growing participation in informal education from mentors, most notably the natural history excursions with Robert Grant near Edinburgh and the botanical and geological fieldwork with John Stevens Henslow and Adam Sedgwick when at Cambridge, also fit a more general pattern in the lives of radical innovators. Where Browne and Gould are only able to see paradoxes and contradictions, and hold on to them uncritically, in the absence of a comparative perspective they miss significant connections. As Chantal Bruchez-Hall points out in her biographical essay on Freud,

> It is difficult for authors of a case study not to become prisoners of their subject. The stronger the lens used by the observer, the greater the possible discovery, and the greater also the danger of becoming so involved in one's case that one forgets to distance oneself from it. At that point, no generalization is possible.[34]

Similar misunderstandings appear in Fölsing's otherwise useful and bulky (over 900 pages) biography of Einstein. Rather than an intimate connection, he assumes a contrast between Einstein's marginal position and his early radicalism in his wonder-year 1905, when he was twenty-six and working full-time as a clerk, third class, at the Patent Office in Bern. For an "explanation" of Einstein's radical innovation, Fölsing lapses into psychological and biological reductionism and chooses the wrong metaphors:

> Although studying rather at the periphery of topical research, he paved the way [for himself] with the certainty of a sleepwalker to the central themes of the principal books and literature of the *Annalen der Physik*. In his letters to [his wife] Mileva it becomes clear that with the obvious instinct of a creative physicist, he knew how to separate chaff from wheat.[35]

Two pretentious and mystifying sentences that do not explain much.

A similar stereotype appears in an online biography of American playwright Tennessee Williams (1911–83) when the author's background is addressed with the following rhetorical question: "Who could have foreseen that this shy, sick, and confused young man would become one of America's most famous playwrights?"[36] A much earlier, anonymous essay on Tennessee Williams that appeared as a *Time* magazine cover story in 1962, however, recognizes the hallmarks of the making of a great artist who capitalized on early adversity.[37] In this particular case, we hear about his difficult relationship with his dominant, brutish father – a traveling salesman who considered him effeminate. But Williams had good relationships with his unhappy younger sister and his mother. He enjoyed a close bond with his maternal grandfather, who read to him Milton, Poe, Thackeray, and Dickens. A destabilizing move from Columbus, Mississippi, to St. Louis, Missouri, meant that he lost contact with his beloved grandfather and mentor. After three years at university in that city, he was put to work by his father as a typist and handyman in the shoe business he had just opened. Odd jobs elsewhere followed, when he had completed his university studies and accepted his homosexuality. Later came literary prizes and the patronage of key figures in the literary world that triggered his first big successes with *The Glass Menagerie* and *A Streetcar named Desire* in the 1940s. As material for these plays, Williams drew on numerous bitter autobiographical experiences.

At the end of his biography of the Dutch writer Maria Dermoût (1888–1962), Kester Freriks sums up, but misses – or takes for granted – the intimate connection between her position of outsider and her innovative work. "Although Maria Dermoût led a retiring life in both the Dutch East Indies and Holland, she conquered a firm place in Dutch literature."[38] The misunderstanding starts with the first word of the sentence. Freriks acknowledges the great international esteem for Dermoût after the publication of her novel *The Ten Thousand Things* in a brilliant translation in 1958.[39] He mentions that *Time* magazine considered the book one of the four best books of that year – along with Nabokov's *Lolita*, Pasternak's *Doctor Zhivago*, and Truman Capote's *Breakfast at Tiffany's*.[40] Freriks sketches an accurate picture of Maria Dermoût's life as an outsider yet he refrains from pointing out that it wasn't *in spite of* her retiring lifestyle in both worlds (including the Dutch literary world, which misjudged her first book, *Nog pas Gisteren* (*Only Yesterday*), that appeared in 1951 after having been rejected by four publishing houses in the Netherlands), but precisely *because of* that advantageous position that Dermoût could, in all her work, get to the heart of the colonial world of the Dutch East Indies. Only after the jubilant American reception of her second book, *The Ten Thousand Things*, set in the Moluccas, was her work widely recognized in her own country.[41]

How did Maria Dermoût become an outsider? She lost her mother when she was not yet one and had to deal with a stepmother and a distant father who managed a sugar factory on a plantation in central Java. These circumstances drove her into the arms and circles of the native servants. Already as a child she could look at the world from both sides. *Only Yesterday* is based on this early experience and testifies to keen observations and a no less attentive ear. As a child, and later as the wife of a magistrate, she kept some distance from "co-Europeans" and had a greater interest in the indigenous world and the interaction between colonials and the subject population.[42] Back in the Netherlands in the 1930s, solitude was again her companion and she stayed away from the established circles of Dutch writers, as well as from the Dutch-Indian subculture. She felt more affinity with the work of the poets T. S. Eliot, W. H. Auden, and W. B. Yeats.[43] Their work, too, resulted from an interaction between two traditions. As Eliot puts it in an interview,

> I'd say that my poetry has obviously more in common with my distinguished contemporaries in America than with anything written in my generation in England. That I'm sure of . . . . It wouldn't be what it is, and I imagine it wouldn't be so good; putting it as modestly as I can, it wouldn't be what it is if I'd been born in England, and it wouldn't be what it is if I'd stayed in America. It's a combination of things. But in its sources, in its emotional springs, it comes from America.[44]

Maria Ingerman (she later took the name of her husband, Dermoût) was born in the Dutch East Indies and grew up as a single child on her father's sugar plantation on Java. She was the daughter of his first wife, whom he had married by proxy from Holland. Six months after the birth of her daughter she died from an unknown illness. Presumably she was poisoned by one of the servants who had been her father's *njai* (concubine).[45] The sugar lord then married a German woman with whom he had no children, The wife remained a somewhat distant mother and governess. Dermoût's first novel, *Only Yesterday*, like all her work, was only completed after the Second World War. Based on notes and sketches made in previous decades, the book consists of what she saw and heard in the Indian world that surrounded her as a small girl. There are subtle references to violence from both sides of the colonial world: sneaky assassinations, the routine of corporal punishment on the plantations, and resistance in the form of arson (so-called sugar-fires), which once forced her, together with her stepmother and on the advice of her father, to take refuge in the mountains.[46] All her work shows the reverse side of *the pax neerlandica*: violence, especially hidden violence. Freriks identifies this aspect competently:

> Readers of her first novel, even professional readers at the time, were blind to the seamy side of the "silence and deep peace" in Dermoût's work. Terror, murder, sugar-fires, poisoning, hatred and violence, divorce, physical punishment of native workers almost to the point of death. These scenes are mostly recorded offhandedly in this book about an "irretrievable" past. This is also Maria Dermoût's "secretive Dutch Indies"; a world of cruelty, sometimes openly crude, often hidden, as the other side of the paradisiacal country.[47]

When she was twelve, Maria went to Holland for education in Haarlem – first to a school for girls, later to a grammar school (gymnasium). Much against her wishes, she lived with a family of a former pastor, whose physical intimacy she hated. She became acquainted with a boy next door, Aldert Brouwer, two years older, who later studied geology in Delft.[48] But this romantic relationship was broken off in December 1905 when her father and stepmother took her back to Java after the end of her father's leave. After only a few months, in August of the next year, when Maria was eighteen, she became engaged to the jurist and civil servant Dermoût, nine years her senior. Presumably she did not want to stay with her father on the isolated sugar plantation in central Java.[49] For her second book, *The Ten Thousand Things*, situated in the Moluccas, she could draw on her own experiences as well as those of her husband, a traveling magistrate charged with criminal prosecutions.[50] Although she was a devoted wife and gave him two children, her relationship with him was also detached, partly because of his long absences in connection with his work as a civil servant.[51] For Maria his traveling created space and time for writing.

Her position as an outsider in two worlds was emphasized further by her broken romantic relationship with her old high-school love, Brouwer, who became a geology professor at Utrecht University. His research took him to various countries, including the Dutch East Indies. She kept in touch with him for the rest of her life. Brouwer, however, who had also married in the meantime, never showed any serious interest in her, even after his divorce from his wife. "All her life Maria Dermoût cherished affection for her former friend . . ."[52] Although they met occasionally – in the Dutch East Indies and later, after her return to Europe, in various places in the Netherlands and Switzerland – this silent love remained unrequited and the short meetings always ended in disappointment.[53] As may have happened to the Anglo-American poet Auden, whom she greatly admired (as noted above), Dermoût's work was inspired by an unrequited love. His lines "If equal affection cannot be / let the more loving one be me" must have strongly appealed to her.

Exclusion, uprooting, solitude, leaving and loss of a dear person abound in Dermoût's life. They induced the creation of a small but innovative oeuvre that also changed our views of both sides of colonial life. For a time, the universal, timeless value of her work remained largely unrecognized. As we have seen, this changed after *The Ten Thousands Things* appeared in the United States in the superb translation of the Dutch-American writer Hans Koning. As one reviewer wrote: "In translation the book is an extraordinary reading experience, an offbeat narrative that has the timeless tone of legend. The book unfolds against the rich, colorful background that author Dermoût knows so well and handles so effectively. The story is pervaded by an ominous undercurrent of violence."[54]

Adversity could also strike highly placed and privileged people. This happened to Francis Bacon (1561–1626), known for his insistence on painstaking empirical research – a major contribution to the great scientific revolution of the seventeenth century. The importance of his discovery is sustained if we recognize that fundamental innovation in science has resulted not only from Bacon's induction method, but also from an understanding of the importance of sharp-witted conjectures and guesses: the formation of hypotheses which can be tested, confirmed, reinforced, or falsified.[55] The work of his contemporary, the astronomer Kepler, is perhaps one of the earliest and perhaps also the most elegant example. Theoretician Kepler could make use of the observations of his former boss, empiricist Tycho Brahe, to discover the elliptical orbits of planets.[56]

Bacon belonged to the British nobility. He was highly educated, and closely connected to both the English and the French courts. When he was eighteen, his father died and left him – as the second son of his second wife – without much of an inheritance. Bacon had to borrow money to finish his law studies. His applications for public office initially failed, in spite of support from influential patrons, including his own uncle. After he had, at an advanced age, reached the influential position of Lord Chancellor, he was, possibly unjustly, accused of accepting bribes. He fell from grace and had to retire on his estate. According to his biographers, Bacon's fall from power had a fortunate side because his house arrest also meant liberation from the social commitments integral to the fulfillment of public office. His exile resulted in a remarkable burst of literary and scientific achievements.[57]

A century earlier, a similar form of exile created distance and insight for Machiavelli (1469–1527). Early in 1513, after the Medici returned to power in Florence, he lost his protector and his position. Suspected of conspiracy, Machiavelli was taken prisoner and tortured. He was set free but forced to retire (with his wife and six children) to his estate near San Casciano, a village not far from Florence.[58] This turn of fate provided the opportunity to reflect on his past activities as a foreign envoy, diplomat, and secretary, and second chancellor of the Florentine Republic. He could also resume his studies of the classical writers and complete his masterwork, which appeared a few years after his death: *Il Principe* (*The Prince*) became the bible of realpolitik – and still "retains its power to fascinate, to frighten and to instruct."[59]

Little is known about Machiavelli's early life. He described his background as follows: "I was born in poverty and already at an early age I learned to deal with adversity rather than to flourish." He came from noble but not rich Tuscan lineage as the oldest son with two older sisters and a younger brother. He received standard, not specialized, instruction, including Latin and mathematics, essential for law study and a career in church or state. Presumably, Machiavelli developed by self-education. "If Machiavelli was an onlooker in that he usually regarded events, and always himself, with some detachment, he was at the same time an avid participant both in public affairs and private relationships."[60] His work in exile on his estate with his wife and six children was also a release from personal distress. This appears from a letter he wrote to his friend Francesco Vettori where he describes how he spends his days on his estate near San Casciano. The letter is regarded as perhaps the most famous letter ever written by an Italian.[61]

Demotion and exile also inspired one of Machiavelli's favorite writers, Thucydides (460–395), to write his *History of the Peloponnesian War* – a prime example of analytic history that is still widely read and studied.[62] An aristocratic general from Athens, Thucydides was demoted and banished for twenty years after he failed to prevent his Spartan opponent Brasidas from taking the city Amphipolis in Tracia. Brasidas arrived there a day earlier. Thucydides wrote his book "not as an essay which is to win the applause of the moment, but as a possession for all time."[63]

Only fragments are known about the life of Thucydides, but this is what he tells the reader in passing in the last sentence of this quotation from Book 5: an observation that attests to great insight and directly links up with the argument of this book.

> I certainly remember that all along from the beginning to the end of the war it was commonly declared that it would last thrice nine years. I lived through the whole of it, being of an age to comprehend events, and giving my attention to them in order to know the exact truth about them. It was also my fate to be an exile from my country for twenty years after my command at Amphipolis; and being present with both parties, and more especially with the Peloponnesians by reason of my exile, I had leisure to observe affairs more closely.[64]

According to classicist Ronald Syme, we can infer several important things from the little that is known about Thucydides.

> Thucydides came to his vocation with signal advantages. First, his time of life. When the war broke out in 431 he was "of an age to comprehend," so he states (v.26.5). His standards tend to be exigent, therefore he was not at this time some mere youth. Let it be assumed that Thucydides was born about the year 460.
>
> His family was among the first at Athens. The father was Oloros, a foreign name. That permits a deduction: Thucydides derives his descent on the maternal side from the family of Mitiades, who married a Thracian princess, the daughter of an Oloros. Therefore, Thucydides is likened to that older Hellas of the aristocratic tyrants and the dynastic families, to the men who were too big for the *polis* of citizens because of their power, their resources, and their fame outside their own cities. The men, it might happened, who are suitable candidates for being thrown out by ostracism.
>
> Next, after birth and station, the education of Thucydides. It falls in a high period of developing intelligence, with the Sophists turning

from speculation about the nature of things to the Science of Man – and with the Greek tragedians. These are twin components in the art and the make-up of Thucydides. He was present at Athens in the first seven years and heard the great debates in the Assembly. Then, in 424, a command in the North. One day he came too late, Amphipolis was lost: exile was the penalty.

Twenty years away from Attica until the fall of the city in the year 404 BC, Thucydides acknowledged the advantage. It enabled him to travel and to see the other side. But there is something more, which he has not said: exile may be the making of an historian. That is patent for Herodotus and Polybius. *If a man be not compelled to leave his own country, some other calamity – a disappointment or a grievance – may be beneficial, permitting him to look at things with detachment, if not in estrangement.* In Thucydides there is estrangement proclaimed by the creation of a style individual, wilful, elaborate, and non-contemporary. Even did the style not avow it, the author parades as a thinker with a method all his own. He is proud, imperious, even didactic. In the first place, hard work and accuracy.[65]

This sketch of the interweaving between Thucydides' life and work, with the emphasis on his exile, was grist to my mill and sums up with a single formulation the core of the argument of this book. How radical innovation in a certain field can be the result of a specific scenario: adversity and privations ("calamities") leading to social exclusion, the status of outsider, estrangement from what is generally accepted or taken for granted – and the raising of questions about established truths. Freed from social restrictions, with no need to be liked by anyone, and learning from two main contemporary intellectual and artistic trends – the philosophers and the tragedians – Thucydides could design a totally new approach, emphasizing strict standards in collecting evidence, carrying out an analysis in terms of cause and effect, propagating political realism, and hence considering relations between nations as based on power rather than law and justice; and trying to account for human behavior in extreme situations: plagues and civil wars. Syme makes it clear that Thucydides' work embraces more than new methods of historical research: it also marks the beginning of a human science, a new way to see the world which, apart from Machiavelli's *The Prince,* Hobbes's translation of Thucydides' *History* (1628) and his *Leviathan* (1651), and Clausewitz's *On War* (1832), had largely been ignored for well over two millennia.[66]

Three fundamentally innovative books on politics and war were written in exile. Because of their timeless insights they still appeal to us: Thucydides' *History of the Peloponnesian War*, Machiavelli's *The Prince*, and Clausewitz's *On War*. They span two millennia. Again the question: why Clausewitz? What was so special about him?

Carl von Clausewitz (1780–1831) was the fourth and youngest son of a poor middle-class family. He grew up in Burg near Magdeburg in Prussia, a provincial nest, a small town seventy miles southwest of Berlin. Clausewitz also "came from the provinces." His grandfather, himself a son of a Protestant (Lutheran) pastor, had been a theology professor. His father had served as a lieutenant in the Prussian army. Clausewitz grew up in a charitable family of disputed nobility on the edge of poverty.[67] In the footsteps of two older brothers, Clausewitz started his military career as a *Junker* in the Prussian army. He was then twelve years old. He spent his teenage years in active military service, saw the conquest of Mainz and exulted with his comrades at the sight of the burning city, behavior of which he later felt ashamed. Along with the campaigns came service in barracks, during which he could read. This was the start of his self-education together with his training at the military academy in Berlin, with General Gerhard von Scharnhorst as mentor.[68] Clausewitz became a major-general and with the Prussian army – and once with the Russian army – took part in four coalition wars against Napoleon. With his patron Scharnhorst he reorganized the Prussian army after the defeat at Jena in 1806, and together with other Prussian officers, he served with the Russians in the Russian campaign (1812–13). In East Prussia he learned a great deal about the employment of popular armies in large campaigns. While serving the Russian Empire, Clausewitz also helped to put together the coalition which would eventually defeat Napoleon and his allies. Joining the Prussian army again, he took part under General von Blücher in the Battle of Waterloo. Afterwards Clausewitz was rebuked because he allowed Marshal Grouchy, who was with his forces near Wavre, to escape to Paris before the Prussians arrived. He was demoted but was allowed to teach at the military academy in Berlin.[69] As so often happens, this adverse experience meant relative isolation and Clausewitz made good use of it. Between 1815 and 1830 he could work on his book *On War*, later proclaimed as "without doubt the most important work ever written by one man about the theory of waging war and strategy." His demotion was partly brought about by his superiors, in particular the Prussian king himself, who was not pleased by Clausewitz's sudden transition (with other Prussian officers) to the Russian army in 1812. The king considered it betrayal.[70]

Clausewitz had an early involvement in court life and was charged with the education of the princes. In 1804 he met Marie Countess von Brühl, who belonged to the high nobility. Six years later he married her, in spite of the considerable difference in social status, a circumstance that had postponed marriage for several years. They had a romantic and intellectual relationship. The marriage remained childless.

Clausewitz did not have a chance to finish and revise his book. In 1830 he had to stop his work when he was mobilized to prevent a potential revolt in the Prussian part of Poland, because Polish patriots in the Russian part were rebelling against the Russian reign of terror.[71] Clausewitz died in 1831 in Breslau (now Wrocław) during an outbreak of cholera when he tried to construct a *cordon sanitaire*. His wife edited Clausewitz's book, completed its last two chapters, and published his masterpiece posthumously.[72]

Adversity could also strike people with an unattractive appearance, small stature, or other physical deficiencies that singled them out from the common run of mortals – as a stigmatized individual and sometimes an object of ridicule. This was the fate of Gottfried Leibniz (1646–1716), who with his contemporary Newton was counted as the co-inventor of calculus – he disputed for years with his English colleague over who had the honor of being first. Leibniz was the first son of the third marriage of a philosopher professor at the University of Leipzig, who died when Leibniz was six years old. His mother raised and educated him and gave him access to his father's library when he was seven. After his studies in mathematics and philosophy at the University of Leipzig, the erudite and widely read Leibniz took time to look for an aristocratic protector. In 1676 he found a position as librarian at the Hanover court of the Duke of Brunswick, who would remain his patron until Leibniz's death in 1716. Leibniz rarely showed up, however, because of his frequent travels, his advice to other princes, and a long stay in Paris, which included discussions with Huygens, whom the French king had appointed director of the Academy of Sciences. Leibniz also visited colleagues at the Royal Society in London and became a member. On his trip from England to Hanover in the fall of 1676 he visited Spinoza in The Hague some months before the latter's death.

We have a written portrait of Leibniz, who also had himself painted on a number of occasions in works which all convey an idealized image of this philosopher, who had the reputation of not always operating in good faith.[73] On his way to Spinoza's house at the Paviljoensgracht in The Hague in November 1676, Leibniz is described as follows:

> He was of smallish frame, with an unavoidable nose and keen, scrutinizing eyes. He carried his head far forward of his hunched shoulders, and he never knew what to do with his arms. His limbs, it was said, were as crooked and ungainly as those of Charon – the old and sulky ferryman of the dead. As he lurched along the leaf-strewn canals of The Hague, his elaborate robes flapping in the autumn wind, he must have looked like an exotic, gilded bird of prey.[74]

Leibniz remained single. He died in the arms of a servant and donated his inheritance to his sister's son. As a vain protégé of crown, church, and nobility, Leibniz remained more courtier than innovating scholar. With all his erudition and mathematical sharpness, he continued believing in the status quo and in a world created by God.[75] Leibniz could not compete with the unassuming, retiring outsider Spinoza, with his austere lifestyle, who, as noted earlier, alongside scientific work made a living by grinding and polishing lenses.[76] In contrast with the tours of Leibniz, modest and amiable Spinoza did not need to travel or to impose on other people. He was already famous before he had published anything. His friends visited him in his refuges and in turn they invited Spinoza to visit them.[77]

Leibniz was not the only famous hunchbacked German philosopher. Physical deformation was also the fate of Georg Lichtenberg (1741–99), author of a collection of famous aphorisms. He was a hunchback because of a malformation in his spine after he suffered from rachitis as a child. He would not grow taller than five feet. Lichtenberg was the youngest of seventeen children. His father was a pastor and taught him mathematics and physics, but he died when Lichtenberg was still at grammar school. At the gymnasium in Darmstadt he was top of his class, because of his "zeal" and "industry." Through intermediaries, his mother obtained a scholarship from the Elector to have her son study at the University of Göttingen, where Lichtenberg was appointed professor of mathematics and physics just before he was thirty years old. Due to his defect, Lichtenberg remained small even by the standards of his time – a circumstance that prompted biographer Bilaniuk to note: "A permanent deformation of his spine in his youth possibly reinforced his propensity for scientific work."[78]

With this observation, Bilaniuk shows how the adversity of a stigma can be dealt with: by connecting with a social sector of companions in distress and ordinary people who do not see physical defects as shameful stains, but regard them as irrelevant and therefore as characteristics that do not overshadow but reveal a person's other qualities, contributing to their development. This is a variant which is absent in Erving Goffman's famous study *Stigma*, which deals with the management of spoiled identity, while the author himself, who was short, successfully dealt with his stigma.

Lichtenberg was known as a zealous, witty, and popular teacher in the many subjects he was in charge of, and this brought him friendships with colleagues beyond his home base and university. During his two visits to England he likewise made himself beloved and became friends with the king, who admired him very much. Lichtenberg is mainly known for the *Aphorismen* he wrote down in what he called his *Sudelbücher* or "scrapbooks." Published posthumously, they reveal how far he anticipated twentieth-century psychology, philosophy of language, and theory of knowledge.[79] It could be added that Lichtenberg, in one of his aphorisms, anticipated Darwin's theory of evolution in which natural selection is indicated as the mechanism for the development of species: "the spider spins its web in order to catch flies. But it does this before it knows that there are flies in the world."[80] One of Lichtenberg's biographers refers to the tradition of writing aphorisms: Montaigne, La Rochefoucauld, Nietzsche, and Wittgenstein.[81] To this series one may add Arthur Schopenhauer. Lichtenberg long remained unmarried, but had many romances, mostly with young girls from poor families whom he employed as maids. Later he married one of them, who gave him six children. He made arrangements to ensure she did not remain without means – she outlived him by forty-nine years.[82]

It is not only Protestant countries like the Calvinist Dutch Republic, later the Kingdom of the Netherlands, that maintain the unwritten rule – and cliché – that you should not judge people by their (outward) appearance. Meanwhile, whether in the past or the present, everybody knows better. It is the first thing people do when they first meet somebody. Looks are everything – in the family, at school, in applying for a job, at work, in the public domain, and not least when looking for a partner. Today, cosmetics is a major industry, as is plastic surgery. Moreover, physical exercise (sports) is one of the most popular leisure activities.

Among radical innovators a deviant appearance is not the exception. Yet when it comes to the physical appearance of their subject, biographers follow the social code, if they refer to it at all. Portraits of innovators are unreliable. Deviant and revolting features are mentioned at best in passing. Readers tend to assume that, apart from caricatures, portraits of their heroes are more or less true to nature.

Celebrated and famous for five centuries, Erasmus had a strikingly small frame, at least according to one or two passing comments in letters from his friends in England and Germany.[83] Yet this does not show on the famous Holbein portraits, nor on any other picture of him. His smallish build may have determined his position in society and, along with it, his actions, greatness, and influence. Born a few years before Erasmus's death, Montaigne dedicated one of his essays to the subject of a small posture. In line with the intention of his work, he started with himself. Montaigne describes himself as rather small of frame. He makes it clear that he is not so much concerned with the physical appearance itself, but the reaction of the entourage: the "looking down" (abasement) and ridicule of the victims, bowed down under social exclusion. The question is how to deal with this. The case of Gogol is instructive.

Nikolai Gogol (1809–52) came from the provinces. As this book argues, this may be an advantage for a prospective innovator. Gogol was born on a small landed estate in Ukraine, then called "Little-Russia." As the eldest son (with three younger sisters and a brother who died early), he was and remained the favorite of his mother, who had had two miscarriages before Nikolai was conceived. She would survive him. Both had a hard time when Nikolai went to college in a town not far from Kiev and lived there with the other students, only coming home during the summer holidays.

We have reliable descriptions of Gogol's appearance, which do not accord with the strongly idealized paintings. First, he had a small frame. At school he was nicknamed "the mysterious dwarf" and also bullied because of his unattractive features. His biographer Troyat mentions his long and drooping nose and how, as a schoolboy, he walked with a stoop and was very thin.[84] At school Gogol kept his teasers at bay with his gift of imitation and satire. "He . . . disclosed all the absurd or petty traits of those around him – as though a magnifying glass stood between his eye and the object of its attention. Faces sagged, noses grew, warts expanded into planets. He was later remembered as an extraordinary actor, particularly in grotesque female roles in school productions."[85]

In the higher classes at school there was a lot of reading, especially of the classics, and with his friends Gogol became an admirer of Alexander Pushkin, ten years older. After his final examinations he went with one of his school friends to St. Petersburg. He wanted to become an actor but had already failed at auditions. His narrative poem, *Hans Küchelgarten* (1829), also was not a success. Gogol collected all the copies and burned them, helped by his servant, a boy he had taken with him from Ukraine. After that he was financed by his mother to go to Lübeck, and returned without success, only to fail once more as an impromptu teacher of the medieval history of Russia at the University of St. Petersburg. Gogol seems to anticipate the heroes of his literary creations – and the witticism and recommendation of his later admirer Samuel Beckett: "Try again. Fail again. Fail better."[86] But a collection of stories in 1831, based on folkloristic materials his mother sent at his request, became a big success and led to friendship with Pushkin, whose protégé he became and who gave him advice, and also suggested the themes for *The Government Inspector* and *Dead Souls*. Gogol also made use of his own defects, including his physical deformities, which he stylized to the point of absurdity, as he did in the story *The Nose*, in which this part of the human body started to lead a life of its own. It was a shame that his most famous story, *The Overcoat*, which Pushkin might have enjoyed for its grotesque realism, appeared after the death of the poet in a duel he himself provoked. Pushkin had a small build and unattractive features, though there is no sign of that on his paintings. He was aware of his appearance. In a gloomy mood, referring to a distant ancestor, he said he was "the ugly descendant of negroes."[87] But the stature and deformities of the famous poet did not prevent his success with women.

This also holds for his contemporary Alexis de Tocqueville (1805–59), who certainly was not ugly, but had a small build (he was 5 feet 4 inches tall). Tocqueville himself claimed his small size "had brought him only advantage" – probably a reference to the womanizing he did not abandon after he married his English wife, even though he knew she suffered from his unfaithfulness.[88] Tocqueville's remark suggests that a small stature (for men) was generally considered a deficiency and supports a popular belief that women may fall for short men because they are better in bed.

To return to Gogol, his reputation and influence as a writer in nineteenth-century Russia appear from a famous, but possibly apocryphal remark attributed to Dostoevsky: "We have all come out from under Gogol's *Overcoat*."[89] The later impact of this short story and Gogol's two novels (of which the second one, *Dead Souls*, remained unfinished) elsewhere in the world can hardly be overestimated. In his Preface to *Dead Souls*, George Gibian writes:

> The twentieth century brought revivals of the socially conscious interpretation of Gogol and a return to the "realistic" conception of his work. The formalist critics and scholars studied his work as masterpieces of artistic composition and analyzed his devices and techniques.

The influence of Franz Kafka and World War I led to an emphasis on Gogol's grotesquerie. Western "literature of the absurd" found spiritual and artistic kinship in Gogol, as did the existentialist movement around World War II.[90]

What Gogol accomplished must be seen in the light of his position as an outsider in nineteenth-century Russia. That position was a very particular one, not only because he was a homosexual and his infatuations remained unrequited, but also because he came from the provinces. According Andrei Sinyavsky and Richard Peavar, his art was born at a crossroads:

> The road that brought Gogol from the depths of Little Russia intersected with Nevsky Prospect, "all-powerful Nevsky Prospect," in the heart of the capital. His art was born at that crossroads. It had the provinces in its blood, as Andrei Sinyavsky puts it, in two senses: because Little Russia supplied the setting and material for more than half of his tales, and, more profoundly, because even in Petersburg, Gogol preserved a provincial's "naive, external, astonished and envious outlook." He did not write from within Ukrainian popular tradition, he wrote looking back at it. Yet he also never entered into the life of the capital, the life he saw flashing by on Nevsky Prospect, where "the devil himself lights the lamps only so as to show everything not as it really looks" – this enforced, official reality of ministries and ranks remained impenetrable to him. Being on the outside of both worlds, Gogol seems to have been destined to become a "pure writer" in a peculiarly modern sense.[91]

With Gogol's art we touch again the theme of this book: radical innovation based on the perspective of the outsider positioned between two worlds – referring, too, to the position and "exotopy" of the anthropologist as ethnographer, as Sahlins puts it: "It takes another culture to know another culture."[92] In a review essay, anthropologist Elizabeth Colson (1917–), retired and living in the hills near her university in Berkeley, looked back at her work: "We live between two worlds and feel somewhat detached from both, but each gains meaning through its contrast with the other."[93]

The *Essays* of Montaigne (1533–92) have been much appreciated since they appeared at the end of the sixteenth century – a rare event in the creation of a totally new genre: resistance to innovation is more common. For more than four centuries his essays have been influential on the work of numerous great writers. New editions and translations of these short *essais*, which are not infrequently about Montaigne himself, still appear. The essays were intended that way: as attempts (*essais*) at self-analysis, intimate and open-hearted – not an autobiography, but an account of his fancies, his imagination, his ideas, his habits. This sounds modest, writes Rosen in a review of the latest edition of Montaigne's work in an English translation, but the project became one of the most ambitious enterprises in the history of literature; and Montaigne himself believed that his project had never been tried before: "His idea of philosophy was not of an effort to reach the truth, but an investigation of the way the mind worked – fallibly, capriciously, unpredictably."[94]

What inspired Montaigne to embark on this work were his persistent feelings of loss after the death of his close friend Étienne de La Boétie when Montaigne was thirty years old. This experience, after three years of passionate friendship, resulted in the periodic solitude and *mélancolie* which accompanied him all his life. Asked about his lasting sorrow, Montaigne replied: "I cannot explain it." Later he wrote: "Because it was him and because it was me." The loss of his kindred spirit led Montaigne to write his essays to fill a void, to remove a deep dissatisfaction that came with the premature death of his friend. He wanted to know himself as his friend had known him.[95] Biographers agree that Montaigne began his work "about himself" to deal with the death of a friend with whom he had shared a specially close and intimate relationship.[96] As Screech puts it, "So at the outset *otium* brought Montaigne not happy leisure and wisdom but instability. Writing the *Essays* was, at one period, a successful attempt to exorcize that demon."[97] Psychoanalysts see a direct connection between loss and creativity. They point to the large number of orphans among creative and famous people, and argue: "all creation recreates what we once loved and then lost."[98] According to this interpretation, the bereaved continue creating because no creation is good enough to replace the (idealized) loved person. However plausible, this proposition is easier illustrated than proved.

After the death of his friend, solitude and alienation drove Montaigne to his project of self-research in his *Essays*, as he also recognized himself.[99] It may have fortified his position as broker between the spokesmen of the fighting parties – Catholics and Protestants – on regional and national levels. In turn, these mediating activities may have reinforced his relativism and skepticism. He remained an outsider, an observer, like Kepler, Rimbaud, and Kafka, who could speak and write about themselves in the third person. Hence Montaigne's *Essays* project, in which he wanted to know himself as his prematurely lost friend La Boétie had known him.[100]

As a firstborn (with three younger brothers) in a country where primogeniture was the rule, Montaigne inherited from his father

"Montaigne": the chateau and estate, located in Périgord, an area northwest of Bordeaux, in the Dordogne. He was then in his late thirties, financially independent, and he would spend the twenty years that remained of his life in writing the *Essays*, secluded with his books in the tower of his chateau. He was well-to-do, largely free from social obligations as a magistrate and city official and as consultant and diplomat connected to the Court in Paris of both Catholic and Protestant kings. The first two volumes of the *Essays* appeared in 1580, and the next volume in 1590, after a trip through Germany to Italy where, in the company of his youngest brother and some friends, he sought healing for his stomach pains in various spas.[101] The last edition, revised and supplemented, was published posthumously by his young friend Marie de Gournay some years after his death in 1592. In this edition of his *Essays*, Montaigne writes in a postscript how much this young woman, an admirer he met four years before his death, had meant to him. His enthusiastic description of Marie de Gournay contrasts with the mainly critical and detached image of women he gives elsewhere in the *Essays*, without making an exception for his mother and his daughter, who barely figure in his work. In the person of Marie de Gournay, Montaigne appears to have retrieved something of the passionate friendship and collaboration he had lost through the death of Étienne de La Boétie.

Montaigne's great-grandfather was a wine trader in Bordeaux. In 1477 he bought the Montaigne chateau and estate and became lord of Montaigne. After courageous military exploits, the family was ennobled. Montaigne had a good relationship with his father, who had been mayor of Bordeaux, an office Montaigne would twice hold himself. He liked his father but was more detached from his mother, who lived with him at the castle and would survive him. Montaigne appreciated company but felt comfortable being alone. An observation at the end of his essay "On Three Forms of Social Intercourse" attests to this detachment: "I find that it is somewhat more tolerable to be always alone than never able to be so."[102]

In his *Essays*, Montaigne also dwells on a number of human deficiencies, not least his own defects. Sometimes these are exaggerated, fitting the design of his book: merciless self-research. About his stature, he mentions that he is somewhat below medium size. He considers himself as small and directly connects this characteristic with social relations. Speaking from his own experience as a civil servant, administrator and adviser at the court, he notes in "On Presumption", "Now my build is a little below the average. This defect is not only ugly but unbecoming, especially in those who hold commands and commissions since they lack the authority given by a handsome presence and a majestic body ... Other beauties are for the women; the only masculine beauty is beauty of stature."[103] Conclusion: If a man has a small frame, nothing good about his head or body can make him beautiful.

Quite a few radical innovators were, according to their contemporaries, small of frame. It was generally considered a deficiency, probably also "ugly" and not infrequently also by those involved themselves. Picasso was painfully aware of his crooked legs and small stature.[104] Hobbes and Darwin were taller than six feet, possibly exceptional because it was specially mentioned. This also holds for the specific statements about a small build for Erasmus, Harvey, Descartes, Newton, Leibniz, Smith, Joseph Haydn, Beethoven, Franz Schubert, Faraday, Pushkin, Tocqueville, Gogol, Maxwell, Ibsen, Brâncuşi, Russell, Igor Stravinsky, Wittgenstein, Antonio Gramsci, Faulkner, Sartre, Capote, Roman Polanski, and Goffman: all of them were not much taller than about 5 feet 3 inches. Harvey (1578–1657), who explained the circulation of the blood and the function of the human heart as a pump in 1628, was the personal physician of two successive British kings. Contemporaries designated him "very small." Faraday (1791–1865) was the youngest son of poor, working-class parents, had little formal training, applied himself to self-education, and became an assistant and protégé of the renowned chemist Humphry Davy. Eventually, he became the father of all electromagnetic theories. Faraday had a strikingly small build – he was not much taller than five feet. Moreover, his head was one size too large for his body, so he looked even smaller than he really was. Faraday also had a speech impediment, which meant he could not pronounce his own name correctly and was bullied at school by his classmates and his teacher. This stopped when his mother sent him to another school.

The American sociologist Erving Goffman (1922–82) was small in stature. He became known and influential through his work on face-to-face relations, social interactions at a micro-level in public domains and closed institutions, including mental asylums, prisons, and old people's homes. In his book *Stigma* we are concerned with people with a physical deformity that determines and puts to shame their social identity, overshadowing all their other characteristics. They include people who are short, ugly, deaf, blind, limping, or who suffer from a speech impediment. Stigmatization involves a public reaction to a physical deviation from what is considered normal, something the stigmatized person is ashamed of and wants to hide.

This form of discrimination can also affect people with a criminal record, or hit them because of illegitimate birth, bankruptcy, or membership of an ethnic minority. People ascribe to them a social identity centered on the stigma.[105] (This is reflected in offensive nicknames that abound in face-to-face communities.)[106]

Goffman also discusses the management of spoiled identity – the subtitle of his book – that is, how people deal with their mark of infamy. Some of them withdraw into a subculture of companions in misfortune. Others join a circle of people for whom it is not the stigma but other distinguishing marks that are are important or significant. Still others make their way into mainstream society and try to make the best of it. As we will see, many radical innovators have a background of stigmatization. Social exclusion closely follows adversity. Nowhere is the relationship more visible.

Goffman's interest in the subject of stigma and stigmatization presumably goes back to his own experience of being a short person. "Presumably," because in his book he remains offscreen. Goffman is no Montaigne. Yet *Stigma* makes clear that its author draws on more than a solid knowledge of the sources on the subject. His inventive use of these sources suggests a great ethnographic familiarity with the subject – an affinity partly acquired through (initially unintended) participant observation, or "fieldwork." If this is indeed the case, Goffman may have ingeniously drawn on his experience of stigmatization and social exclusion and elaborated on it in numerous innovative publications on the behavior of people at a micro-level when it comes to unwritten rules of behavior regarding private territories and the protection and violation of those rules and territories. In this way, Goffman opened a road for himself to a new field of research and acceptance in a respected enclave of science. He found in academia a niche and environment in which his stigma was all but irrelevant and where his initially shadowed qualities came into light and could be further developed. Goffman must have noticed early on that in this environment he was not the only person who "deviated" from the norms of physical integrity that were in force outside of this "protected workplace." In the hall of knowledge other priorities were in force, other qualities took precedence.[107]

Goffman was indeed far from being the only one. The present book investigates an entire company of radical innovators, who were all inspired by adversity and exclusion, made good use of it, and opened new roads in their respective fields. Physical defects have received little attention in the history of science, if they were noticed and registered at all. It was not fashionable, *bon ton*, politically correct, to dwell on them. Portrait painters followed the same unwritten rule. There are, of course, exceptions. Caricatures are such an exception. Another exception and eye-opener is the observation of a biographer of Lichtenberg, already cited, indicating his physical shortcomings – his hunched and dwarfish build – and suggesting these defects might have reinforced his tendency to scientific work. An early intellectual start under the supervision of his father was decisive. For Lichtenberg, too, his deficiencies paled in the light of his scientific capacities, including those of teacher, charmer, conversationalist, writer of aphorisms, and wit. There has been hardly any investigation not only of adversity in the form of physical defects, but also of the paradoxical effects and the use that can be made of them. In a way, and in more than one sense, quite a few of the radical innovators reported on in this book were considered "misfits."

Contemporaries describe Beethoven (1770–1827) as rather small of stature. He had a large head and thick, bristling, coal-black hair; his forehead was broad, heavily underlined by fluffy eyebrows. He was solidly built and had short, thick fingers. He sometimes moved clumsily around the room, knocking things over. He was short-tempered, but always apologized. Some contemporaries found him "ugly," even "repelling," but many saw "the animation and expressiveness of his eyes, which reflected his inner feelings to an extraordinary extent – now flashing and brilliant, at other times filled with an indefinable sadness."[108]

It is unlikely that stature and outward appearance played a role in the making of the composer. They were overshadowed early on by his qualities as a virtuoso pianist and as a composer after his entrée in Vienna as the protégé of various aristocratic families to whom he dedicated his work.[109] In Beethoven's career, another physical defect was decisive in the development of his art: the extremely painful and paradoxical blow of the gradual loss of his hearing. His growing deafness, which started even before he was thirty, to his chagrin increasingly isolated him from his friends after he had turned forty. Yet he also realized that this provided more time for composing and freedom to experiment. The result was not only his best work (*Missa Solemnis*, the late string quartets), but also his most innovative work. This is why people still consider Beethoven the greatest composer of all time.[110]

From his earliest youth onwards, Ibsen (1828–1906) had to deal with successive calamities – to begin with, the rumor about his illegitimate birth. This literary giant, strikingly short, also came from the provinces. Ibsen grew up in Skien, a Norwegian coastal town, a small community southwest of the capital. His father was a well-to-do merchant from a prominent lineage in which trade and shipping had an important place. His mother had the same background. As a boy Ibsen heard the whisper that he was not the son of his father, but born from his mother's relationship with a former lover. When Ibsen was eight, his father's firm went bankrupt. The family had to leave the big house in the center of Skien and be satisfied with a summer house in the periphery.

Social degradation, worsened by the presence of a depressed and often drunk father and a mother who sought comfort in religion, led Ibsen to leave before he was fifteen. There was no money to continue his education and he had to support himself. He found work as an assistant to a pharmacist in a town with the ominous name of Grimstad. Further trials and errors followed. A romantic relationship ended badly: when he was eighteen he made a servant girl, ten years older than he was, pregnant. Ibsen had to contribute to the boy's education until he was a teenager. He never saw the child. An attempt to study at university failed and Ibsen set himself to write for the stage. His plays were not a success. Later he found a place as a stage manager in Bergen and was entrusted with preparing and staging performances, including plays he had written himself. Dissatisfied with the reception of his work, he took up the same position in the capital. As in Bergen he learned a lot, but his efforts met with little response and appreciation. The public wanted to be entertained and did not want to see serious stage work. Disappointed, Ibsen left for voluntary exile in the company of his wife and with a scholarship from the king (as a reward for a reasonably successful book). He settled first in Italy and later in Germany, where he lived with his wife and son at various locations to work on his pathbreaking plays, most notably *A Doll's House* (1879) and *An Enemy of the People* (1882).

Contemporaries from Ibsen's time in Bergen later remembered his small build and believed he was conscious of it and suffered from it. A girl who was a friend when he was twenty-five narrated thirty-six years later:

> When he was alone with you he could suddenly start to talk in a frenzied, ruthless torrent of words – paradoxes and wild truths, so that one walked bewitched beside the little man as he exploded savagely against all conventions. He sometimes said that he was a lonely person, and would always be a lonely person, whom no one believed in and no one, no one in the world, cared about. But there were other times when he would be quite silent and spent long periods shut up like a book. He was usually melancholy.[111]

Ibsen's mother-in-law, the Dane Magdalena Thoresen, gave a description of Ibsen's appearance around 1858 when he married her daughter: "Henrik Ibsen was a silent and withdrawn person to whom no one got closer than he, Ibsen, wished. This strong reserve became the weapon with which he kept clear the ground around him . . ." In the same memoir, Magdalena Thoresen mentions that as a young girl she had once met Søren Kierkegaard.

> It now occurs to me that there was a striking similarity between these two great spirits. Outwardly the resemblance was small: Søren Kierkegaard was long-striding and gangling, while Ibsen took short paces and had a squat build of a miner. What similarity there was must, therefore, have lain deeper; and so it was. I have never seen in any other person, male or female, so marked a compulsion to be alone with themselves.[112]

But there were also people who had quite different memories of Ibsen, from the time before he was married and was working as a pharmacist's assistant in Grimstad. One of his friends remembered the cheerful meetings with Ibsen on Sundays in the waiting room of the pharmacy. During one of these sessions, Ibsen asserted with some passion that he and his wife, if he ever had one, should live on different floors and not address each other as "Du."

> This was at that time his ideal of marriage . . . Gradually people began to notice this intelligent and witty young man, and the waiting room of the apothecary's shop soon became, especially on Sundays evenings, a favorite meeting place, to which friends were continually introduced. It was always fun, with Ibsen as the centre-point of the grateful circle, for he bubbled with humour, and, admittedly, with sarcasm too, and despite the poverty of his circumstances he was always in an excellent temper. He possessed to a high degree the elasticity of youth.[113]

Ibsen remained voluntarily in exile for twenty-seven years. He crowned this period of a retiring lifestyle with a series of plays, which provided western stage literature with a new "realistic" foundation. Moreover, his work did not fail to have its intended effect on society at large. His apprenticeship in Norway over a period of about ten years paid off, and extended further back to his early youth of adversity and self-education. In his plays, which appeared between the end of the 1870s and the beginning of the 1890s and were immediately translated from Danish (the language then also spoken in Norway), Ibsen denounced established opinions and customs, reaching back to experiences of adversity and exclusion during his childhood and early youth: illegitimacy, financial and economic machinations, vicissitudes, poverty, social degradation, hypocrisy, and the subordinated position of women and the abuse of control over them under the mask of protection. Indicative of the tenor of his work are the ironic titles of his plays, including *The Pillars of Society* (1877), *A Doll's House* (1879), and *An Enemy of the People* (1882).

"The master of modern theater," also called "The master of Realism," Ibsen became one of the five greatest dramatists in history, "realizing general truths through the most scrupulously detailed particulars."[114] Together with the Swedish playwright Strindberg, he changed the face of European theater in the last decades of the nineteenth century. They did not particularly like each other, did not visit each other, but continually kept an eye on one another – a classic example of *Doppelgängerscheu*.

In their work both Ibsen and Strindberg followed in the tracks of Schopenhauer (1788–1860) and Gustave Flaubert's *Madame Bovary* (1856). After his attention was drawn to this, Ibsen admitted – after some time – that he had learned a lot from Kierkegaard (1813–55). In relative isolation, both Scandinavian writers, Ibsen and Strindberg, brought into question mainstream norms and values. They examined in a modernistic, naturalistic manner the everyday reality behind the facades of family and community, Ibsen drawing on his experiences in small provincial settings, Strindberg starting from the disastrous marriages that followed his miserable childhood and adolescence.

August Strindberg (1849–1912) was the son of a barmaid and a businessman who married shortly before his birth. It was the second marriage of his father, and Strindberg had older half-brothers. He was four years old when his father went bankrupt (but later recovered) and thirteen when his mother died. After a year, his father married the maidservant. The boy and the stepmother, who also figured as a governess, did not get along. Just like his Norwegian counterpart, Strindberg failed on various fronts before he found a niche in litera- ture and became the author of the masterwork *Miss Julie* (1888)[115] and the self-analytical autobiographical novel *The Son of a Servant* (1886). To understand why the works of Ibsen and Strindberg were innovative and still speak to us, one cannot overlook the early adver- sity and social exclusion of their authors – destabilizing experiences on which they critically capitalized for their art in self-chosen exile.

Among various innovators, exile could take different forms: as a punishment, as in the cases of Thucydides, Machiavelli, Bacon, and Clausewitz, or more or less voluntary, arising from a search for freedom and solitude, Ibsen being a telling example along with several other innovators.

When the Spanish Civil War began, experimental filmmaker Luis Buñuel (1900–83) left Spain, first supporting Spain's Republicans from Paris and then taking refuge in the United States. There he tried to survive with his wife and children, relying on his friends for jobs in the world of theater and film. Buñuel's reputation suffered from the accusation that he had been a member of the Communist Party at the beginning of the 1930s, a time when he was at odds with his fellow surrealists, whom he reproached for having a middle-class mentality. The allegations came from the artist Salvador Dalí, his former friend and co-creator of *Un Chien Andalou* (1929), the film they had made together in France more than ten years earlier. During the making of a second film, *L'Age d'Or*, they fell out because of a passing remark from Buñuel that offended Dalí.[116] Dalí's accusations appeared in a book he wrote, and Buñuel was forced to resign from his job as film editor at the Museum of Modern Art in New York. He took refuge in Mexico, where he made various films (recently rediscovered) until his breakthrough with *Los Olvidados*, which won him the prize of Best Director at the 1951 Cannes film festival. In the next decades there followed a series of innovative feature films made in France and Spain, with predominantly French and Spanish actors, most of them in the unique style – parodic and ironic, often documentary – that became his trademark: *Viridiana*, *Diary of a Chambermaid*, *Belle de Jour*, *Tristana*, and *The Phantom of Liberty*.

Buñuel was a radical firstborn from a well-to-do, liberal family in Calanda, a village in the hinterland of Zaragoza, Aragon. Buñuel, too, came from the provinces. He received his primary education at a college run by Jesuits, who taught him French and Latin. This experience made an impression and later provided him with a target for his films: all forms of organized religion and superstition. After he had taken courses in various disciplines at the University of Madrid, he followed his father's advice and chose not entomology (although insects would interest him his whole life) but agrarian studies. He could combine this with biology, which would be useful because his father owned land. After his studies he traveled and worked briefly on the stage, and then directed his interests to the making of surrealist films. Although his parents were slightly disappointed, they supported him. His films were a *succès de scandale* and remained classics. This also holds for his *Tierra sin Pan* (*Land without Bread*) of 1932, also entitled *Las Hurdes*, a short ethnographic documentary, in surrealist style, about rural poverty, illness, and ignorance in a peripheral and backward area in Extremadura, south of Salamanca. For a long time, the film was banned in Spain. After *Los Olvidados* (also critically received in Mexico City, where it was shot), there followed surrealist masterpieces directed against the hypocrisy of the clergy and bourgeoisie.[117] The published text of *Viridiana* (1961) is provided with an epigraph, a programmatic statement by Buñuel: "For me, the morality of the bourgeoisie is its immorality, and we have to fight it. It is a morality based on our very unjust social institutions, including religion, the fatherland, the family, the culture, and finally everything that is called the 'pillars of society.'"[118]

The sources Buñuel drew on were those of formal education. His teachers told him that they kept nothing hidden from their students, and he blamed them for not mentioning the work of Darwin and de Sade, which he learned about only later from his friends.[119] He considered that these writers taught him as much about human behavior as his studies had about the behavior of insects.[120] "In de Sade I discovered a particularly subversive world in which really everything figures: from insects to human manners and customs . . ."[121] For Buñuel, de Sade presented a figure of endless fascination, writes Evans, especially because of de Sade's longing for completely unconditional freedom. When he refers to de Sade's liberating influence on his own work ("The imagination is free, man is not"),[122] "the work of deconstruction begins, for, however potent the ideal, the reality surely escapes few of the constraints of ordinary human thought and behavior."[123]

First alone and later with his family, living at the intersection of different languages and cultures often brought adversity, but it also provided Buñuel with the distance and the alienation which made him doubt the fundamental values of western civilization. As Evans puts it: "underlying [all his films] is a profound sense of exile, a theme characteristic of almost all his work . . . Exile, of course, has its many advantages, through distance creating awareness of the realities not only of one's adopted homeland, but also of the country left behind."[124] Clearly, as noted above, this observation links up with the point of view and experience of anthropologists who study other cultures.

In contrast to Buñuel, we have to understand the innovating achievements of another great filmmaker, Ingmar Bergman (1918–2007), in this case against a background of adversity at home. Both made controversial films. Yet their mainsprings differed, like the circumstances in which they grew up. As a sickly child in Stockholm, Bergman suffered under the regime of a tyrannical older brother and moral blackmail and corporal punishment from a stern and implacable father, who was a pastor. The situation in which he found himself corresponds to Sulloway's theory on the effects of birth order and sibling rivalry as key factors in radical innovation. From the 1960s to the end of his life, Bergman lived most of the year secluded in his house on Fårö, one of the Baltic islands. He considered it a place of self-exile.[125] Exile, including self-exile and seclusion in one's own country, was far from uncommon in the lives of radical innovators, in particular among artists. Spatial retirement reflected their marginal position in society and was at the same time a constituent part of their habitus.

Forced exile among scholars afflicted Thucydides, Erasmus, Machiavelli, Bacon, Galileo, Hugo Grotius, Descartes, Hobbes, and Clausewitz. Other scientists, including Curie, Einstein, Malinowski, Wittgenstein, Lévi-Strauss, and many more, left voluntarily. They included those who left when confronted by the imminent establishment of a police state, as happened in the 1930s with the exodus of intellectuals from Western Europe to North America. Among early examples of artists who had to leave their hometowns we find Dante Alighieri (1265–1321), who had to leave Florence for political reasons. Under adverse circumstances as an exile in various Italian cities, he found inspiration for his innovative work and his contribution to the development of the Italian language. Together with other innovators, Dante is an example of novel production at a later age. Dante lost his mother when he was twelve, just before he fell in love with Beatrice, a girl from the same town whom he could not marry because both families had assigned them other partners. This arrangement did not prevent Beatrice from becoming an inspiring ideal and playing a principal part in Dante's further life and work. In this case, too, loss and creativity go hand in hand.

Exile as a source of inspiration and imagination also affected Miguel de Cervantes (1547–1616). After his military career, which included service with the Spanish fleet in the Mediterranean, where he distinguished himself at the Battle of Lepanto, he was taken prisoner and sold as a slave in Algiers, where he remained for five years. Back in his own country, he was imprisoned again because of debts. While in prison in Seville, he started writing his masterpiece, *Don Quixote*. The book was an instant success, not least because of its language: the satirical novel of chivalry changed the colloquial language of the country.

Differently from Montaigne, his serene fellow countryman in Périgord two centuries earlier, de Sade (1740–1814) did not spend most of his time at the Château de Lacoste in Provence, with which his name is closely connected. The radical moral relativist spent many years in other, involuntary, places of seclusion. De Sade was born in Paris as the only child of well-to-do and influential aristocratic parents and was raised by an uncle who was an abbot. After grammar school and lycée, de Sade received a military education and took part as a cavalry officer in various campaigns in Germany during the Seven Years' War, in which the French army fought against Prussia. Shortly afterwards he married, but seldom lived at home. He was repeatedly accused of "libertinage" and intermittently imprisoned in various places of detention in France. He wrote most of his novels and plays in these locations. They still count as radically innovative and controversial, but have been finally included in the mainstream series of the Bibliothèque de la Pléiade. At first de Sade was convicted for (alleged) criminal acts, and later on for his libertarian writings as well. He started writing after his first year of detention at Vincennes, when he was allowed books, paper, and pen. He was able to continue his work in prison in the Bastille, and also during his confinement at Charenton, where he wrote plays for the local stage and performed them with other inmates of the institution.[126]

De Sade's work anticipates insights of psychopathologists and those of twentieth-century anthropologists who claim that every human social order is essentially arbitrary and that there is no inevitable social pattern. From another point of view, de Sade's philosophy, in which "Nature" appears as personified, reified, and all-powerful, approaches Darwin's theory of evolution, according to which the struggle for life is most severe between individuals and varieties of the same species. As Guillaume Apollinaire put it, de Sade, twenty-eight years a prisoner, remained "the freest soul that ever existed."[127]

The following artists voluntarily settled away from home, definitively or for shorter or longer periods: Euripides, Beethoven, Ibsen, Conrad, Rilke, James Joyce, Ezra Pound, Eliot, Van Gogh, Brâncuşi, Stravinsky, Beckett, Gombrowicz, Buñuel, Czesław Miłosz, and Polanski. Other pioneers remained in secluded locations in their own country: Montaigne, Spinoza, Newton, Darwin, Mendel, Brontë, Flaubert, Cézanne, Marcel Proust, Lampedusa, and Perelman. Some of them we have met before. Others require further attention.

After having been at sea for almost twenty years, Joseph Conrad (1857–1924) published his first novel, *Almayer's Folly*, in 1895.[128] He was then thirty-seven and had just married an English woman. They lived together in England, later with their two sons, in various villages in the Kent countryside, where between 1898 and 1910 he wrote his best work. Inspired by the work of Schopenhauer, Flaubert, and Guy de Maupassant (all of them unmarried), Conrad, already bilingual, had learned English only after the age of twenty. How hard he found it to write in English is apparent from a letter to his literary agent and friend Edward Garnett, who encouraged and supported him: "I had to work like a coal-miner in his pit, quarrying all my English sentences out of a black night."[129] Amid his many difficulties – gout, recurrences of malaria, an acute sense of displacement – "the will to continue remained unflagging."[130]

Conrad is considered the first modernist writer. As an outsider in several ways and helped by literary friends, he renewed the language and the narrative structure of the English novel. His impact was enormous, most specifically on Eliot, Eugene O'Neill, Faulkner, Ernest Hemingway, and Graham Greene. Hemingway considered Conrad his "father," and declared, "From nothing else that I have ever read have I gotten what every book of Conrad has given me."[131] A recent biography acknowledges that Conrad's work has also enriched the fiction of more recent writers, including William Golding, Gabriel García Márquez, V. S. Naipaul, John le Carré, and Coetzee.[132]

Conrad was one of the first writers to give a voice to the claims and aspirations of non-western peoples. His own lack of a homeland led him to appeal to a wider audience and his statelessness is reflected in the large variety of national types who appear in his fiction.[133] Knowles and Moore give examples and begin with Almayer and Willems – as the main characters in his first two novels – *Almayer's Folly* and *An Outcast of the Islands* (1896). In a letter to his relative Marguerite Poradowska in Brussels, Conrad describes Willems as "an ignorant man who has had some success but neither principles nor any other line of conduct than the satisfaction of his vanity."[134]

Adversity can inspire creativity. As one of Conrad's biographers puts it: "Artists are skilled at converting apparent liabilities into assets." Watts continues:

> In Conrad's case, the fact that he was writing in a foreign language can clearly be related to one of the most striking features of his supreme works, *Heart of Darkness* and *Nostromo*. Repeatedly these texts manifest a linguistic scepticism which anticipates the subsequent concerns of philosophers like Wittgenstein, Sartre and Derrida. Conrad sardonically depicts the contrasts between word and fact, notion and nature, creed and deed, preaching and practice. And since Conrad's art, at best, constantly aspires to the condition of paradox, what he offers is a critical anticipation of that later scepticism.[135]

The Secret Sharer is one of Conrad's most inspired and multilayered stories in which he lives up to his power of description of human dilemmas. Schwarz summarizes Conrad's influence as follows:

> Focusing on the problems of how we understand, communicate, and signify experience, he anticipated essential themes in the philosophy, linguistics, criticism, and literature of our era. He understood the potential of the novel for political and historical insights and thus enlarged the subject matter of the English novel. When he dramatized the dilemma of seeking meaning in an amoral universe, he addressed the central epistemological problem of the twentieth century.[136]

Conrad was born Józef Korzeniowski in the Russian part of Polish Ukraine. He was the only child of artistic and patriotic parents who belonged to the *szlachta*, the landed Polish gentry. He lost his mother when he was seven, after his father was sent with his wife and child to a Russian penal colony because of his intellectual patriotic resistance against the Russian regime in that part of Poland.[137] After two years, his mother died from exhaustion and tuberculosis. Back in Poland, Conrad followed his father to Lviv and Kraków, where he read the European classics his father translated to make a living. After the death of his father when Conrad was eleven, his uncle Tadeusz Bobrowski, his mother's brother, took care of him and in fact became his guardian. He was a well-to-do landowner and belonged to the Polish gentry. He was a widower and had no children. Bobrowski later granted his nephew's long-cherished wish to go to sea. Conrad was not yet seventeen when he left Poland in 1874 and arrived in Marseille with letters of introduction from his influential uncle. Bobrowski continued to support Conrad financially and encourage him with good advice until his death in 1894. Later that same year, Conrad's first novel appeared, which he dedicated to his uncle and benefactor, with whom he had corresponded for more than twenty years, and whom he had also occasionally visited. Bobrowski had worked for years on his own memoirs. After they were published in 1900, they provided Conrad with an important source for *A Personal Record* (1912).[138]

Not all single people portrayed in this book led a strictly celibate life. Although Galileo was never formally married, in his Padua years he had a relationship with a Venetian woman, Marina Gamba, who lived in his house and bore him three children. After he moved to Florence for a better position at the university, his young son stayed with the mother. When she married, the son joined his father in Florence, while the two daughters had entered convents. The unmarried Descartes had a relationship with a Dutch maid, with whom he had a daughter to whom he was much attached. She died young. Lichtenberg long remained unmarried, but had many romances. At an advanced age he married a servant girl, who gave him six children.

The painter Paul Cézanne (1839–1906) was born in Aix-en-Provence. His parents married when he was five years old. Cézanne may have suffered at school from the stigma of his illegitimate birth. Later, in Paris, where he had studied art, he lived with Marie-Hortense Fiquet, an artists' model he had met in 1869, and they had a son. Cézanne wanted to hide both facts from his father, a self-made banker in Aix. His father had already been displeased with his son's choice of career – he would have preferred him to finish his law studies. Yet he accepted his son's decision, and supported him financially. The year 1886 did not look promising for Cézanne, who was living with Hortense and their son in semi-poverty, only rarely able to sell his paintings. Moreover, he had fallen out with his close friend Émile Zola, with whom he had grown up in Aix and who had always helped him financially. After Cézanne offended him at his friend's house in front of other visitors, Zola published a novel about a failing artist in whom everyone could recognize Cézanne. Later that year, Cézanne married Hortense to satisfy his father. Soon afterwards, his father died and bequeathed Cézanne a considerable inheritance, which solved his financial problems. He was now well-to-do, independent, and the owner of the family house, Jas de Bouffan, in Aix.

After they were married, Cézanne and Hortense lived separately, "together but apart." While Hortense mostly lived in their house in Paris, Cézanne remained in Aix, first in Jas de Bouffan, and later in Les Lauves on the other side of the city, in a house with a view of Mont Sainte-Victoire, which he immortalized. Cézanne's affinity with Provence also appears from his paintings of local architecture, his portraits of local people, and many still lives.[139] The long series of paintings Cézanne made of Hortense may testify to their uncommon relationship.[140]

Cézanne's road to prominence was laborious. He was not admitted to the École des Beaux-Arts and had to be satisfied with the Académie Suisse, where he met the painter Camille Pissarro, nine years older, and they became close friends. Along with academic training, self-education was important. It included frequent visits to the Louvre museum, where he studied the great masters and copied them. Meanwhile he learned a great deal from his friend and mentor Pissarro, who introduced him to fellow impressionists in the artists' village of Auvers-sur-Oise, near Paris, where Cézanne lived for some time with Hortense and their son.

The official Salon in Paris had little appreciation for Cézanne's work. For almost twenty years he remained a *refusé* and was hardly known in France. This changed at the beginning of the 1890s when his work was discovered by the young and ambitious art dealer Ambroise Vollard, an outsider to the established art world with a good sense of timing. With the help of Cézanne's son, who looked after many of his father's paintings in Paris, Vollard organized Cézanne's first solo exhibition in the fall of 1895. It was a great success and marked a turning point in the life of the painter, whose work now became known and sought after. The exhibition would also prove to be a turning point in painting and in modern art as a whole. Vollard organized a second show in the spring of 1898 of sixty of Cézanne's paintings, which was similarly successful.[141]

Who was Vollard and why did he have so much success? Vollard was an outsider in more senses than one. He was young (twenty-nine) and came from La Réunion, a French colony in the Indian Ocean. He began studying law in Montpellier and then continued in Paris, where he developed a growing interest in art. After training not very successfully at two galleries, he decided to become an art dealer himself. He was new to this field and little bothered by the burden of established opinions and social pressure. He had an understanding of the slow movement in French appreciation at the time toward more primitive, provincial, and native forms of art. Vollard had his own gallery in the Rue Lafitte, the center of the modern art trade. As a biographer phrased it, "His aggressive, daring tactics of settling right in the middle of his rivals was largely spurred on by his status as a socially marginal person in the capital, a colonial outsider. Even physically he stood out. His friends emphasized his exotic aura and his athletic stature (over six feet)."[142] "He spoke with a particular Creole accent . . ."[143] Vollard was a smart businessman who operated according to the principle of "buying low and selling high." He also showed work by Édouard Manet, Paul Gauguin, Van Gogh, Edgar Degas, Auguste Renoir, and Pablo Picasso. The unmarried Vollard was an excellent cook and host, and the kitchen attached to his gallery became a meeting place for the Paris avant-garde in the Belle Époque.

We know about Rilke's great appreciation of the retrospective of Cézanne in Paris in the fall of 1907, less than a year after the painter's death, an exhibition the German poet visited almost daily. He wrote about his experience in his famous *Briefe über Cézanne*, to his wife, the sculptress Clara Westhoff, a former student of Rodin, who lived in Worpswede, an artists' village not far from Bremen. Looking back on his life in the 1940s, Picasso described the impact of Cézanne's work on twentieth-century painting: "Cézanne was my one and only master. I spent years studying his paintings . . . Cézanne was like the father of us all."[144] The international stature of Cézanne today is evident from the prices fetched by his paintings. In February 2012, the Museum of Modern Art in Qatar acquired Cézanne's *The Card Players* for 250 million dollars, the highest price that had ever been paid for a work of art.

Cézanne's life comprised almost all the elements of a scenario that produces radical innovation: the stigma of illegitimate birth, a tense relationship with his father over his career choice – a theme we encountered earlier in the life of Galileo – rejection by the École des Beaux-Arts in Paris, his own dissatisfaction with his first paintings (and destruction of these experiments), refusal of his paintings by the Salon for years, ending in the semi-official Salon des Refusés, other difficult issues with his parents from whom he had to hide his relationship with Hortense and the existence of their son, a falling out with his close friend and supporter Zola, who made fun of him in one of his novels, and finally his split with Hortense. For Cézanne all these adversities and exclusions paid off. Most of these troubles created separation and seclusion, which enabled him to make a breakthrough in his field, initially with help from a mentor who encouraged him, and his friends, including Zola, and his father, who both supported him financially. At a later age, his work was discovered by chance through the fortunate arrival and intervention of Vollard after a serendipitous encounter with one of Cézanne's paintings in a store. Vollard approached Cézanne's son, organized a successful exhibition in Paris, and rescued the painter from oblivion.

Along with striking differences, Van Gogh (1853–90) shared various characteristics with his contemporary Cézanne. Comparing cases may contribute to a better understanding of radical innovation. Both painters came from the periphery: Provence and Brabant, respectively. Both started drawing early and both were educated in informal ways: self-education, frequent visits to museums, mentors, and friends. As firstborns, both had difficult relationships with their parents and were inclined to solitude and wanderlust, going back and forth between more or less the same locations. Both painters had a slow start, with very little public attention, and peaked relatively late. For different reasons, each felt mistreated as a child. Cézanne may have suffered from his illegitimate status: his parents only married when he was five. When he was a child, Van Gogh's mother considered him unmanageable. Vincent left home before he was twelve, when he was sent to a boarding school in Brabant. This was not uncommon at the time. As a Protestant pastor, his father belonged to the local elite and had to be an example in Zundert, their village on the periphery of the predominantly Roman Catholic Brabant, not far from the Belgian border. For the young Van Gogh, residence at the boarding school meant a continuation of his loneliness and "the beginning of a lifelong banishment," as he later put it. This exile also meant the continuation of his long and solitary walking trips, collecting insects. His interest in observing the environment came at the cost of learning to deal with other people, who in turn found him "strange." This made him spend more time on solitary activities, including reading and writing letters. The exception was his early friendship with his brother Theo, four years younger, to whom Vincent was genuinely devoted.[145] Their later correspondence tells us about the close brotherly devotion and feedback given by Theo, without whose care we would probably never have heard of Vincent. According to recent research by Claudia Kammer into the work of Van Gogh, the painter was not a "genius" but a passionate, single-minded worker – entirely in line with other pioneers discussed in the present book. Kammer's painstaking and detailed analysis of his paintings and drawings proves that Van Gogh did not have a "natural talent" and had problems teaching himself the basic elements of his art. He did so by carefully looking at the work of predecessors whom he admired. Van Gogh also experimented a great deal – another characteristic of pioneers.[146]

According to Sulloway's theory of birth order, Cézanne and Van Gogh were firstborns who, following conflict with parents, would be expected to rebel against them and, like "functional laterborns," become radical innovators. The problem with this argument is that Van Gogh, without the friendship, encouragement, financial help, and mediation from his brother Theo, probably would not have become an innovative painter. In this historical friendship between two brothers, demonstrated by their great correspondence, there is a lack of the sibling rivalry Sulloway considers necessary, if not key, for radical innovation to occur. Sulloway strongly insists on this point: conflict with parents is fueled by rivalry between siblings.[147] Collaboration between brothers receives only lip service from Sulloway: he acknowledges that it exists in his passage on Hamilton's theory of kin selection – social altruism between close kin[148] – but does not provide any examples and falls noticeably silent about the lifelong friendship and collaboration between the brothers Charles and Erasmus Darwin. There is much more to be said for considering the radicalism of both Cézanne and Van Gogh in the light of their adversity and social exclusion and their painstaking roads to the summit of their art – with substantial support and encouragement from a loving brother (art dealer Theo van Gogh), a faithful friend (Émile Zola), and a shared connoisseur and patron (Ambroise Vollard).

What also strikes us about these two painters is their geographical mobility, their itinerant, wandering lifestyle: traveling from one place to the next and back again. In this, they are certainly not alone among radical innovators. Staying on the move can be related to their desire for space and freedom, keeping a distance from what is generally accepted and wanting to escape the social pressure that, in the end, emanates from any group of people. Wandering overlaps with (voluntary) exile, exemplified by Thucydides, Dante, Erasmus, Cervantes, Descartes, Leibniz, de Sade, Tocqueville, Andersen, Gogol, Rimbaud, Rilke, Wittgenstein, and Ibsen. The Norwegian dramatist worked outside his homeland for almost three decades, and stayed at different locations in both Italy and Germany. Wittgenstein said he could only be productive "in exile." Max Weber traveled several years with his wife in Italy and elsewhere in Europe after he resigned his position at the University of Heidelberg to recover from his illness. In this period of adversity and retirement, he developed his thesis on the connection between Protestantism and the development of modern capitalism. It is widely believed that Descartes lived in Amsterdam, but how much time did he actually spend in that city during the twenty years he remained as a voluntary exile in the Dutch Republic, before he left for Stockholm and died there within a year? In reality, he only lived a few years in Amsterdam. Apart from Amsterdam (between 1629 and 1636 with interruptions in Leiden and two years in Deventer), his biographer Gaukroger mentions the following locations: Breda, Franeker, Dordrecht, Utrecht, Leeuwarden, Egmond, Santpoort, Endegeest, and Egmond-Binnen.

In the few years when he wrote his "visionary" poems, Arthur Rimbaud (1854–92) was continually on the road – and continued after he stopped writing when he was nineteen. Traveling and wandering had become, he said, his "passion." Rimbaud was born in Charleville, a border town in the French Ardennes. Like many other innovators, Rimbaud came "from the provinces" – from the periphery. Together with a brother two years older, and two younger sisters, he lost his father, a captain in the French army, who disappeared after his leave. His family never heard from him again:

> One day in September 1860, Captain Rimbaud left to join his regiment in Cambrai. He never returned. Arthur was about to celebrate his sixth birthday. His mother was thirty-five. She was unhappier than she had

ever been, marooned in a seedy neighbourhood with four demanding children and an excruciating personality: a combination of intransigence and acute awareness of what other people were thinking. To lose a husband when he was still alive was an unmentionable humiliation. She decided that from now on she would be known as "Widow Rimbaud."

Rimbaud often evokes this abandonment in his poetry. *Like any personal disaster, it was not the event of a single day but the atmosphere of a whole life.*[149]

The shock of the loss is invariably depicted through the mother's eyes and presented as that of the pain of sexual deprivation: "The regret of thick, young arms . . . / The gold of April moons in the heart of the sacred bed!"[150]

At school Rimbaud excelled and won numerous prizes. If he was not in the library or writing poems, he took long solitary walks through the Ardennes. Two early and surprising poems attest to his great skill – "Le dormeur du val" and "Au cabaret-vert." When he was fifteen he showed some of his poems to the new young teacher Izambard, who encouraged him, advised him, lent him books, and later, through others, put him in touch with the poet Paul Verlaine, who invited him to come to Paris. The brothers in art became friends. Verlaine left his young family and the two embarked on long wanderings that led first to London and later to Brussels, where, after a violent conflict, they parted ways. In the summer of 1873, at his mother's farm in Roche near Charleville, Rimbaud wrote *Une saison en enfer*. The next year in London, he revised and completed *Illuminations*. After these efforts he wrote no more poems.[151] He was still not yet twenty.

Rimbaud resumed his solitary treks, on foot as usual. Searching for a job – *any job* – led him through Europe, Asia, and Africa, and back again to Europe, interrupted only by short visits to his mother and sister at home at the farm in Roche. He had an adventurous voyage as fusilier in the Dutch colonial army to Java, but shortly after arrival in the Dutch East Indies he deserted. After more wandering, he signed on as a deckhand with a British ship in the port of Semarang, and traveled back to Europe.[152] Rimbaud left for Austria, and later he went to Germany and Scandinavia. Always on the lookout for a job, he joined a small group crossing the St. Gotthard Pass in the Alps in November 1878, to arrive in Genoa and continue further to Alexandria and Cyprus, where he worked as an overseer for a British firm. After a fatal incident, he slipped away to Aden and afterwards to Harar in Abyssinia (now Ethiopia), where he worked as a trader for a French company. Following hard years, Rimbaud fell seriously ill and had to return to France, where he was admitted to a hospital in Marseille. After a long and difficult sickness, Rimbaud died in the presence of his caring sister Isabelle on November 10, 1891.[153]

Attempts have been made to explain Rimbaud's penchant for long solitary walks (and the revolutionary character of his poems) as a search for his father, who had left home never to return. There was also the severe regime of an ambitious, authoritarian, heartless mother, who insisted on good results at school and engaged a mentor to teach her promising, already successful son. Unintentionally, she contributed to his rebellion – first at home, then elsewhere – and to the innovative poetry of an outsider, someone who declared: "Je est un autre" – "I is an other." As a sixteen-year-old schoolboy, Rimbaud drew up a manifesto for poets and sent it in a letter of May 13, 1871 to his teacher and mentor Izambard with the famous key sentence, "The poet makes himself a seer by means of a long, immense and rational derangement of all the senses." This call was further illustrated with his poem "Le bateau ivre." "Derangement of all the senses": extreme alienation as a necessary condition for radical innovation.[154]

It would be wrong to regard Rimbaud's long, solitary walks and wanderings, which developed after the loss of his father and the subsequent severe reign of his mother, only as a personal "passion," as he phrased it himself.[155] They are part of a more general pattern of loss and solitude, pointed out earlier in Darwin's case after the early death of his mother and the failing care of his surrogate parents.[156]

Similar patterns appear in the life of the British primatologist Jane Goodall (1934–). From an early age, she grew up without her father, who mostly lived abroad as a professional racing driver and officer in the British army. He visited his family in Bournemouth only occasionally, and even less after a late divorce. Jane remembered that "he touched her only once" when she was a little girl.[157] The space that developed offered the opportunity for solitary pursuits, including long walks, collecting, reading, and playing with domestic animals and taking care of them – activities that did not require the presence of other people.[158]

Moreover, Goodall suffered from a moderate form of prosopagnosia, or face blindness, a neurological condition that makes it difficult to recognize faces, including the faces of familiar people, like friends, relatives, neighbors, and colleagues, especially when they are encountered in unfamiliar contexts.[159] This genetic defect, with its neurological basis, hinders the initiation and maintenance of social relations and may lead to social exclusion. Face blindness may go together with topographical blindness. This was the case with Jane Goodall, who told Oliver Sacks (who also suffered from both afflictions) that she often could not recognize individual chimpanzees from their faces, but

> once she knows a particular chimp well, she ceases to have difficulties; similarly she has no problem with family and friends. But, she says, "I have huge problems with people with 'average' faces . . . I have to search for a mole or something. . . .I can be all day with someone and not know them the next day."[160]

Apart from specific marks, context was also important for recognizing faces – for both Goodall and Sacks. As Sacks explains:

> Parties, even my own birthday parties, are a challenge . . . I have been accused of "absentmindedness," and no doubt this is true. But I think that a significant part of what is variously called my "shyness," my "reclusiveness," my social "ineptitude," my "eccentricity," even my "Asperger's syndrome," is a consequence and a misinterpretation of my difficulty recognizing faces.[161]

Already as a child, Van Gogh, too, was considered "strange," an opinion later shared by his younger sisters and other members of the family. He was also a child who missed a feeling of belonging with his parents. Apparently his family did not consider the possibility that the latter was the cause and the former the effect, or that they interacted – and nor did his biographers. Not without reason did the painter himself speak about his "lifelong banishment." One of Rimbaud's biographers indicates a similar interaction:

> As a result of the lack of warmth and affection at home, Rimbaud had been, from his earliest years, of a solitary disposition; his sisters were too young for companionship and his brother too loutish. His mental development was so far in advance of that of boys his own age that for real intimacy he needed friends many years older than himself. And so, even at school, he remained solitary in the midst of the friends who liked him; these were friends with whom he played, but he could not have confided in them, they could not have shared his inner life.[162]

Comparing these cases also throws light on the situation in Darwin's youth: the early loss of his mother was not adequately compensated for by his older sisters who functioned as foster parents and even less by a depressive, authoritarian widower father, who vetoed any reference to his deceased wife. To deal with this situation Darwin developed in his relations with his sisters what he called his "doggedness," which, as he later recognized, helped him in his scientific work. Fortunately his older brother Erasmus, who seemed less affected by the death of his mother, took care of his younger brother and encouraged his early intellectual interests. Later he assisted him by word and deed. Curiously, Darwin omits to mention the friendship and the considerable intellectual support of his brother in his autobiography and only declares: "I do not think that I owe much to him intellectually."[163] If mentioned at all, his biographers do not try to explain this.

Exile, early loss of parents, illness, physical defects, minority status, and other forms of adversity among radical innovators have led to social exclusion, solitude, and alienation from generally accepted views and practices. They have created space and distance from everyday social intercourse and the pressure inherent in any social setting. Space and freedom following adversity are often not identified and their possible effects have likewise been neglected. Dutch psychiatrist Witte Hoogendijk was seven when he lost his father (also a psychiatrist), who drowned at sea in a sailing accident. Looking back to that period, he says in an interview: "The death of my father had an enormous impact on me. It cannot be any other way . . . it also opened an enormous space, precisely because he was not there."[164]

Space definitely opened new roads for Polish writer Witold Gombrowicz (1904–69) when he found himself with other Poles in Buenos Aires during a cultural visit in late August 1939. War had become imminent and their ship was ordered to sail back to Poland. At the last minute, Gombrowicz decided to disembark. Within days German military forces had invaded his country and Gombrowicz would remain an exile in Argentina for well over two decades.[165] Already an outsider in his homeland three times over (member of the Polish gentry, sickly, and homosexual), which had an impact on his writing, as his 1937 novel *Ferdydurke* attests, Gombrowicz must have recognized the vantage point of exile in a country where he knew nobody and did not even speak the language. He observed: "I was nothing so I could do anything."[166] This sense of unlimited possibilities, despite severe poverty, especially during the war, inspired all his further work. "I was suddenly in Argentina, completely alone, cut off, lost, ruined, anonymous. I was a little excited, a little frightened. Yet at the same time, something in me told me to greet with passionate emotion the blow that was destroying me and upsetting the order I had known up to now."[167]

In this ambiguous and controversial figure of Argentina as both "something that is simply unshaped" and "a genuine and a creative protest against Europe," we will find all the crucial aspects of Gombrowicz's aesthetics: Argentina, like other cultures that Gombrowicz considered "minor," became an ally in the struggle with the domination of European culture, with the automatism of forms, with the mechanization of modern life . . . Argentina offered Gombrowicz not exactly an escape but the possibility of a second beginning, and thus of a certain distance from *form* in its manifold cultural manifestations: nationality, aesthetics, morality, religion, social status, [sexuality, and] personal identity. It enabled a passionate "protest against Europe" without congealing this protest into a program, artistic or otherwise.[168]

Being unknown and without money, Gombrowicz lived under circumstances that were not easy. Especially during the first years of his exile he often lived in poverty and depended on charity from the substantial Polish community in Buenos Aires. To get something to eat, he attended funerals of totally unknown people. His situation improved after the war when he found a job in the Banco Polaco, where he worked between 1947 and 1955. Meanwhile he had made friends with younger Argentinian writers who helped him translate *Ferdydurke* into Spanish.[169] His most important works – *Trans-Atlantyk*, *Pornografia*, and the three-volume *Diary* – were written during his exile in Argentina, which lasted until 1963. Up to then, fragments had appeared in French and other languages. A scholarship from the Ford Foundation in 1963 allowed him to spend a year in West Berlin.[170]

Illness prevented Gombrowicz from returning to Argentina and he found residence in an abbey near Paris in 1964. There he met Rita Labrosse, a Canadian student of modern literature. Suffering from asthma, he moved with her as his secretary to Vence in southern France. Gombrowicz wrote frankly about his homosexuality (he liked adolescent boys) and his experiences in his semi-autobiographical style – as part of his struggle with the automatism of established forms and his preference for ambiguity, in-betweens, and "immaturity." About six months before he died in the summer of 1969, he married his Canadian friend. Already for a while, Rita had been visiting Poland annually at the invitation of a circle of admirers of Gombrowicz's work, now translated into well over thirty languages.[171]

Travel and wandering offered radical innovators opportunities for developing new perspectives, fitting their detached lifestyle, their leanings toward solitude – away from social constraints. Being on the road was a large part of the life and work of Rainer Maria Rilke (1875–1926). He was a single child of a well-to-do middle-class family belonging to the German-speaking minority in Prague. His parents separated when Rilke was nine and he moved with his mother to Vienna. He attended a military academy in lower Austria. He thoroughly disliked the school, and after four years, when he was fifteen, he left because of his health. Tutoring prepared him for university entrance exams and he studied art, literature, and philosophy in Prague and Munich. As a young man he had twice traveled to Russia – in the summers of 1899 and 1900 – with the much older Lou Andreas-Salomé, his mentor and first love, whom he had met in Munich in 1897, when he impressed her with some of his poems. They visited Leo Tolstoy on his estate and met other writers. In 1877, Lou Salomé had married Carl Andreas, professor of West Asian languages at the University of Berlin, when he was forty-one and she was twenty-six, on her condition that their marriage would remain celibate. On the first trip to Russia she went with both her husband and Rilke; on the second tour she traveled alone with the poet.[172] Later, their ways would part, but she and Rilke always remained close friends and stayed in touch, keeping up an extensive correspondence.[173] During a visit to the artistic circle in Worpswede near Bremen in 1901, Rilke married the sculptress Clara Westhoff, who had studied with Rodin in Paris. They had a daughter but separated within a year. They remained in touch, mostly through correspondence.

In the early 1900s, Rilke worked for some years in Paris as a private secretary to Rodin and collected material for a biography of the sculptor, from whom he learned that there is no harm in hard work: "Il faut travailler toujours, et il faut avoir patience" – always work hard, and be patient. Rilke understood that the artist should not just wait for inspiration, but that steady application would summon up inspiration and preserve it. Even more important, Rilke learned from Rodin's work, and a few years later from Cézanne's paintings, to look at the world around him "objectively" and "let things speak for themselves." This resulted in New Poems (referred to as "thing poems"), in which Rilke found a new way of looking at the things around him and also a new voice. His famous poem about the panther behind bars in the Jardin des Plantes attests to this fundamental turn.[174] Rodin's impact on Rilke went hand in hand with the effect on him of the Cézanne exhibition in October 1907 in Paris, a place he visited almost daily. He reported his discovery – his new way of looking at things – in a series of letters to his wife in Worpswede, describing his enthusiasm about the revolution in painting and art accomplished by Cézanne's work.[175]

After his extended sojourn in Paris, during which he also wrote the semi-autobiographical novel *The Notebooks of Malte Laurids Brigge*, Rilke traveled through Spain, the Mediterranean, North Africa, and Europe. He moved through the Alps from one castle to another – remote locations offered him by aristocratic patrons and friends. Invited by his benefactor and friend Princess Marie von Thurn und Taxis, he stayed at her Duino castle, located on the Adriatic coast near Trieste. There he began writing *Duino Elegies* in 1911–12, finishing them ten years later in a curious overlap with his second major work of poetry, *Sonnets to Orpheus*, which he had just started.[176] In a burst of energy, both works were completed in February 1922, when Rilke was living in the thirteenth-century Château de Muzot in the western Alps, which his patron Werner Reinhart had bought, renovated, and put at Rilke's disposal.[177] The *Duino Elegies* were dedicated to his patroness Princess Marie von Thurn und Taxis.

Although Rilke sought out the company of women, not all of them mistresses, and throughout his life several took care of him, housing, feeding, and in some cases funding him, as described by Banville, Rilke could still write in an early letter to his mentor, friend, and former love Lou Salomé and confess his ruthlessness: "In one poem of mine that succeeds there is much more reality than in every relationship and affection I feel . . . [W]hat are those close to me other than a guest who doesn't want to leave?"[178]

Yet Rilke had another side as well. He could also, if necessary, empathize with the unhappy fate of others, as happened in the "Letters to a Young Woman" he wrote between 1919 and 1924. This admirer of his work, named Lisa Heise, had asked him for help at a difficult stage of her life: after a failed marriage she was living alone with her child somewhere in northern Germany. Although she was totally unknown to him (and he would never meet her), he is fairly outspoken and tells her that writing letters is one of the most beautiful and productive means of human communication. He also tells her about the consolation art can offer, gives her advice, and describes in some detail his secluded life in the small Château de Muzot.[179] At this time Rilke was friends with the mother of a son who would later call himself Balthus (1908–2001), later to become a famous painter under that name, who likewise preferred to live and work in this area. With other artists Rilke was among the early sponsors of Balthus, "the painter who avoided the avant-garde, but made a great impression on that same avant-garde" with his paintings of sweeping local landscapes and adolescent, prepubescent girls, as in the still controversial *The Guitar Lesson* of 1934.[180]

101

Rilke and other innovating artists and scientists who preferred a withdrawn and solitary life, such as Beethoven, Darwin, Flaubert, Conrad, Einstein, and Kafka, wrote numerous letters to friends they rarely or never saw. The letters were important, more important than actual meetings. In October 1907, Rilke wrote a letter almost every day to his wife, Clara Westhoff, in Worpswede about the paintings in the Cézanne exhibition in Paris. There were days when his contemporary Franz Kafka (1883–1924) sent no fewer than four letters to Felice Bauer, his fiancée in Berlin – with a total of about 500 letters and postcards over a period of about five years.[181]

Kafka's letters to Felice and those of other writers reveal that they were not only written about their work but also as part of their work, as finger exercises, and to secure and maintain their retiring lifestyle. As a reviewer observes, "Kafka's correspondence with Felice has all the earmarks of his fiction: the same nervous attention to minute particulars; the same paranoid awareness of shifting balances of power; the same atmosphere of emotional suffocation – combined, surprisingly enough, with moments of boyish ardor and delight."[182]

People have also pointed at the effect of a fiancée at a distance. Felice lived and worked in Berlin. After their first meeting on August 13, 1912 at the parental home of Kafka's friend Max Brod in Prague, and after the start of their correspondence in the fall of that year, Kafka wrote his first masterworks in November and December: *Das Urteil* (*The Judgment*), which he dedicated to Felice, and *Die Verwandlung* (*The Metamorphosis*). Meanwhile he worked on his novel *Der Verschollene* (*The Man Who Disappeared*). He would see Felice only in the spring of the following year. Her first letter came at the end of September as a response to his first letter a week earlier – more than a month after their first, unromantic encounter in Prague – and he bombarded her with numerous letters: "the correspondence immediately took on an almost boundless character – with two, three, four letters a day – keeping pace with the production of his masterworks."[183] For Kafka, writing meant everything. Friendships, engagements had to yield to it: "Because the longing for writing always has the upper hand."[184] In one of his letters to Felice, Kafka spells out this point: "for the existence of the writer is really dependent on his writing desk. If he wants to escape madness, he really must never move away from his desk; he has to hang on to it with his teeth."[185]

Obviously, the letters served to keep his bourgeois fiancée at a distance: Felice in Berlin, Kafka in Prague or traveling, or staying weeks in a sanatorium for his health. There he met other, often younger, women, with whom he had mostly short romantic relationships, as with the youthful "Swiss" girl, G.W., whom he met in the summer of 1913 during a stay at a spa near Lake Garda. It involved a brief affair that remained in his mind for years, but Kafka never wanted to talk about it.[186]

Apart from significant differences, we find also striking similarities with the life of the writer Heinrich von Kleist (1777–1811). Kleist, too, kept his fiancée at a distance and traveled with other women through Europe, until he agreed with one of them, Henriette Vogel, who suffered from a terminal disease, that they should die together. The pact was executed at the Kleine Wannsee in Berlin: Kleist shot Henriette first and then himself.[187] On Kafka's first visit to Felice in Berlin, he made a pilgrimage with her to Kleist's tomb.[188] His priorities were obvious. In a letter to Felice he explained: "I do not have a literary interest. Literature is what I am made of."[189] Kafka might have agreed with another writer he admired, similarly unmarried and similarly with a great need for solitude: Flaubert, who wrote in one of his letters: "Je suis un homme-plume. Je sens par elle, à cause d'elle, par rapport à elle et beaucoup plus avec elle [I am a man of the quill. I feel through it, because of it, in relation to it, and much more with it]."[190]

Biographers emphasize Kafka's plural outsidership as the key to a better understanding of the writer and his work. Born in Prague, Kafka lived most of his life in this city and belonged to Prague's German-speaking Jewish minority in a city where people spoke Czech. He was also an agnostic, non-confessing Jew: "What have I in common with Jews?" he asked himself in that typically self-disparaging tone of the German-Jewish community in Prague which he made into an art: "I have hardly anything in common with myself, and should stand very quietly in a corner, content that I can breathe."[191] Kafka found himself in a position where he did not belong to any group, people, tradition, or culture: all of them had become dubious, questionable.[192]

Kafka was a firstborn and had, as is well known, a troubled relationship with his father, who never missed an opportunity to humiliate him. He gained a degree in law, and worked at an accident insurance company, where he was much appreciated. Poor health forced him to visit spas at the seaside or in the mountains. The retreats were brightened by romantic encounters at these locations. His position as outsider was also tempered by ties with friends, of whom Max Brod was the most important and loyal. Kafka's profession brought him in touch with workers who were seriously wounded in accidents caused by the introduction of new industrial equipment in the process of industrialization that occurred around 1900 in

Bohemia.[193] This position provided him with material for his literary work. Moreover, he remained unmarried and continued to live at home with his parents, and in this respect, too, he was an outsider. Kafka got on well with his youngest sister, Ottilie ("Ottla"). He visited her at her farm in Zürau, went on holidays with her, and lived for a while (the winter of 1916–17) in her little house in the old city walls of Prague, where he wrote stories in his collection entitled *Ein Landartz (A Country Doctor)*.[194] Although Kafka often fell in love, he remained a hesitant, reluctant lover of successive girlfriends and fiancées. He had good looks and was described as tall (around six feet), slender, lean, dark, always meticulously dressed and groomed, modest, charming, and funny; an interesting conversationalist – an attractive young man.

As noted above, Kafka's first fiancée was Felice Bauer, but there is no sign of a falling in love or even a flirtation.[195] Moreover, Kafka may have been complying with his parents' wishes: he was about thirty years old and it was time to look for a woman to marry. During a period of five years (1912–17), Kafka broke off the engagement twice, "because I believe that marriage will endanger my work as a writer," he wrote in his diary.[196] Numerous letters kept his fiancée at a distance. The real reason was his fear of intimate contact with women who wanted to marry and have children. It was a distance that was absent in brothels and in short romantic encounters – infatuations like the one with the "Swiss" girl in the summer of 1913 at Lake Garda. That same summer Kafka wrote in his diary on July 23: "The exploded sexuality of women. Their natural impurity." Three weeks later, after the summer with Felice, follows the famous observation: "Coitus as the punishment for the happiness of being together. Possibly life as an ascetic, more ascetic than single, this is the only way for me to tolerate marriage. But what about her?"[197]

Kafka's third engagement in 1919 to the attractive, good-looking Czech Julie Wohryzek foundered a year later in spite of matrimonial promises from Kafka. He broke off the relationship because of his involvement with Milena Jesenská, the Czech translator of his work, unhappily married in Vienna. Kafka had briefly visited her and had been "intimate" with her. Milena strongly insisted that this meant the end of the engagement with Julie Wohryzek.[198] Yet the relationship with Milena was also short-lived and was soon restricted to an extended exchange of letters. Once more, Kafka pleaded illness and his "Angst."[199] This fear applied much less to fleeting romantic contacts and relationships with prostitutes. By nature they excluded a lasting relationship and expectation of marriage and a family. These involvements with women could not, therefore, threaten his freedom to write, but they could inspire him. Quite a few female figures in his stories and novels have "features of whorish subordinates."[200]

The only woman Kafka lived with was Dora Diamant, whom he met in the summer of 1923 at a spa on the Baltic Sea, a year before his death.[201] They lived in a rented house in the Grünewaldstrasse in Berlin, where Kafka read her stories by his favorite writers, Kleist and E. T. A. Hoffmann.[202] Kafka was then already seriously ill. Dora was very dedicated to him and they made plans and preparations to leave and settle in Palestine.[203] His worsening tuberculosis, however, ruled out these plans and in the spring of 1924 Kafka had to be transported to a sanatorium near Vienna, where he died in June of that year.[204]

One of the results of the comparative research for this book points to the mainly unmarried status of radical innovators. The few who were married had partners who took care of the household and the children (Kepler, Bach, Darwin, Freud, Conrad, Einstein). In other cases their marriages remained childless and their partners acted as assistants or colleagues (Lavoisier, Clausewitz, Weber). Still other radical innovators were single at the time of their breakthrough (Boerhaave, Keynes, Watson, Goodall). All these cases illustrate a dedication to a calling and a passion for their work. Kafka was no exception.

Like other radical innovators, Kafka made use of his shortcomings for his work, in which alienation and fear predominated and in which he "realistically" and selectively uses his experiences in his parents' house, at work, while traveling, and with the women he met in brothels and coffee houses, where they can be recognized, often in subordinated positions.[205] Wagenbach emphasizes the importance of Kafka's use of autobiographical materials in his novels and stories, and argues that discussions about "realism" in Kafka's work have to take these into account if they are not to go off-track. The theme of most of the narratives concerns relentless relationships of authority – a relationship Kafka often experienced with his father. He looked up to him and considered him a real man: big, strong, authoritarian, and openly proud of what he as a man had accomplished – and looking down on his skinny, fragile, sickly son, who was highly educated and had an important job, but was still unmarried and lived with his parents. Around 1912 it seemed that a change was imminent for the almost thirty-year-old bachelor. The relationship with Felice, which started in the second half of that year, and was maintained for the time being through numerous letters from Kafka, was possibly brought about by his parents' pressure. This also held for his first visit to Felice in Berlin in the spring of 1913 – eight months after their first meeting at the family house of his best friend, Max Brod, in Prague. For five years, in his relationship with Felice, Kafka tried to overcome his aversion to marriage and family; then, for another year, with fiancée Julie Wohryzek and friend Milena Jesenská. It cannot be said he failed for lack of trying.

In breaking off these engagements Kafka always raised the same reasons: his illness (tuberculosis) and his literary work meant that founding a family was impossible. As he indicated in a long, explanatory letter in November 1919 to Julie Wohryzek's sister: "Marriage and children are for me the highest good, in a certain sense, but I cannot possibly marry. . ."[206] The women with whom he corresponded, and whom he probably would have liked to marry, he needed for his work – as a source of inspiration. The same holds for the relationship with his father – a model for the power relationships in his tales. Kafka continued living at home because it suited him. The greater part of his work was written in Prague under claustrophobic conditions: "I live with my family, with the best and most loving people, stranger than a stranger."[207] Three years before his death he described in his diary his position between "work" and "life": "I have only rarely crossed this borderland between solitude and community, I have settled myself there even more than in solitude itself."[208]

Kafka's exaggerated conscientiousness, which sometimes made him socially awkward, also found a place in his writing, where he could indulge in his extreme attention to style.[209] The result was "prose like shards of glass. It was meant to be lucid, and it was intended to cut."[210] Barely twenty years old, he wrote in a letter to a friend: "A book must be the axe for the frozen sea within us."[211] Because of Kafka's perfectionism, only a few stories were published during his lifetime. He had also indicated that all his manuscripts should be destroyed after his death. He considered most of them unfinished – again a result of his painstaking devotion to his art. As is well known, his executor and best friend Max Brod ignored the request.[212]

Biographers seem unanimous in their judgment of Kafka: no other writer had a more innovative influence on postwar literature, and no writer was as much of an outsider and so estranged, not only from any group, people, and tradition, but thus also from himself. Kafka's work links up with the heritage of Hoffmann, Kleist, and Gogol, in which he recognized himself and where we find the same alienation and dissension. In this respect his work anticipates or speaks to an epoch of global displacement, to a more general experience of deracination and exclusion, not only among numerous migrants in a myriad of diasporas, but also among countless ordinary people, as the obsession with "identity" and "authenticity" attests.

A lonely parsonage on the edge of a village in the heather-covered hills of western Yorkshire represents the setting and the inspiration for the writing of *Wuthering Heights*. It is an ethnographic novel whose narrative complexity and "symbolism" – from its first publication in 1847 under a (male) pseudonym – have given rise to hundreds of essays and books.[213] In her introduction to the text, Stoneman argues that the reception history of this novel reflects the history of literary criticism over the last 150 years. She adds that *Wuthering Heights* has been translated into twenty-six languages and, at the beginning of the 1990s, was the third most borrowed book in British public libraries and available in twenty-seven editions in the United Kingdom. With the book's multiplicity of meanings, all this made *Wuthering Heights* a classic.[214]

Adversity dominated the early life of the author, the young Emily Brontë (1818–48), who was not yet thirty and single, and who remained living with her widowed father, two sisters, a younger brother, and her aunt, the younger sister of her deceased mother. Confining herself to an area with which she had an inseparable bond, she together with her siblings read the books and periodicals provided by their father. Moreover, they told each other fictional stories and wrote poetry and novels to pass the time. To get their novels published, the sisters had to use male pseudonyms. This marks their position as outsiders in terms of gender. Emily did not leave us much information about herself. She died a year after the publication of her book, which she had written without the knowledge of her sisters and brother. The most important source of written information about Emily is Charlotte, two years older, who first edited the text and then tried hard to get her sister's manuscript published. Her letters to a friend formed the basis for Elizabeth Gaskell's *Life of Charlotte Brontë*, which appeared in 1857.

> As a personal friend of Charlotte, writing only a year after Charlotte's death and only eight years after Emily's, Elizabeth Gaskell was able to visit their home and talk to their father, servants, friends, and neighbours. A novelist herself, Gaskell was painfully impressed by the solitariness of the Brontës' Parsonage home, at the very top of the steep village, surrounded on three sides by the graveyard, and swept by tumultuous winds from the moorland behind.[215]

The Brontës were not completely cut off. Their father also wrote himself and had educated his children and provided them with a

stream of literature and periodicals. In addition, the three Brontë
sisters had also been teaching assistants at local schools and had also
planned to found a school themselves. To this end Charlotte and
Emily went for some time to a boarding school in Brussels to learn
French and German.

Emily was very much a loner, including toward her two sisters.
The ethnographic precision of her novel, the narrative techniques and
the local dialect she used, the geography, her sense of place, and the
organization and presentation of her materials attest to literary erudition and to sociological and psychological insight. Her professional-
ism lifts the book far above the genre of the provincial novel – then
and now:

> Each technical device contributing to the celebrated complexity of
> narration in *Wuthering Heights* has its precedents in modern fictional
> practice from Cervantes down to novelists contemporary with Brontë.
> The time shifts, the multiplication of narrators and narrators within
> narrators, the double plot, the effacement of the author, and the
> absence of any trustworthy and knowing narrator who clearly speaks
> for the author are used strategically in *Wuthering Heights* to frustrate
> the expectations of a reader such as Lockwood. They are used to invite
> the reader to move step by step, by way of a gradual unveiling, room by
> room, into the "penetralium" of Brontë's strange vision of life.[216]

With *Wuthering Heights* Emily Brontë demonstrates a great
familiarity with the customs, language, and social relations of this
rural society in Yorkshire; contrasts between gentry and peasants set
the tone in social relations and events taking place in the framework
of complementary oppositions between the two houses, Wuthering
Heights and Thrushcross Grange, and the two families, the Earnshaws
and the Lintons, with their corresponding contrasts, ambitions, and
lifestyles – including those between the characters of Catherine and
the adopted outsider Heathcliff.[217]

Early loss of parents is not unusual in creating the driving force
for pioneering achievement. As the fourth daughter of a clergyman,
Emily Brontë lost first her mother when she was three and then, some
years later, two older sisters when she was not yet seven. She grew
up with a sister two years older, a sister two years younger, and a
brother one year older. These four children played at being productive artists in a relatively isolated area – "in the provinces" – where
they followed mainly informal instruction, first from their father, and
later through self-study. Possibly Emily felt the loss of her mother as
a three-year-old more acutely than her younger sister Anne, who was

young enough to adapt easily to her mother's sister, who looked after the household and became a substitute mother. Already as a child Emily went off on her own; she liked nature and took long walks over the moors. Of all the children, Emily suffered most from homesickness when they were away: as a pupil at school, in the short period she acted as assistant-teacher in the area, and later with her sister Charlotte at the boarding school in Brussels. All these circumstances, most notably the long period of informal education at home with her father as mentor, and later experimenting with story-telling and writing stories with her siblings, can help explain why Emily was able to make a breakthrough in literature with a book that still appeals to many readers across time and place: not only as a story about *un amour fou*, but also by its plurality of meanings and deep structure, which still speak to the imagination of the modern reader.[218]

As we have seen, the early loss of a parent or other dear one is an event that can determine the shape of an entire life.[219] All original creations can be considered as re-creations of what was once loved and then lost – a mother, a father, a friend: Montaigne's *Essays*, Darwin's *Origin of Species*, Rimbaud's poems, Proust's *In Search of Lost Time*. This connection has also been found in the work of Edgar Allan Poe (1809–49). He was the second child of artistic parents, whom he lost before he was three years old. His father had left the family earlier and Poe slept in the same bed as his sick mother. One morning he woke up to find his mother dead beside him. Poe was adopted and educated in Richmond, Virginia, by the family of a well-to-do merchant, John Allan, from whom he acquired his middle name. He grew up as their only child, and in 1815, when the Napoleonic Wars were over, he traveled as a six-year-old with them to Europe. After a short stay in Scotland, the family left for London, where Poe went to school. After five years they returned to Richmond. When Poe was eighteen he failed at university and left the family after an altercation with his foster-father about debts and career choice. In Poe's case, the loss of his mother carried more weight than birth order. Poe had an older brother but did not grow up with him.

The loss of his mother, whom he venerated, dominated Poe's life and his work. In his explanation of the theme and plot of his most famous poem, "The Raven," he observed: "The death then of a beautiful woman is unquestionably the most poetical topic in the world, and equally is it beyond doubt that the lips best suited for such topic are those of a bereaved lover."[220]

Poe also had a close bond with his foster-mother. Later he lived with his aunt and her thirteen-year-old daughter, Virginia, whom he married in 1836. As in his stories and poems, the relationship with the beautiful Virginia, who died early, remained in all likelihood romantic and platonic – a celibate marriage.[221]

With three detective stories Poe introduced a new genre in western literature. In "The Purloined Letter" Poe shows that nothing is less obvious than what is right in front of us – both figuratively and literally. With this point of view he anticipated modern philosophy of language and the exotopy of the ethnographer, as well as the epistemological implications of anthropological research. Anthropologist Sahlins refers to an observation by colleague Ruth Benedict: "the last thing an intelligent fish would be likely to name is the water in which it swims." Comments Sahlins: "How much can the participants know of the culture by which they know?"[222] A century after Poe, Wittgenstein noted, "The aspects of things that are most important for us are hidden because of their simplicity and familiarity. (One is unable to notice something – because it is always before one's eyes.)"[223]

Poe's innovation is the creation of the detective C. Auguste Dupin. As a well-to-do bachelor living on his own as an outsider, Dupin discovers, tracks down, and brings to light things that are too obvious to be noted by ordinary people, including the police. The purloined letter in Poe's eponymous story, a possession of great value to various people, is not tucked away or hidden in the office of the thief, but lies on his desk in plain sight along with other things; it is thus missed by the police who look everywhere in vain for something they assume is *concealed*. Missing something obvious is sometimes called the "purloined letter effect" in tribute to Poe. Just like Dupin, detectives in popular culture are frequently single and asexual, marks that metonymically indicate their position as an outsider. Examples abound: Arsène Lupin, Sherlock Holmes, Hercule Poirot, Miss Marple, Tintin, and Adrian Monk. Georges Simenon's Maigret is indeed married and a police inspector, but acts in the stories as functionally single, just like the contemporary unmarried Sicilian colleague, Commissario (Inspector) Montalbano.

Outside America Poe's work was first praised in France, where the poet Charles Baudelaire was fascinated by Poe's personality, his poems, stories, and literary theories. He rendered Poe a great service by translating his work so excellently that in some cases, according to some experts, the translations exceed the original. As would happen a hundred years later with Faulkner, Poe first had a fruitful effect on French literature and, because of that, later influence on English and American literature. It is no exaggeration to say that the detective story was Poe's invention and that generations of this new genre descend from Poe's "The Murders in the Rue Morgue," passing by Sherlock Holmes.[224]

Poe's work also inspired other French-speaking artists, in particular the Belgian surrealist painter René Magritte (1898–1967), who was a great admirer of Poe's preoccupation with a combination of the real and the artificial. This is reflected in Magritte's painting *Le Domaine d'Arnheim*, echoing a Poe title, and *La Réproduction Interdite*, which features a copy of Poe's *The Narrative of Arthur Gordon Pym of Nantucket*.

Hans Christian Andersen (1805–75) was born as the only child of poor parents in the poorest section of Odense, then Denmark's third city. His father was a shoemaker in his late twenties and his mother was an illiterate washerwoman just a few years older than her husband. His father read books to his son and reading soon became Andersen's favorite activity, along with playing with a puppet theater his father built for him. His mother also told him folktales. Both parents made it clear to him that he was a special child and they contributed more to his education than the schools Andersen attended in Odense, where he stood out by his unusual physique: he was tall and gangly, with long, thin arms and legs, big feet and a high voice that emphasized his girlish appearance, for which he was bullied at school and at work.

Andersen's early artistic interests hardly brought him in touch with other children, either. He had few friends. In class he was a dreamy child and showed little interest in what the teacher had to say. Taken out of school after the early death of his father when he was eleven, he never learned to spell correctly (not unlike his contemporary Melville) and worked in a factory, where he gave a rendering of his soprano voice. The workers listened attentively but harassed him afterwards to check if he was a girl or a boy. His mother took him to other workplaces. When he was fourteen Andersen left for Copenhagen with the money he had earned with his "performances" as a singer at the homes of well-to-do families in Odense. He wanted to become a singer and actor – and also to escape from what he called his roots as a "swamp plant." In Copenhagen, because of his soprano voice, he obtained a position at the Royal Choir School, but after a year his voice broke and he was dismissed. He then performed irregularly as a dancer and actor, and appealed to a former girlfriend from Odense who was also living in Copenhagen. She supported him financially and also persuaded her friends to help him out. Through another friend he was put in touch with an established writer who offered him lessons in Danish and German. The friend also organized a subscription fund. A former friend from Odense was a librarian at the university who allowed Andersen to borrow books without payment. Andersen became an avid reader and understood that, from a social point of view, writing was a winning card.

Decisive for his later development was his contact with a highly placed and influential benefactor and patron, Jonas Collin, who had trust in him and provided him with funding to follow a secondary education, which he completed under difficult circumstances. At this school, too, he did not fit in because he was much older than his classmates and did not like the director in whose house he lodged.[225]

Initially Andersen published verse. A comic fantasy, in the style of E. T. A. Hoffmann, about his daily walks from his house to his private tutor and back, called "A Walking Tour," drew attention. A scholarship from the king enabled him to travel to Italy and write a novel, *The Improvisatore*, which became a big success. In the same year, 1835, the first installment appeared of his fairy tales, followed by new collections which established Andersen's reputation as the creator of a new literary genre, and eventually made him a world-famous writer while he was still alive. The poor orphan boy from the periphery was now widely celebrated, recognized, and invited everywhere, including to the Royal Danish Court to drink tea with the king and queen. Elsewhere in Europe, too, he was a guest in distinguished circles and received like a prince. Written both for children and grown-ups, his tales criticized hypocrisy and satirized class society. In the course of time, they were translated into more than one hundred different languages.

Biographer Wullschlager notes a direct connection between Andersen's position as outsider and his innovative literary achievement: how he made use of his adversity and social exclusion for the composition of his tales. She describes how, with the charm of an innocent and promising child, he could turn people from all walks of life into friends and mediators. This took place in the age of Romanticism, a time of great social contrasts when a child of humble background might be considered unspoiled, innocent, and promising, and thus in need of protection and encouragement. Andersen's ability to be eagerly alert to chances and take the initiative, convincing influential people of his talent and zeal, casts doubt on the social awkwardness often ascribed to him. Even before he was eighteen, he was already aware of his potential and drive when he noted in a letter of 1823: "If anyone can become a poet through the events of his childhood, then I will become one."[226] He would show this in his most autobiographical and most famous tale, "The Ugly Duckling," which reflects every episode in Andersen's odyssey. Before writing the story, in one day (in November 1843), he had, so he said, thought about it for a whole year.[227]

Andersen's bisexuality reinforced his position of outsider.[228] He fell in love several times, first with women, later with men, mostly people with whom he had relations of friendship. His infatuations remained unrequited and Andersen never married. Wullschlager believes that it wasn't physical passion but artistic sensitivity that dominated these relationships.[229]

Andersen's stories brought about a turn in the nature of fairy tales. He initiated a new genre for both children and grown-ups, in which he ridiculed establishment customs and conceptions. Some titles of these tales have become general concepts: "the ugly duckling," "the emperor's new clothes." In "The Little Match Girl," "The Steadfast Tin Soldier," and "The Nightingale," Andersen builds on the work of E. T. A. Hoffmann, who introduced an interweaving of dream and reality and of life and automata – themes that return in the work of Poe and Lewis Carroll.

The influence of E. T. A. Hoffman (1776–1822) reaches far into the twentieth century. His tales about doubles, split personalities, and the supernatural not only provided a source for Andersen, Poe, Gogol, Nathaniel Hawthorne, Carroll, Robert Louis Stevenson, and Kafka, but also influenced the work of Freud on the unconscious and his essay "The Uncanny" ("Das Unheimliche," 1919), in which he extensively cites from Hoffmann's *Die Elixiere des Teufels* (*The Devil's Elixir*). Hoffmann, who also played the piano and composed music, inspired various composers with his tales, including Jacques Offenbach, Léo Delibes, Pyotr Tchaikovsky, and Paul Hindemith. Because of his influence on Andersen, Wullschlager provides a minibiography of Hoffmann, paying attention to his grotesque appearance, the circumstances in which he grew up, and his strikingly peripatetic existence, and she celebrates his artistic manysidedness.[230]

Ernst Hoffmann was born in 1776 in Königsberg, eastern Prussia, as the youngest son. His parents were first cousins and both had degrees in law. The father was a lawyer, but also a poet and an amateur musician. When Hoffmann's parents divorced a few years after his birth, the father left with his oldest son and Ernst remained with his mother and other relatives on his mother's side: a grandmother and her three unmarried children, his uncle and two aunts, all of them charged with his education. Hoffmann would later regret the separation from his father, but remember the love of his aunts and render this in his tales – which were also inspired by his personal experiences in an unsettled career after he began studying law in

113

Königsberg (now Kaliningrad). As a child between five and twelve, Hoffmann received instruction in drawing and music. For both he showed great interest and ability, as is clear from his caricatures, brilliant piano playing, and many compositions. He became close friends with a classmate, Theodor von Hippel, with whom he also studied in Königsberg. Hippel would remain loyal to Hoffmann all his life and help him out at critical moments – of which there were quite a few.

Wullschlager describes Hoffmann as "short and ugly as a caricature: a huge head, a shock of black curls, a big nose, thin lips pressed together, tiny hands and feet," but omits to note the extent to which Hoffmann's appearance played a role in his life, imagination, and work – precisely because we are concerned with a writer with a strongly divided inner life, who is skillful at fabricating caricatures of people in positions of authority and tales about doubles, mirror images, shadows, and human/animal figures. His diaries are full of references to doubles and "divided self-images": "I imagine that I see myself through a multiplying glass – all the forms which move round me are myselfs [ichs]."[231]

After an affair with a music pupil ten years his senior, who was married and had children, Hoffmann had to leave Königsberg when he was eighteen. He found a job with another brother of his mother, a jurist in Glogau (now Głogów) in Prussian Poland. After his exams, in 1798, he left for Berlin with his uncle, who was appointed to a court. Hoffmann finished the third round of his exams and went to Posen (now Poznan) for a position as civil servant at a court. After his marriage in 1802 to Misha, the daughter of a member of the municipal council, he left for another city in Prussian Poland. Finally, his friend Hippel provided him with a position of civil servant in Warsaw, where he did well until the end of 1806, when Napoleon took the city and disbanded the Prussian administration. At the age of thirty, Hoffmann was without work and without money.[232] He left for Berlin, also occupied by French troops. Loans from friends kept him alive and it was at this time that he wrote one of his best compositions.

Between 1808 and 1813 Hoffmann worked in various positions with a theatrical company in Bamberg. He also gave music lessons, fell in love with his pupil Julia Marc, and wrote music reviews for the *Allgemeine Musikalische Zeitung*. His articles on Beethoven were well received, in particular by the composer himself. A year later his breakthrough followed with the publication of *Ritter Gluck*, a story about a man who met the composer Christoph Willibald Gluck (1714–87), or believed he had met him (or that he was himself Gluck), more than twenty years after the death of the composer. The theme refers to the work of a novelist known as Jean Paul (1763–1825), who invented the term "Doppelgänger" (double) and subsequently greatly influenced Hoffmann and also became one of his earliest admirers. Later, Hoffmann became director of an opera company and traveled back and forth between Dresden and Leipzig to avoid the dangers of war from Napoleon's troops. After the end of the attack on Dresden, Hoffmann visited the bloody battlefields around the city and wrote a report on it. In the aftermath of Napoleon's defeat in Russia, Hoffmann returned to Berlin in 1814 and was appointed as Councillor of the High Court of Justice in Berlin. In these years he wrote his most important works.

Paradoxes and contrasts marked Hoffmann's life. In spite of his senior position, he was often without work and suffered poverty. His unsettled career was largely due to the Napoleonic Wars: once he had settled somewhere, he had to leave and was without work. Paradoxes also existed between his role as an official and that of an artist. In his work he satirized the established bourgeois order of which he was himself a part. Contrasts also existed between his private life and his public role. He had a satisfying marriage but in Bamberg he maintained an unconsummated love for his former music student, Julia Marc. She was only thirteen when Hoffmann started the lessons, but when she turned sixteen she married a rich businessman from Hamburg and Hoffmann never saw her again. However, she continued to inspire him and was the model for a number of his heroines. Wullschlager adds:

> out of his own harrowing experiences of isolation, failure, and madness, he started a new genre, the supernatural short story in which sanity and insanity, dream and reality are indistinguishable, and where man's greatest struggle takes place not against the external world but within his own mind – Hoffmann points straight to Freud. He wrote by night, and was sometimes so terrified by his bizarre creations, such as Coppelius and the life-sized doll in "The Sandman" . . . that he woke his wife for reassurance. . . . By forty-six he was dead from drink, disappointment and poor nerves, and something of an icon among literary young men. Many nineteenth-century authors – Gogol, Pushkin, Dostoevsky – acknowledged their debt to him.[233]

As noted above, and to acknowledge Hoffmann's impact, other names should be mentioned here, including that of Kafka, perhaps the greatest innovator in western literature. Together with Kleist, Hoffmann was his best-loved writer. He gladly read Hoffmann's works to Dora Diamant when they lived together in Berlin during the last year of his life.[234]

Lewis Carroll (1832–98) came from a well-to-do family of officers and pastors in the north of England (Yorkshire) – once again an innovator "from the provinces." His father married a cousin and became a country clergyman, known as very conservative and High Church. Carroll was an eldest son, the third of eleven siblings. He had a hereditary affliction. Apart from epilepsy and deafness in one ear, he suffered from a mild but troublesome stutter, as well as from micropsia and macropsia: seeing large objects as smaller and vice versa. Shortly before his death, he wrote in a letter that the stutter was what had caused him the most suffering in his life. Apparently, he had always been bullied for it and his shyness arose from this early form of social exclusion. His bitter experiences at Rugby School (where he excelled and won awards) are only mentioned in letters to his family, where he says that "the nights were worse," and later, looking back at this period in his life: "From my own experience of school life at Rugby I can say that if I could have been thus secure from annoyance at night, the hardships of the daily life would have been comparative trifles to bear."[235] He went on to Christ Church, his father's old Oxford college. Along with his religious studies, which made him a clergyman, he excelled in mathematics and was appointed to teach mathematics and logic at Christ Church, publishing a number of specialized texts under his own name, Charles Lutwidge Dodgson. For his children's books, he invented the pen name of Lewis Carroll by translating his first two names into Latin as "Carolus Ludovicus," transposing them, and loosely translating them back into English. Carroll started writing early, but the work for which he is best known only came when he was in his thirties. *Alice's Adventures in Wonderland* and *Through the Looking-Glass, and what Alice found there* originated from stories he told children and he was urged to publish them. Carroll thus added a new dimension to the genre of stories which Andersen had pioneered: not only for children, but also for adults – funny, absurd, timeless, the *mundus inversus* of Wonderland and Mirrorland.[236]

Physically, Carroll differed from his predecessors Andersen and Hoffmann. He did not have their unattractive features and was good-looking: of medium height, slender, and well groomed – not unlike Kafka – with an attractive, modest appearance.[237] Nor did Carroll have the wanderlust of Andersen and Hoffmann. Although he traveled by train through the whole of England and liked to take long walks, he was a more withdrawn, somewhat shy figure who stayed where he had studied and taught. His trip to Russia in 1867 with a friend was an exception. As a clergyman and member of an Oxford college, he remained single, reserved, and a deeply religious Victorian academic.

Yet hiding behind this composure and outward dullness was a revolutionary mind. *Alice's Adventures in Wonderland* (1866), a book for and about children, made effortless fun of establishment practices and beliefs, as well as of the laws of logic. It appealed to the openness and the imagination of children who were not yet adapted adults. The black romanticism and humor of Hoffmann gave way to the dry humor and absurdism of Carroll. Biographers have pointed at the paradoxes in the life and work of the writer, and have been surprised at the attention and love for children from a person who did not have children himself. They asked themselves how an unmarried man, withdrawn inside college walls, could catch the attention of children, fathom and address their feelings, and produce stories that belong to the most popular classics in the English language.[238]

Carroll had a particular weak spot for prepubescent girls. As Cohen writes in his biography:

> For him ... female children embodied the essence of romance: he admired their natural beauty; he valued their spontaneous utterances; he treasured their untrammeled innocence; and he devoted his time, energy, and imagination to amusing and edifying them. He loved to make them laugh, he invented games to play with them, he encouraged them, plied them with gifts, photographed them – he worshiped them.[239]

This is not an exaggeration. A large part of Cohen's biography of more than 500 pages consists of detailed descriptions of numerous meetings he sought with children (mostly through their parents) over a period of about forty years: from 1855, when he was in his early twenties, till a few years before his death in 1898.

> [W]ith children, his favorites, he was particularly inventive. He could laugh with them at the absurdity of the adult world in which they were compelled to live and mature. He mastered the key to a world of frivolity that enabled his child friends, and later a world of child readers, to banish worry, sorrow and fear, and, at least for a transitory minute or hour, to laugh hilariously.[240]

His biographer asks himself: How did Carroll become fascinated by children and why did he remain interested in them all his life? A later thought occurs to him and a casual remark on the last page of Cohen's biography provides an important indication: "Perhaps his failure to correct his speech impediment was the overarching symbol of his entire life. He learned to live with his stammer; he knew what it permitted him to do, what not . . ."[241] As Carroll indicated shortly before his death, his speech impediment interfered especially when he *read* in public and not, or not so much, in conversations with friends or in speaking in public.[242] Earlier in this biography, we read that children considered him very differently than adults, and it is stated later that he was entirely at ease with them, as they were with him, that they found him well spoken, friendly, open-minded, and open-hearted.[243] No wonder that children were such a large element in his life.

In line with the argument of this book, Carroll found a niche for his speech impediment in the company of children and flourished: if his "hesitation" happened at all in their company, it was less pronounced and was not considered a hindrance. Sometimes he made use of an imminent "hesitation" in his story, presenting it as a breathing space and to postpone the point.[244] Among children and good friends he found a place for his impediment, a place where all his qualities (and these were not minor) could be given form, put at their disposal, used to please them.[245] While he felt excluded among adults, as a successful entertainer he was included in the company of children.[246] His marginality in the world of grown-ups linked up with that of children, whom he could therefore amuse with his stories about another, upside-down world – a *mundus inversus* – the world of Wonderland and Mirrorland where other rules prevailed. Carroll also capitalized on still other defects – used and made subservient to his art. His genetic defects of micropsia and macropsia (seeing large objects smaller and small objects larger) were used to give form to the topsy-turvy world in his fiction.

This chapter started with the assertion that wealth, class, intelligence, talent, erudition, and advanced formal education have not been the decisive factors in radical innovation in science and the arts. The great differences in background between Darwin and Wallace, who both pointed to natural selection as the mechanism of evolution, already suggest a different approach: what, apart from the striking differences, did they have in common that might explain their simultaneous discovery of natural selection? It is especially the *differences* between these two leading scientists that make us aware of the decisive *similarities* in their backgrounds: the early adversity and social exclusion that brought about a passion for collecting and led to scientific research. This applies to all the innovators who figure in this book. They form a colorful company, but along with their diversity one finds a striking similarity in their early seclusion and alienation brought about by assorted calamities. These experiences formed the spur for radical innovation in their respective fields: they created the space and freedom for noticing chances and making good use of them.

Nearing the end of this chapter on adversity, we direct our gaze at an artist who in the early twentieth century brought about a revolution in sculpture, with no noticeable support or encouragement from relatives, friends, or mentors – except for a single anonymous benefactor and later feedback from occasional teachers at art schools.

The Romanian Constantin Brâncuşi (1876–1957) came from the provinces: he was born in a peasant village in the southern Carpathians not far from the city of Tîrgu Jiu in the Oltenia region. The area is known for its rich tradition of folk art, especially wood carvings of ornaments for houses and tools. From seven years old, as the youngest son, he had to tend sheep for the poor family in which he grew up. At an early age, Brâncuşi showed his ability in wood carving, but suffered from the teasing of his older brothers and his father's tyranny. To escape the situation he ran away from home several times. After the death of his father he left the parental home for good and worked as an assistant in restaurants and shops, first in Tîrgu Jiu, later in Craiova, where he also had time for wood carving and, studying on his own, learned to read and write. Among other things, he built a violin, which caught people's attention. When he was eighteen, his employer collected money to enable him to study at the local art school. After his final exams, when he was twenty-two, he obtained a scholarship to study at the School of Fine Arts in Bucharest, where he took lessons in modeling and anatomy. In this period he made his first important works, including the sculpture of a man whose skin had been removed to show the muscles underneath (*Écorché*). Although made as a study, the work anticipated later efforts to reveal "the very essence of things," and not make just a copy of their outward appearance. Later, in Paris, Brâncuşi would produce one of his most famous sculptures, *The Kiss*, in which the two people and the act have been adjusted to the material and not vice versa.[247]

In 1903 Brâncuşi traveled, largely on foot, as he said, from Bucharest to Paris, where he would go on to join a circle of avant-garde artists and intellectuals. He stayed with a Romanian friend, worked in restaurants, and took lessons with Antonin Mercié. Impressed by Brâncuşi's work, Rodin invited him to work as his assistant. Only a few months later, Brâncuşi left with the now famous words: "Nothing can grow in the shadow of a great tree." His work now gathered pace, with minimalist sculptures which did not tend to abstraction (a characterization he rejected), but toward what he called the "essence." He increasingly carved sculptures in wood, stone, or marble, though he was still making them in polished bronze, with the long controversial work *Princess X* (1916) as an example.[248] This meant a return to a way of working that was really his own: less foundry work, but cutting into the material itself to reach the "essence of things" instead of rendering outward forms. This probably sounds vague, but each sculpture carved in this way belongs to his revolution in modern sculpture. Brâncuşi had almost immediate success, not only in France, but especially in the United States, a country he visited several times and where much of his work was bought by museums and private collectors.

Brâncuşi was small in stature, single, charming, surrounded by beautiful, often rich, women. He remained a mysterious figure. Initially he was very sociable and hospitable, fond of his friends (who included some famous Romanian émigrés) for whom he prepared Romanian dinners and played the violin, for he was an accomplished player. Later he adopted a more withdrawn lifestyle. Dressed in the traditional outfit of a Romanian farmer, he led a simple, ascetic, retiring life in his Paris studio. Brâncuşi had a wide interest in science and art. He detected the miraculous in many things, and he also believed that his whole life had been miraculous. In 1952 he became a French citizen in order to help a Romanian married couple, who had taken care of him, and to leave his studio and work to the Musée National d'Art Moderne.[249]

Coming from the provinces appears to have been a particular advantage for a striking number of radical innovators in science and the arts. If anything, it put them in the position of an outsider. Peripheral origin led to questions and doubts about what is generally believed, trusted, and accepted. This also affected James Clerk Maxwell (1831–79), a Scot who became a mathematician and physicist known for his discovery of electromagnetic fields, following in the footsteps of Faraday and anticipating Einstein's discovery of special relativity. Maxwell was a single child and grew up on a landed estate in Scotland belonging to his well-to-do father, who later sent him to the Edinburgh Academy. Small of build, James was in a higher class for his age and was made fun of because of his odd outfit, with homemade shoes, and his accent. This earned him the less than flattering nickname of "Daftie," and the accompanying marginalization and social exclusion. Two years of social isolation came to an end when he befriended two students who shared his interests. The three remained friends for life.

Sometimes a radical innovator looks back on his student days and reflects on the consequences and effect of coming from a peripheral area. More than twenty years ago, the French sociologist Pierre Bourdieu (1930–2002) gave an account of this experience in an interview with Loïc Wacquant, one of his former students. Bourdieu grew up as the only child of a postman in a peasant community in the Béarn, a region in the extreme southwest of France in the foothills of the Pyrenees. He went to school in Pau and later studied in Paris at the prestigious École Normale Supérieure. Although he was educated in this breeding ground of the French intelligentsia, Bourdieu declares that he did not feel at home in the university world:

> During my studies at the École Normale Supérieure I felt ill at ease. I might recall the description that Groethuysen gives of the arrival of Rousseau in Paris or what Nizan says in *Aden, Arabie* about his experience at the École Normale: they recall word for word the memory of what I felt when I was there – proof that that experience was not unusual and connected with a social route. *In France, the fact that one comes from a distant province, especially when the area is located south of the Loire, confers on a person certain qualities which correspond to those in colonial situations. There exist more or less subtle forms of social racism which produce a certain clarity: the fact of being continually reminded of your strangeness prompts you to notice things that other people cannot see or feel.* Having said that, it is true that I am a product of the École Normale who has forsaken the École Normale. But you have to come from the École Normale to write such things about the École Normale without creating the impression that you are motivated by resentment.[250]

These are interesting sociological observations. Yet, diverted by the issue of resentment, Bourdieu neglects the great advantages this early social exclusion and discrimination brought him as an outsider in the university world. This vantage ground was already evident at an early stage of his ethnographic research among the Kabyles in Algeria, and in his long essay on celibacy among peasants in the Béarn, his region of origin. Later, Bourdieu said that in these researches he developed key concepts (such as "symbolic violence" and "masculine domination") in his sociology which only later, after publication of his best-known work, *Distinction* (called "an ethnography of France"), became important and influential.[251]

The next chapter links up with the now familiar social context in which radical innovators found their place in the sets of social relations necessary to have historical effect.

121

— 5 —

CHANCE AND NECESSITY

Clearly risk taking is necessary for large success – but it is also
necessary for failure.

> Taleb, *Fooled by Randomness* (2007: xiv)

For all their passion for solitary work, pioneers in science and the arts
remained dependent on other people. These included parents, other
relatives, patrons, benefactors, teachers, mentors, and friends, as
well as intermediaries and sponsors to secure recommendations and
the reception of their work. Most of these circumstances could not
have been anticipated. But when the chances presented themselves,
they could be seized, windows of opportunity could be recognized
and provide a niche. In previous chapters these preambles to radical
innovation have already been traced and noted. It is now time to
shed more light on these sets of institutional and conjunctural relationships from the available biographical materials and get a better
understanding of the role of chance and necessity in radical innovation in science and the arts. A substantial collective biography may
help to specify what has to be explained. On this scale the subject
has hardly been explored, let alone systematically investigated. Nor
have pioneers themselves, as far as one can tell, greatly emphasized
the role of chance and necessity in their careers, probably for fear of
detracting from their own merits or reputations. Erasmus is one of the
few exceptions.

As we saw, the parents of Erasmus sent him to a famous Latin
school in Deventer. It was one of the few places in the northern
Netherlands of which he, discriminated against as an illegitimate
child, had good memories.[1] When he was twelve or thirteen, both
parents died from a plague in Rotterdam. His foster parents sent him

for further education to a monastery in 's-Hertogenbosch and later to Gouda. Erasmus liked the monastic ideal better than the practice. Nevertheless he found some kindred spirits there and made some good friends. It was also where he started his career as a writer through self-study. The occasion to leave the monastery presented itself when the Bishop of Cambrai offered him the position of secretary. Huizinga writes that Erasmus received this offer because of his reputation as a Latinist and man of letters, for the bishop had in mind a trip to Rome, where he hoped to acquire a cardinal's hat. At about twenty-five years old, Erasmus now set foot on a common and sought-after career path: that of an intellectual in the shadow of the greatest.[2]

Because of frequent moves and other discomforts, the work with the bishop was disappointing. Moreover, the trip to Rome was canceled. Erasmus found consolation in completing his *Antibarbari*, a play in the form of dialogues between friends in an atmosphere of idyllic repose and civilized conversation. For Erasmus to become the writer he wanted to be, aristocratic patrons and friends, including printers and publishers in Paris, Venice, and Basel, were indispensable. It was his best friend, Jacobus Battus, who mediated for him and persuaded the bishop to provide Erasmus with a grant to study theology in Paris.

But residence in Paris did not please Erasmus much either and he did not finish his studies. Huizinga observes that it was far from easy to make a living from intellectual work at the time, and not always respected. Erasmus had to rely on either church prebends or financial support from distinguished patrons – and if possible, from both.[3] But a prebend was not easy to obtain and the patrons were unreliable and often disappointing. Publishers only paid famous writers substantial fees. So Erasmus gave lessons to rich young men. With one of them, a young English lord, he left for England at the latter's request. Meanwhile, his friend Battus had found a protector for him: Anna van Veere.[4]

During his first visit to England, Erasmus made many friends and he had the good luck to be presented to the royal family. On his way back to Paris in January 1500, however, he had to hand over his savings of twenty pounds at the customs in Dover because of a new rule that forbade the export of gold and silver. This setback, writes Huizinga, injured him on two fronts: financially, because the meager support from his patron was not enough to live on; and psychologically, because it violated his feeling of self-worth – "his mental balance and his dignity."[5] To make sure of some income, Erasmus, immediately after his return to Paris, started teaching students and collecting, writing, and publishing his *Adagia* (proverbs), on which he would work for much of his life in a long series of revised and expanded editions. With a sense of the irony of history, Huizinga observes, "Yet this mishap had its great advantage for the world, and for Erasmus, too, after all. To it the world owes the *Adagia*; and he the fame, which began with this work."[6] Less accidentally, perhaps, the *Adagia* contains a short entry on the proper way to acquire a Maecenas, or patron. Erasmus's argument comes down to a brilliant sociological sketch of the crucial importance of patronage in societies where, as we now recognize, the central power of states remained weak.[7]

In the meantime, Erasmus studied Greek in Paris for three years, and would later return to England and find there new friends and patrons, including the personal physician of Henry VII, an Italian from Genoa who was looking for a teacher to accompany his sons on a trip to Bologna where Erasmus would be charged with supervising their university studies.[8] In the summer of 1506 the traveling group stayed two months in Paris, where Erasmus took the opportunity to have some of his work printed. He was now a well-known and favorite author, "gladly welcomed by the old friends and made much of."[9] In Italy Erasmus enlarged his network of friends and colleagues. First he spent a year in Bologna under his contract with the young students. Later he went to Venice, where he stayed eight months with the famous printer and publisher Aldus Manutius, who received him cordially, generously offered him board and lodging at his father-in-law's, and printed a much enlarged version of his *Adagia*. "With great temerity on my part," Erasmus testifies, "we began to work at the same time, I to write, Aldus to print."[10]

In those days printers and publishers were often themselves scholars who could put a library at the disposal of their guests. Their firms were nodes in international networks of writers in which Latin was not only the language in which they wrote, but also the lingua franca through which they corresponded and communicated. On his way back over the Alps to England, Erasmus let his thoughts roam over the world as general folly, "folly as the indispensable element making life and society possible and all this put in the mouth of Stultitia – Folly – itself (true antitype of Minerva), who in a panegyric on her own power and usefulness, praises herself."[11]

Once arrived in London, he first stayed in the house of Thomas More, "that most witty and wise of all his friends, with that curious name Moros, the Greek word for a fool, which so ill became his personality,"[12] writing *The Praise of Folly* in a few days. He stayed with friends, living in Cambridge. On his way back five years later, he

124

visited his Maecenas, Lord Mountjoy, in Calais. The destination of the trip, via Antwerp and Louvain across the southern Netherlands, where he called on various friends and patrons, was Basel. He stayed with the publisher Johannes Froben, and shortly after his arrival in August 1514 started on having his manuscripts printed.

> There such pleasures of fame awaited him as he had never yet tasted. The German humanists hailed him as the light of the world – in letters, receptions and banquets. They were more solemn and enthusiastic than Erasmus had found the scholars of France, England and Italy, to say nothing of his compatriots ... Soon the work for which he had come was in full swing. He was in his element once more, as he had been at Venice six years before: working hard in a large printing-office, surrounded by scholars, who heaped upon him homage and kindness in those rare moments of leisure which he permitted himself.[13]

At Froben's place he also met the painter Hans Holbein the Younger, who made a number of matchless portraits of him during the several years Erasmus stayed in Basel, and also illustrated *The Praise of Folly*. Their collaboration would extend their lasting fame.

Through his work, Erasmus became better known and more famous. Offers of stipends, annuities, and university chairs flowed to him from all points of the compass. But he did not accept any of them. He wanted to go on with his work and not break contact with the great printing houses. It "would have meant a postponement of his life-work."[14] It had become an honor for a Maecenas to add a celebrated scholar to his domain – and Erasmus would certainly have been a jewel in the crown of more than one of them. In patronage the distinction of the patron not only radiates out to his protégé, but in this case we also see the opposite: the intellectual authority and the prestige of the learned client enhanced the esteem and prestige of the patron. Erasmus's contemporary Machiavelli also understood this, as witnessed by his famous letter to Lorenzo de' Medici, to whom he dedicated his book *The Prince*.[15]

Almost a century later, we see the same thing happen with Galileo, who dedicated his pamphlet *Sidereus Nuncius* (1610), the report of his discovery of the four moons of Jupiter with the use of a telescope, to Grand Duke Cosimo II de' Medici.[16] In this way he hoped to obtain the latter's patronage for a favorable appointment at the University of Florence, which, along with teaching, would give him more time for research and publishing than he was allowed in Padua. By also naming the new "planets" after the Medici ruler, Galileo accomplished a "masterstroke" in elevating himself from the level of an obscure professor of mathematics at the University of Padua to the status of the most wanted client in Italy.[17] For much of his adult life as mathematician and "philosopher," Galileo remained attached to the Medici court. This experience made him familiar with the patronage system to the extent that later biographers suggest that the social legitimacy Galileo acquired in this environment contributed to the intellectual legitimacy of his innovative theories.[18]

Patronage is a special form of reciprocity between socially unequal persons and has also been called "lopsided friendship," thus recognizing both the personal and the instrumental aspects of the relationship. Moreover, the relationship is "multistranded," that is, the partners depend on each other in more than one way.[19] There are numerous examples of patronage in which the word "patronage" is not used and people speak of "friends" while still recognizing the hierarchical patron–client character of the relationship. Both parties are strongly interdependent. We cannot understand their relationship without the informal and reciprocal exchange of goods and services – and not least, honors and favors. According to some historians, patronage was "perhaps the most pervasive institution of preindustrial society."[20] Yet patronage also figures in the modern world, albeit in more hidden forms, where people likewise speak of "friends" who exchange services and cannot refuse favors. Earlier, in the eighteenth-century Dutch Republic, members of the urban upper class (*regenten*) practiced so-called "contracts of correspondence" (mutually preferential treatment, also called "patronage") in appointments for public office. Today both the terminology and the practices have acquired pejorative connotations. Similar forms are now differently defined and conceptualized, and described in terms of networking, cooptation, sponsorship, lobbying, old boy networks, and reciprocity in other informal circuits. Friendship – in the sense of "friends of friends" – still animates the modern world of politics, science, sports, arts, and literature.

As mentioned above, the German poet Rilke can serve as an example of a pioneer who was supported by well-to-do patrons who enabled him to write and publish. For several years from about 1910 onward, he enjoyed the protection from his maecenas, Princess Marie von Thurn und Taxis. It was at her castle Duino, situated on the northern Adriatic coast, that (with long intervals) he wrote his *Duino Elegies*, which he dedicated to her, as he had done before with other work. Twenty years older than Rilke, this Austrian princess "was not only patroness and helper in need, but at the same time the liveliest and most sensitive woman friend and mother-figure of exceptional

126

rank."[21] She was not the only patron of Rilke, who spent a great deal of his adult life traveling from one great house in Europe to another to write.[22] In the last years of his life he settled in the small Château de Muzot, located on the Rhône near Sierre in the Swiss canton of Valais. This place was put at his disposal by the married couple Werner and Alma Reinhart, who first had the medieval tower renovated and rented it to him, and later bought it for him.[23] Rilke observed of his seclusion at Muzot in the Alps that "its solitude and high and exceptional silence continue to favor many a productive hour."[24]

Radical innovators often existed by the grace of patronage. We are concerned here with young people who were usually considered promising or "talented." Following severe adversity, they fell outside accepted social frameworks after the early loss of parents, parental neglect, minority status, illness, exile, bankruptcy, or poverty, and had to find a niche in the margins of society and therefore had to look for protection or sponsorship. It sometimes happened that they obtained this support without their knowledge. As mentioned before, for Newton to go to Cambridge rather than working on the family farm as his mother wished, it took at least three people to intervene and to convince his mother to give her permission: the headmaster of Newton's school; his mother's brother, a local clergyman who had a degree from Cambridge; and the brother-in-law of the pharmacist in whose house Newton was living, Humphrey Babington, a clergyman in the area and also a fellow at Trinity College, Cambridge, who had taken a liking to Newton and would later become his protector at Trinity.[25] Nearly two centuries later, similar events affected Mendel, who was supposed to take over the family farm in a small village in Moravia. His two sisters helped out: the elder one asked her husband to buy the farm, and the younger one gave Mendel part of her inheritance to let him finish gymnasium. In a similar vein, we would probably never have heard of Darwin without decisive interventions and chances being seized: if his botany professor – his mentor and patron John Stevens Henslow at Cambridge – had not recommended his protégé as "naturalist" on the trip with the *Beagle*, and if Darwin's uncle – a mother's brother – had not acted as intermediary and persuaded Darwin's grumbling father to agree to the trip, which, as we know, would eventually become a turning point in Darwin's life as well as in our perspective on life on earth.[26]

The decisive role of fortuitous circumstances in the making of radical innovators has long been neglected, not only in popular culture but also in the history of science and cognitive psychology, where the preoccupation with "talent," "intelligence," "personality," and the cliché of the "isolated genius" has until recently had the upper hand and seemed nearly ineradicable. Cognitive psychologist Robert Weisberg convincingly deconstructs the notion of "genius" in *Creativity: Genius and Other Myths* (1986). He demonstrates that radical innovators in science and the arts were not more intelligent or gifted than other people. Their achievements are the result of an early start, dedication, feedback from mentors, prolonged exercise, acquiring skills, and a basic knowledge of their field.[27]

A confirmation of these findings is offered by a similarly comparative essay by K. A. Ericsson et al. (1993), which demonstrates that what is crucial to attaining *perfect performance* in sports and music is not talent but development of skills in an early learning period of about ten years, which he calls *deliberate practice*, under supervision of a mentor who provides feedback. Ericsson assumes that this also applies to scientific work and the arts. What people call "talent" is empirically difficult to demonstrate, and what is seen as talent is not prior, but can be the result of *deliberate practice*. To prove this point, various cases are presented of people with "anti-talent" who, through prolonged exercise, or deliberate practice, under the supervision of a mentor, surmounted their handicaps and reached exceptionally high achievements. The essay mentions the example of Wilma Rudolph, who recovered from polio as a child through prolonged and intensive training, and as a twenty-year-old won three gold medals in athletics at the Olympic Games in Rome in 1960.[28] Another example of "anti-talent" is the career of the American dancer and choreographer Martha Graham (1894–1991), who despite her short stature and prejudice from men, revolutionized the world of ballet.[29] Ericsson's essay on the development of skills through sustained deliberate practice in order to reach perfect performance unfolds a perspective that touches on the blessings of adversity in science and the arts.

Yet the image of the lonely genius still occasionally arises phoenix-like from its ashes, as happens in the work of Michael Howe, *Genius Explained* (1999). There is, of course, no reason not to use the word "genius" as long as one realizes that it does not explain anything. The term amounts to nothing more than a label, a romantic, idealized attribution to a person who has achieved something particularly outstanding that lies beyond the reach of ordinary people, whether we are talking about leading violinists or scientists. The work of so-called geniuses is the result of sustained hard work, dedication, and the development of skills rather than talent or other innate qualities. On the other hand, some pioneers did contribute to the cliché of the lonely genius with an egocentric self-fashioning, ignoring the contributions of other people, including those of their own mentors. It is to one of these that we now turn.

Even the amiable Darwin did not escape from failing to appreciate the significant contributions made by other people when he summed up his work in his autobiography. Most notably he neglected to acknowledge substantial contributions of his former professors. His mentor at Edinburgh University, the zoologist Robert Grant, the teacher who took his protégé on excursions and expeditions and thus laid the foundation for Darwin's scientific work, is only mentioned in passing. As one biographer observes, "The importance of the collaboration with Grant can hardly be overrated."[30] Similarly, his older brother and best friend Erasmus helped him through the first year in Edinburgh and encouraged him with his studies. Himself unmarried and living in London, whenever he was needed, for his whole life he was always on his brother's side. After Darwin's return from the voyage on the *Beagle*, Erasmus introduced him to his network of intellectual friends in London. Yet Darwin mentions in his autobiography that they were so different that "I do not think that I owe much to him intellectually."[31] Darwin apparently also forgot to mention that his brother had recommended and lent him a copy of Malthus's *Essay on the Principle of Population* – the key to his evolution theory – when he noted in his autobiography:

> In October 1838, that is, fifteen months after I had begun my systematic enquiry, I happened to read for amusement Malthus on *Population*, and being well prepared to appreciate the struggle for existence which everywhere goes on from long-continued observation of the habits of animals and plants, it at once struck me that under these circumstances favourable variations would tend to be preserved, and unfavourable ones to be destroyed. The result of this would be the formation of new species. Here, then, I had at last got a theory by which to work.[32]

The entire genre of the autobiography not only suffers from what the author still can and wants to remember, but especially from all that has been forgotten. We have seen that Enzensberger considers the genre of the autobiography as inherently unreliable: "Wahr beschreiben können eine Person nur andere [A true description of a person can only come from other people]."[33] With this phrase Enzensberger endorses the important epistemological point (in anthropology): "It takes another culture to know another culture."[34]

In his autobiography, Darwin acknowledges the role of his mentor and patron Henslow at Cambridge, "a circumstance which influenced

129

my career more than any other ... was my friendship with Prof. Henslow." But Darwin is thrifty with praise. As in his judgment about his brother, we hear at the end of the paragraph in his auto-biography that Darwin does "not suppose that anyone would say that [Henslow] possessed much original genius."[35] This unnecessary posthumous kick came from a former friend who had the reputation of always walking with Henslow during expeditions and who had learned a great deal from him; Henslow was the man who had "made him" and had recommended him for the trip with the *Beagle*.[36]

At the end of the second volume of her biography, Browne indi-cated the superficiality of Darwin's autobiography:

> in choosing which memories to record in words, in selecting the anec-
> dotes, he was constructing himself in the shape in which he wished
> to know himself and be known by. . . . He believed everything he
> had attained was the result of his own industry. Looking back, he
> reckoned he learned nothing at school; nothing from his father, who
> considered him "a very ordinary boy"; nothing from two universities
> except that which was performed under his own steam. Everything
> accomplished on the voyage was through his own hard work. . . . There
> was a decidedly self-congratulatory element to this. He could not even
> believe that the subject of evolution had been "in the air." . . . Darwin
> was incapable of seeing himself as others saw him. In an oddly engaging
> manner, he remained a stranger to himself.[37]

Numerous remarks of Darwin reveal his paradoxical unworldliness – paradoxical partly because of his five-year trip around the world and his contacts with people from all walks of life. Yet, as he repeatedly emphasized, work meant everything to him. Consequently his social contacts rarely developed into social relationships. His correspond-ence to obtain information for his lifework involved contacts all over the world, as well as contacts with people in his own area with whom he compared notes about the results of artificial selec-tion, an important analogy for his investigations of natural selec-tion (which, of course, he did not mention to his informants). His voluminous correspondence kept people at a distance. His friends were colleagues with whom he could talk about his work. Even his relationships with his most intimate friends, geologist Charles Lyell and botanist Joseph Hooker, and later Thomas Huxley, had a strongly instrumental side. Their personal life hardly interested him. In this respect, Darwin could go to extremes. For example, he could not be persuaded to visit his friend and mentor Henslow on his deathbed, even though he had been the most loyal student of the man "who had made him." He also ignored the request of his closest friend, Hooker, who was the son-in-law of Henslow, to attend the funeral.[38] Darwin also managed to avoid the funeral of his father and later also that of his mentor, friend, and protector Lyell, on similarly unconvincing grounds: his illness, missing the train. Where social obligations were at issue, Darwin usually appealed to his chronic illness. Merely the prospect having to attend these public occasions made him feel unwell.[39]

Darwin never made a secret of standing with his back to society: everything around him, including members of his family, was subservient to his work. This was already clear from the tenor of his private notes on marriage mentioned earlier. Purely businesslike, functional, down-to-earth considerations made him decide for marriage with Emma, his cousin with whom he was not in love, but liked a lot.[40] What held less for Emma, strongly held for other people in his circle: they were all amiably used to make his work possible. In all his egocentrism he remained the formal English gentleman – including in his autobiography, as Browne rightly points out.[41]

Darwin's fundamental dependence on his friends also appears from the reception history of his work. In the spring of 1858, there was a threat he might be forestalled by Wallace with the arrival of his letter in the post, enclosing a revolutionary paper on the evolution of species. Darwin recognized a blueprint of his argument in his nascent magnum opus on natural selection, and made an urgent appeal to his most loyal friends, Lyell and Hooker. With Darwin's approval, they found an elegant solution in the form of a joint publication, with which Wallace, out of easy reach in the Moluccas, turned out also to be happy.[42] The course of the further reception of the discoveries of Darwin and Wallace also depended on a number of accidental circumstances. After reading Wallace's paper, Darwin himself spoke of a "coincidence": "I never before saw a more striking coincidence," although later it transpired that there were also significant differences between the two theoretical schemes. Moreover, Darwin had neglected the extent to which "evolution had been in the air" for quite a while and had ignored Lyell's warning to finish his book on natural selection to avoid being forestalled. The receipt of Wallace's paper had serendipitous effects on both Darwin and Wallace. First, it forced Darwin to write *The Origin of Species* (instead of completing his greater work on natural selection). Here, along with the mechanism of natural selection (a term Wallace did not use), he also now emphasized the working of the "principle of divergence," which had fulfilled a key function in Wallace's paper, along with the concept of the "struggle for life."[43]

After completing *The Origin of Species*, Darwin could once more rely on his established friends Lyell, Hooker, and Huxley for its launch, and they acquitted themselves of this task with great effect: the book sold out in a single day and Huxley successfully presented it in a series of public meetings in various places in 1859 and 1860. Finally, the success of the book radiated out on to Darwin's colleague and co-discoverer Wallace, who, from being a still largely unknown outsider, was incorporated into an established circle of leading scientists. In this way, his unintended preemptive coup had an unintended effect. Even so, the joint publication of their papers and notes in alphabetical and chronological order in the *Proceedings of the Linnean Society* in 1859 implied Darwin's priority: it was Wallace who supported Darwin. As Wallace's biographer phrased it: "Thus Wallace – from the perspective of history – was relegated to a secondary role in the greatest scientific revolution of modern times."[44]

The paradoxes marking Darwin's life do not end at this point. Quite a few people have raised the question of how a person who was chronically ill, and had therefore to periodically interrupt his work, could collect so much data as convincing proof for a "materialistic" theory that gave chance alone the role of divine providence and made biblical authority yield to the working of the laws of nature. Darwin's chronic illness had two sides: his illness interrupted his work, but it also made his work possible because it provided him with an excuse to restrict socializing and carry on with his work.[45] It is difficult to imagine how the enormous production and high quality of Darwin's work (let alone his huge correspondence) could have been realized otherwise.

Darwin may have been an extreme example – and therefore possibly a revealing case – of radical innovators for whom "things were more important than people," to paraphrase an insightful observation of the evolutionary biologist William Hamilton.[46] It is precisely in the passionate devotion to collecting specific facts and the search for the theory that best fits them, which hardly leaves room for other activities, that we find the quintessence of the habitus of the pioneering scientists and artists portrayed in this book. Their dedication can be demonstrated and understood in the light of early adversity and social exclusion. What some radical innovators claim to have "accomplished under their own steam" appears to have been an illusion, however, in view of the encouragement, help, feedback, and protection from other people. No less unusual was their selfishness, which confirmed and may have reinforced the still prevalent picture of the "isolated genius."

Such "antisocial" features testify to a habitus of social and spatial seclusion that originated in early social exclusion following destabilizing adversity – often early parental loss or parental abuse. Pioneers found a niche in social exclusion after having chosen activities that did not require the presence of other people: a place in science or the arts where they could flourish. In this way, solitude and seclusion could become blessings – as in Einstein's famous "precious solitude" and Rodin's motto "always work, and have patience" that inspired the young Rilke. Both Rodin's conception of work and Cézanne's paintings made the young Rilke change his worldview and move toward more "realistic" writing – no longer waiting for "inspiration."[47]

Many pioneers remained unmarried because of their total involvement in their work. As argued above, those who were married were no exception because their partners (or other people) took care of domestic chores. They included Kepler, Bach, Darwin, Curie, and Freud. Marriages that remained childless also fit this pattern. As happened with Lavoisier, Clausewitz, and Max Weber, and in a handful of other cases, the wife was more than an assistant and functioned as a colleague, sparring partner, and provider of feedback, and in some of these cases wives edited and completed work left behind by their partners and ensured its posthumous publication. Some pioneers married late or later, after their breakthrough in their field. They fall into the category of single pioneers, including Boerhaave, Watson, Goodall, and Hamilton.

Unlike Darwin, Einstein never made a secret of the support, assistance, and contributions of his colleagues and friends, most notably Mileva Marić (before she had a child), Marcel Grossmann, and Michele Besso, along with two members of their short-lived discussion club "Akademie Olympia," Maurice Solovine and Conrad Habicht. They were all a few years older than Einstein. With Besso in particular he remained a personal friend for his entire life, playing music together from their days in high school in Aarau. Strong personal ties also existed between Einstein and Hendrik Lorentz (1853–1928), although their opinions on ether differed. A generation younger, Einstein admired Lorentz and regarded him as a father. He often visited him in Leiden and at his house in Haarlem. At Lorentz's funeral in 1928 Einstein showed his admiration for "the greatest and most noble-minded man of our time." For the commemoration of Lorentz's hundredth anniversary in 1953 he wrote: "He meant more to me personally than anybody else I have met in my lifetime."[48] Very much like Darwin, however, Einstein never publicly acknowledged the influence of other scientists on his work.[49]

What distinguished Einstein from Darwin was his personality. Einstein was charismatic, had a sense of humor, and could have fun with his friends. Darwin was socially awkward and avoided appearing on public occasions. The mere thought of attending a social meeting upset him. The question very much arises as to whether Darwin could enjoy anything except his work: to one of his sons he said he only felt comfortable when he was at work. Where work was concerned, there were also differences in reception history. While Einstein's breakthrough was recognized and praised relatively quickly, including outside his own circle (although not always understood), Darwin's *The Origin of Species*, although readable and lucid for everyone, long remained controversial both within his own circle and outside it. Even his longest and most loyal friend and mentor Lyell needed several years before he could, not without a proviso, agree with Darwin's theory – a circumstance that made Darwin ill and shows us one side of his personality: the behavior of a child who does not get his way. Among numerous millions of people Darwin's work is still controversial because of the materialistic implications of a theory in which chance takes the place of God's rule. Even more important: for Einstein God did not disappear totally from the stage and remained hidden behind the scenes in the form of laws of nature. As Einstein phrased it: "God does not play dice."[50] Darwin might have agreed with this thought but lacked savoir faire and the art of coming up with one-liners. Fortunately, he could rely on his friends, most notably Huxley, who effectively took on Bishop Wilberforce after his attack on Darwin's work at the public discussion of *The Origin of Species* in June 1860 in Oxford. The bishop had asked: Was Huxley related on his grandfather's or grandmother's side to an ape?[51]

For a better understanding of what makes pioneers in science and the arts, this chapter addresses the necessity of protection and the decisive role of chance in the circumstances under which protection and further help could be offered, noted, and grasped. It sometimes happened that decisions were taken without the knowledge of the lucky ones themselves – and gratefully accepted. This also illustrates the role of serendipity and necessity: seizing chances that unexpectedly come up for grabs. As we have seen, this happened to Newton as a seventeen-year-old schoolboy when he was offered the chance to go to Cambridge instead of following his mother's wishes and working on her farm.[52] As noted earlier, similar forms of protection happened to the ten-year-old Copernicus after the death of both parents, when he was adopted by his mother's brother, the future Bishop of Ermland (now Warmia), who offered him and his older brother the opportunity to study in Kraków and Bologna. Because Nicolaus Copernicus was successful and returned to Poland after his studies, he remained his uncle's protégé and favorite. In return he became his secretary and personal physician at the bishop's seat in Heilsberg (now Lidzbark Warmiński). This was not far from the cathedral in Frauenburg (now Frombork) on the Baltic coast, where the bishop had earmarked the position of canon, which allowed Copernicus, alongside his other obligations, to work on his masterpiece.

Once again we see the importance of reciprocity in the system of patronage, which Copernicus's contemporary Erasmus wrote about in passages concerning the maecenas and patronage in his *Adagia*: "The first thing a young man should do is to provide an outstanding specimen of his work as a pledge that what is given him will not be wasted."[53] Speaking about one of his own protectors in England, Erasmus writes, "I do not know whether he has regrets about me as his protégé, but I have certainly not repaid to my own satisfaction his kindnesses with my services to him, and I do not think I will ever be able to do so."[54]

Much later, the young Beethoven, too, would seek aristocratic protectors when he arrived in Vienna and performed in their houses as a piano virtuoso and as music teacher for their children. He would further commit himself to his patrons by dedicating compositions to them and in this way immortalize their names. His "Waldstein" Sonata of 1804, for example, was dedicated to his friend Count Ferdinand von Waldstein, and the three middle-period string quartets (Opus 59), dubbed the "Russians," are also called the Razumovsky Quartets, because they were dedicated to the Russian ambassador to Vienna, Count Razumovsky, and because Beethoven incorporated some Russian folksongs in them. Three of the last series of five string quartets, the so-called Galitzin Quartets, were dedicated to his former protector, Prince Nikolai Galitzin.[55]

Identifying and making use of any chances offered was decisive for obtaining patronage. They were the spur to continued radical innovation, as in the life of Kepler, Galileo's contemporary and correspondent. His mentioned zeal at a local Latin school on the periphery of the state of Württemberg was drawn to the attention of the Elector. This resulted in a place as a theology student at the University of Tübingen, which had to provide the new cadre for a state that had turned Protestant. Kepler had the great luck to have a teacher in mathematics and physics who encouraged his interest in astronomy and became his mentor. After finishing his studies, mentor Maeslin also arranged for Kepler's appointment as a teacher of mathematics at a secondary school in Graz. Kepler found time to write his first masterpiece, *Mysterium Cosmographicum*, which he sent to Maeslin.[56] His mentor, who had supervised Kepler during the writing process, arranged publication. He also brought the book to the attention of the Danish astronomer Tycho Brahe (1546–1601), who managed the imperial astronomical observatory near Prague and accepted Kepler as his assistant. The rich aristocratic Tycho neatly matched the poor, myopic Kepler, who was to provide the theory to make sense of the astronomic observations of the Danish scholar.[57] After more than a year of somewhat laborious cooperation, Tycho died suddenly and Kepler, appointed as his successor, could make use of the Dane's observations and continue his work. At first without a telescope, but later, after 1610, with the help of this improving instrument, Kepler completed his work in 1618 with his third law of the elliptic orbits of planets. More than half a century later, Newton concluded the Copernican revolution with his universal law of gravitation.[58]

Biographical information about these four pioneers appears in Koestler's classic, *The Sleepwalkers: A History of Man's Changing Vision of the Universe* (1964). Koestler recognizes that history is contingent: there is no plan underlying world history, and it is the same for the careers of innovating scholars. His choice of the metaphor "sleepwalkers" is less fortunate, however, and perhaps even misleading. But Koestler does recognize the zigzag patterns in the minds and work of his four heroes: Copernicus, Kepler, Galileo, and Newton.[59] He thus acknowledges trial and error as the sole method in scientific research that can lead to a new point of view. This method comes down to taking risks, guessing, and testing – a method Peirce recommends and calls "abduction." When you fail, try again: experimenting is a hallmark of radical innovators.

"Blindness" is perhaps a more fitting metaphor, not as a quality of pioneers, but as a characteristic of the long-term historical processes to which the research of pioneers belongs: long-term developments that evolve in an unplanned way, "blindly," that is, without a premised goal, but nonetheless taking shape in a certain direction and resulting in the design of a more encompassing model.[60] At the end of his book on the structure of scientific revolutions, Kuhn notes, "The analogy that relates the evolution of organisms to the evolution of scientific ideas can easily be pushed too far. But [with respect to progress through revolutions] it is very nearly perfect . . . the resolution of revolutions is the selection by conflict within the scientific community of the fittest way to practice future science."

To which he adds, "the entire process may have occurred, as we now suppose biological evolution did, without benefit of a set goal, a permanent fixed scientific truth, of which each stage in the development of scientific knowledge is a better exemplar."[61] Thirty years later, German philosopher and physicist Stefan Klein took a more decisive step and argued that

> natural and cultural development are both a play of combinations. Here as there, novelty arises when familiar starting materials are put together in a surprising way. The histories of nature and culture travel in step and in both cases the results are not foreseeable. Both proceed without a goal ... In both nature and culture permanent innovations are no luxury but a vital necessity to keep pace with a changing environment. Those who do not experiment cannot develop and will be pushed aside by agile competitors. Both evolution and human creativity lead to growing diversity ... Which way of life and which ideas finally succeed is only determined by competition. Development in both nature and culture would be inconceivable without chance.[62]

The so-called Copernican revolution took shape in stages during the sixteenth and seventeenth centuries: from Copernicus's mathematical model of heliocentrism via Galileo's observations of planets revolving around the sun and Kepler's discovery of the elliptic orbits of planets, to Newton's discovery of the universal law of gravitation which showed how these celestial movements kept everything in place.[63] A similar development can be traced in biology. With the concept of "natural selection," Darwin followed in the tracks of a long discussion on "transmutation," culminating in a development in scientific thought on the evolution of species. This process also evolved in fits and starts ("blindly"). Only in retrospect – with the benefit of hindsight – can its direction and structure be detected and understood. It remains to be seen to what extent the history of science, in its most common form of the history of ideas, will succeed in discovering the structure of these long-term developments instead of endlessly describing its separate stages in ever increasing detail – while the developments themselves indicate a movement toward more encompassing and simpler models. As Einstein suggested on more than one occasion, the best thing that can happen to a physical theory is that "it should of itself point out the way to the introduction of a more comprehensive theory, in which it lives on as a limiting case."[64] Earlier, in 1901, he mentioned to his friend and colleague Marcel Grossmann, "It is a glorious feeling to perceive the unity of a complex of phenomena which appear as separate entities to direct sensory observation."[65]

137

Returning to the role of patronage in the family networks of pioneers, the position of a mother's brother as protector of his sister's son deserves special attention, in particular where there is adversity. The help of the mother's brother in the various cases mentioned above – Copernicus, Newton, Darwin, etc. – was not an exception but part of a more general pattern of specific reciprocal obligations between kin. Anthropologists have found that in various tribal cultures, past and present, the mother's brother is the respected, favorite uncle. He feels responsible for the well-being of his sister's son and devotes his energies to him. Conversely, a nephew may, if need be, call on his mother's brother for help. In some tribal societies, marriage with a mother's brother's daughter can be preferred or even prescribed for his sister's son.[66] Recall that Darwin married the daughter of his uncle on his mother's side. Both families were enthusiastic. Such endogamous marriages were far from uncommon, keeping resources within the local gentry, as Browne rightly points out.

This form of social altruism – a less loaded term than "nepotism" – is not strictly tied to time and place. It has been described in widely different societies, without, however, producing a satisfactory explanation, at least not in anthropology where the subject drew a great deal of attention until the late 1960s, when it all but disappeared from the agenda. The concept of "inclusive fitness" (later called "kin selection"), coined by British evolutionary biologist William Hamilton, may throw new light on the issue of the close bonds between a mother's brother and his sister's son. According to the working of the principle of kin selection, a maternal uncle can be more altruistic than a "father" because he has more reason to trust his genetic relationship with his sister's child than with a child of his own – his wife's child – and in this way there is greater certainty in the reproduction of his genes.[67] A marriage of cousins between a mother's brother's daughter and his sister's son may reinforce this presumed genetic effect. Interdisciplinary research may clarify the issue and help us understand the close bonds between an uncle on the mother's side and his sister's son, as well as the related, frequent marriage pattern in both its preferred and prescribed varieties.

Further research may also help explain why, in the youth of some prospective pioneers who were hit by parental loss, a maternal uncle acted as guardian, advisor, or benefactor in the life or career of his sister's child after the death of (one of) the parents. Apart from those already mentioned, this also happened with Melville, Conrad, and Camus, while Einstein and Kafka also had close bonds with their mother's brother when they were students. With a father who was often absent and later divorced, Jane Goodall, too, depended as a child to some extent on her mother's brother, a physician and surgeon who lived in London and regularly visited the family (of six females) in Bournemouth. He was unhappily married and had no children himself.

Mothers' brothers who acted as stand-in parents or supported their sister's son were indeed often unmarried, widowers, or did not have children themselves. This was the case, as we saw, with Lukasz Watzenrode, the future Bishop of Ermland, who took care of his sister's four children (including the ten-year-old Copernicus). In similar fashion, the widower and childless Tadeusz Bobrowksi, brother of the deceased mother of Polish writer Joseph Conrad, took care of his nephew after his father's death from his eleventh to his sixteenth year. He continued to support him financially and provide him with good advice even when Conrad had enrolled as a mate in the British merchant navy.[68] Siegfried Löwy, the brother of Kafka's mother, was an unmarried country doctor who became the model for the main character in Kafka's story *Ein Landartz*. He was his favorite uncle. Löwy was a witty man with a large library, and he had a great influence on Kafka, who stayed with him as a teenager during his high-school vacations.[69] Camus's father was killed in the first months of the First World War and his mother's brother, Étienne Sintès, paid for his nephew's studies, and appears as a model in various places in his work.[70] Melville's mother's brother, Peter Gansevoort, acted as a support and refuge for his young nephew after his father's bankruptcy and early death.[71] In regard to Einstein, there were early intellectual contributions from his uncle on his mother's side, a trader in grain who lived in Brussels.[72]

As already outlined, Copernicus, born and brought up in Toruń in Poland, was ten years old when he lost his parents. His mother's brother, Lukasz Watzenrode, shortly to become Bishop of Ermland in 1485, took care of his sister's four children: Nicolaus, Andreas (four years older), and their two sisters. Pending the completion of their university studies, Uncle Lukasz arranged stipends for both nephews as canons in absentia at the cathedral in Frauenburg (now Frombork), a Polish town on the coast south of Königsberg, "a remote corner of civilized Christianity," as one biographer phrased it.[73] For the elder daughter of his deceased sister he found a place as a prioress at a Cistercian monastery in his domain; for the younger he arranged a marriage to a Polish nobleman. It would be an anachronism to see these arrangements as illegitimate favoritism. As mentioned earlier, what is regarded as "nepotism" today was then, under totally different circumstances, a moral obligation. Moreover, the cathedral's investment would turn out to be to the benefit of the institution[74] after the brothers completed their studies at the universities of Kraków and Bologna in the 1490s. In the Polish city, the brothers, like their uncle before them, became members of the German student fraternity – an indication that their mother language was German – presumably also the colloquial language in Toruń, the Hanse town on the Vistula River where Copernicus grew up and went to school. Moreover, the surname of their uncle and patron, Watzenrode, has a distinctly German ring.

Andreas was an adventurer who failed miserably. Because of his zeal and achievement, Nicolaus became his uncle's protégé. He studied medicine, canon law, mathematics, and astronomy, the latter in Bologna with the famous astronomer Domenico Navarra, in whose home he lodged and whom he assisted with his astronomical observations. Copernicus also learned Greek in order to read the works of Aristarchos of Samos and other forerunners of heliocentrism in their original versions. After his study of medicine in Padua and his doctorate in canon law, and after more than ten years mostly spent in Italy, he returned to northern Poland. He established himself as his uncle's secretary and personal physician. He also accompanied him on his diplomatic travels in connection with the disputed status of the princedom of Ermland on the Polish and German border. In this way he reciprocated the generosity of his benefactor, who had acted as his patron after the early loss of his parents.

In his free time Copernicus read the books on astronomy he had brought with him from Italy and also worked on a short sketch that became known as *Commentariolus*, which anticipates his main work, *De revolutionibus orbium coelestium* (*On the Revolutions of the Heavenly Spheres*), which appeared in print toward the end of his life, not without outside help. He had circulated a brief summary in manuscript form among friends. Copernicus already writes here about three revolutions or rotations of the earth: around the sun every year, around its own axis every day – hence sunrise and sunset – and a slight, but continuous, rotation around its poles, which explains the changing direction of the earth's axis.[75] Moreover, he used his knowledge of Greek acquired in Italy to translate into Latin the aphorisms of a seventh-century Byzantine historian and poet, Theophylactus Simocattes. It was published in Kraków in 1509 and dedicated in homage to his uncle, guardian, patron, and benefactor, Bishop Lukasz Watzenrode.[76]

There are striking parallels and similarities with the work and life of Erasmus, who had also learned Greek (in Paris at the beginning of his career) in order to translate Greek texts for his *Adagia* (proverbs). As we have seen, in one of them Erasmus points to the obligations of the protégé toward his Maecenas.[77] At the printer and publisher Aldus Manutius in Venice, who was a friend of Copernicus's Greek teacher in Bologna, the paths of Copernicus and Erasmus had crossed. Copernicus visited the publisher, probably for books, in 1503 just before his departure for Poland. After his work in Bologna, Erasmus stayed eight months in 1508 with Aldus to prepare a new and larger edition of his *Adagia*. Erasmus was not always satisfied with what he produced. For the rest of his life he would revise, correct, and expand his work on the *Adages*, writes William Barker, who refers to this time with Aldus as marking Erasmus's working style – an "example of the text that grows by accretion."[78]

Like other pioneers, Copernicus preferred academic training in its informal mode where the teachers were also mentors, especially when it concerned his real interests in astronomy and Greek. He took these courses in his free time alongside the studies in canon law and medicine that qualified him for his work as his uncle's assistant and later (after his uncle's death in 1512) in his role as a secular canon at the cathedral in Frombork where he acted as physician and was also charged with administrative tasks and diplomatic service. His astronomical work in the cathedral tower, with a splendid view of the Baltic Sea, was done in his free time.[79]

Other pioneers, too, had to combine their work with other activities to provide for their livelihood. Einstein worked full-time at the patent office in Bern for a period of seven years, which included his "wonder year," 1905. By chance, the job at the patent office dovetailed with his theoretical work.[80] In order to make a living, Spinoza ground lenses, refusing financial support from his friends.[81] Along with his experiments with peas at the monastery in Brno, Mendel taught at a local high school, kept bees, and did innovative work in meteorology.[82] As a student, Kepler had moved from astrology to astronomy, but still made horoscopes for his patrons when they were seeking perfect timing for their military and political exploits.[83] Newton had to be drawn away from his work on alchemy and Arianism by his colleagues Robert Hooke and later Edmund Halley, who encouraged him to return to his work on celestial motion. Their persuasion eventually resulted in his breakthrough discovery of centripetal forces and the universal law of gravitation.[84] In other cases, the real work fed on other closely related activities, as with Wittgenstein's teaching, when he raised questions and discussed and dictated texts to students, on the basis of which entire books were eventually achieved, most notably *The Blue and Brown Books*.[85]

141

For all Wittgenstein's tendency to solitude, he strongly depended on discussions with friends who would ask critical questions that more than once made him fundamentally change his mind.[86] The economist Keynes was also involved in other professional activities, including working for the government, which had a decisive impact on his theoretical work. He participated in the peace talks between the Allied Powers and Germany in 1919 and criticized the onerous terms imposed on Germany after it had lost the war and had to face losses of territory, foreign occupation, and retribution payments. Keynes foresaw revenge and another war, but was not listened to. Again, in the Great Depression following the financial crisis in 1929, Keynes pleaded in vain for government investment in infrastructure to fight mass unemployment. Only much later was he proven right on both scores.

Returning to the fate of Copernicus's book, it was more from fear of making himself ridiculous by mistakes in his calculations than being hit by ecclesiastical sanctions that he long lingered over the publication of his *De revolutionibus orbium coelestium*.[87] It was obvious that publication would not take place without help from outside. It was the young and enthusiastic Georg Joachim Rheticus, professor of mathematics and astronomy at the (Protestant) University of Wittenberg, who visited Copernicus in Frauenburg. It was only after great persistence that Copernicus was moved to have his book published. That finally happened in Nuremberg in 1543, shortly before the death of the author – who failed to acknowledge the considerable efforts and services of Rheticus in the editing, publishing, and reception of the book.[88] In the introduction, Copernicus dedicated his book to Pope Paul III and did not mention the Protestant Rheticus, whose name was also absent from elsewhere in the book.[89] It would not be the last time that a radical innovator would omit the names and contributions of important supporters.

Heliocentrism remained controversial long after the publication of the *Revolutionibus*, insofar as it was reprinted and read. Both ecclesiastical and secular authorities forbade discussion of the subject in word and writing other than as hypothesis. This did not prevent Kepler (whose teacher Maestlin in Tübingen was a Copernican) and Galileo, independently of one another, looking for further proofs of the Copernican worldview. Only with the invention of the telescope in 1610, which became available in ever more advanced models, could the evidence be found. In the 1680s, and building on the work of his predecessors Copernicus, Tycho, Kepler, Galileo, and Huygens, Newton could complete the Copernican revolution with the universal law of gravitation. Newton not only showed that the earth revolved around its own axis and that the planets in elliptical orbits revolved around the sun, as Kepler had established with his three laws, but also *how* celestial motion took place – the mechanism that made planetary movements possible.[90] Newton's laws of motion and gravitation not only offered an elegant explanation for a large quantity of astronomical observations that had accumulated since the days of ancient Babylon, but also represented fundamental steps in the development of modern physics.[91]

In his position as canon, Copernicus remained unmarried. His place in the chapter did not, however, prevent him from having a mistress: Anna Schillings, probably a distant relative. She acted as *focaria*, meaning both housekeeper and mistress. Copernicus's superiors reprimanded him more than once and the chapter promised amendment. But nothing changed in the situation, which was not unusual at the time, as the double meaning of the term *focaria* indicates.[92] These further shades of general solitude as a basic feature of the unmarried status and the most striking feature of the habitus of pioneers were also found elsewhere. Quite a few unmarried innovators were by no means celibate and lived for years with a woman. While he was professor of mathematics at the University of Padua, Galileo had a relationship with his housekeeper, Marina Gamba, a Venetian woman with whom he had three children. When Galileo returned to Florence in 1610 to work under the patronage of the Medici family, Marina remained in Padua with her four-year-old son, while the two daughters joined their father and later became nuns. Later on, the son also moved to his father's house in Florence.

After an earlier visit to Breda in 1618, where he chanced to meet his future mentor, the Dutch mathematician Isaac Beeckman, René Descartes lived much of his life in various places in the Dutch Republic as an exile of sorts. He remained unmarried but maintained a relationship with his servant girl, with whom he also had a daughter who died when she was five.[93] As mentioned above, the German philosopher Georg Lichtenberg also remained unmarried for a long time, but had many romances. When he was in his early forties, he lived with his young servant girl, his "flower girl." A year after her early death in 1787, he met Margarethe Kellner, likewise a young girl of working-class background. He took her into his service and later married her to make sure she had a pension after his death. She gave him six children and survived Lichtenberg by almost half a century.[94]

Einstein's place in a wide-branching network of relatives and later as a student of mathematics and physics at the Polytechnic Institute in Zurich and in his work at the patent office in Bern, where he was surrounded by congenial friends, offered him numerous chances in the run-up to the exceptional achievements in his wonder year of 1905, when he was twenty-six. The early part played by his parents and uncles was significant, as well as his Jewish background. Einstein knew early that he was "different." He went to school as a child of assimilated Jewish parents, first in Ulm, where he was born, and later in Munich, where his father and uncle had an electrotechnical firm in an epoch when the population was switching to electric lights in the larger cities. Einstein's grandfather on his mother's side had provided a large part of the money needed. After the family's move to Munich, Einstein went to a local Roman Catholic school and soon understood that, as the only Jew, he differed from his seventy classmates, who were mostly anti-Semitic. On the way to school and back he was sometimes molested. It did not upset him, and he did not complain, but he realized that he was different. There was a memorable occasion when the teacher of religion came into the class one morning and showed the pupils a large nail, telling them that a nail of this kind was used to crucify Jesus. Thereupon numerous classmates pointed their fingers at Einstein.[95] This experience emphasized his "difference" and would not have reinforced his already scanty trust in authorities.

His father's and uncle's electrotechnical firm so close to home brought Einstein in touch with technology and science early on. His uncle, who lived in the same house, introduced him to the foundations of mathematics. Earlier, when he was five, his father had given him a compass. It intrigued him that something could move without any visible cause. His musical mother gave him violin lessons. He would remain faithful to the instrument all his life and often play in ensembles, first with his mother and later with his best friend, Besso – preferably Mozart and Beethoven sonatas, which tells us something about his early level of accomplishment: "His violin, on which he improvises for hours, will be his faithful companion."[96] This sideline seamlessly links up with his tendency to "precious solitude," forming the core of his habitus as a radical innovator. Playing and practicing the violin does not require the presence of other people. It is a preeminently solitary practice. Leading violinist Jascha Heifetz (1901–87), also called "the violinist of the century" and considered the embodiment of perfection by many, emphasized the importance of daily practice rather than talent when he said, "If I do not practice one day, I know it; two days, the critics know it; three days, the public knows it."

Following a Jewish custom, Einstein's parents provided him with a mentor to discuss with him what he had read. In Einstein's case it was a medical student, who visited him weekly and also joined them at dinner.[97] Einstein's mother's brother, Caesar Koch, the grain merchant in Brussels, contributed to the informal education of his nephew and surprised the ten-year-old by sending him a toy steam engine.[98] Later, in 1895, when Einstein was sixteen, he sent this uncle a copy of his first scientific essay, entitled "On the investigation of the state of the ether in a magnetic field." It was the first step to his article ten years later on the "electrodynamics of moving bodies" or his special relativity theory.[99] As early as 1901, Einstein had mentioned to the mathematician Marcel Grossmann – one of his close friends, sounding boards, and guardian angels – that "it is a glorious feeling to perceive the unity of a complex of phenomena which appear as separate entities to direct sensory observation."[100]

Missing out on an important public tender, in which the anti-Semitic climate in the city presumably played a role, the electrotechnical firm went bankrupt in 1894. This led to Albert's parents and his younger sister moving to family in Milan and later to nearby Pavía, where they found temporary shelter with relatives who ran a similar firm. Initially Einstein remained in Munich in a boarding house to finish high school. He did not like it very much and after a few months he left by train to join his parents in Milan. Through friends, they found lodgings for him with other students in Aarau near Zurich, where he could complete his last year and matriculate in mathematics and physics at the Zurich Technical Institute. His maintenance during the four years of university studies was taken care of by well-to-do relatives in Italy with a monthly allowance of a hundred francs.[101]

Study and reciprocal help within a network of relatives constitute two major and closely related Jewish traditions. The effect of these strategies by a minority suffering discrimination and persecution did not remain unnoticed. After their official emancipation in the course of the nineteenth century, it resulted in a relative over-representation of Jews in science and the arts – the few fields from which they had not been excluded.[102] This had earlier been the case with commerce, which was long stigmatized in Indo-European culture and remained a profession "without a name" – as the term "negotia" (derived from ne-gotium, that is, not leisure) reminds us – and was assigned to members of minorities or strangers.[103] Einstein made good use of these windows of opportunity and he was not the only Jew. Discrimination, the resulting specialization, and emancipation in the second half of the nineteenth century meant there were relatively high proportions of Jewish students and teachers in the natural sciences and, from the early twentieth century onward, a steady over-representation of Jewish scientists among winners of Nobel prizes in these disciplines.[104] During the same period, a similar development took place in the performing arts, with a steady over-representation of Jewish leading violinists from the late nineteenth century onward.[105] Most of them had a background in central and eastern Europe, where discrimination against Jewish minorities long persisted and classical music remained, under the protection of aristocratic families, one of the few channels for upward mobility and Jewish emancipation.[106]

There are also examples of social exclusion because of a minority position where few or no relatives were available to help out. People had to set out and search for chances on their own. In these cases, too, accidental, serendipitous encounters proved decisive.

The French anthropologist Claude Lévi-Strauss, born in Brussels, grew up with assimilated Jewish parents in Paris, where the family's vaguely conceived Jewish identity would play a decisive role, according to biographer Wilcken, who notes that Lévi-Strauss learned early what it meant to have a Jewish-sounding name in a still fundamentally anti-Semitic culture. At school, he was bullied by other children, who called him "a dirty Jew." He reacted, he said, "with a punch."[107] When Lévi-Strauss turned eighty he gave a long interview to Didier Eribon. "When pressed, he spoke of his sense of his own Jewishness, not in religious or ancestral terms, but as a state of mind. Being a part of a traditionally persecuted group brought a heightened awareness and a sense that he would have to overachieve in order to have a chance to compete fairly."[108]

Lévi-Strauss, writes Wilcken, has often been portrayed as a hermit, not least by himself: "I don't have much of a taste for socializing. My initial instinct is to avoid people and go back home." This agrees with what he earlier said in the same interview recorded in Wilcken's biography: "I realised early on that I was a library man, not a field-worker.[109] At this point Wilcken moves to protect the French savant against himself and against the later received opinion of anthropologists on the supposedly scanty merits of Lévi-Strauss as an ethnographer. His fieldwork in Brazil in the 1930s indeed had its limits, writes Wilcken, yet together with guides and anthropologists he traveled more than a thousand kilometers by train, on horseback, and on foot in the Mato Grosso at a time when travel in the hinterland was difficult and dangerous. Lévi-Strauss was a gifted writer and photographer who, with few resources, made iconic portraits of a series of Brazilian Indian groups. More than sixty of these pictures are included in his best-known book, *Tristes Tropiques* (1955), which opened the door to a new genre in anthropology. Rather than a fixation on the minutiae of a single group, which often makes ethnography outside of a circle of specialists unreadable, Lévi-Strauss produced lively descriptions of the richness and variety of the indigenous cultures of the Caduveo, Bororo, Nambikwara, Mundé, and Tupi-Kawahib, which were still little known. Much has been said about the briefness of his stays among these peoples, but anthropologists can spend ten years in the field and end up not mentioning anything of importance. Moreover, Lévi-Strauss was a good observer and, even more important, an intelligent analyst of his own observations.[110]

Lévi-Strauss's publications on indigenous Indian cultures in the late 1930s drew the attention of French and American anthropologists and opened up an expanding interest in South American Indians. His contributions to professional journals earned him a certain reputation, including recommendations and invitations he could make use of and flee the country with numerous other Jewish refugees. He left Vichy France by boat from Marseille as late as 1941 to find work in New York.[111] On board he got into conversation with surrealist André Breton, with whom he shared an interest in primitive art, and they became friends. Lévi-Strauss settled in New York and was inspired by the artists and scholars he made friends with (among them another refugee, the Russian linguist Roman Jakobson) to lay the foundations of a revolution in anthropology. This materialized after the war, first with a new view on the subject of kinship, *Les structures élémentaires de la parenté* (*The Elementary Structures of Kinship*) (1949),[112] and the introduction of new genres, including *Tristes Tropiques*, and later with the structural analysis of myths, *Mythologiques,* in the 1960s. In *Le totémisme aujourdhui* (1962) Lévi-Strauss opened a new line of research for the study of animal symbolism with the one-liner "animals are good to think with." Following Arnold van Gennep, "totemism" refers to a form of classification: it comprises a code in which social differences are articulated with analogous differences in nature – differences in nature are used to stress differences between social groups.[113] Lévi-Strauss repeatedly emphasized that his "structuralism" was not a theory, but a method.

Lévi-Strauss's achievements are far from minor, especially if one realizes that he himself had not studied anthropology. We have seen before that this can also be an advantage, even for anthropologists, who on account of their field are already outsiders. This also holds for some other innovators in anthropology, including Franz Boas, Marcel Mauss, Bronisław Malinowski, and Edmund Leach. Lévi-Strauss learned the profession and fieldwork from his wife, Dina Dreyfus, a French anthropologist with whom he traveled to Brazil in the early

1930s for her to teach sociology at the University of São Paulo. He also learned a great deal from Dreyfus's Brazilian colleagues who joined them in ethnographic expeditions to the interior of the country. Radical innovation tends to arise, as argued in this book, from people who come from outside – and have been educated by informal means in the field in which they make a breakthrough.[114] Lévi-Strauss belonged to a persecuted minority and found himself a refugee in exile in the midst of other companions in distress, among them inspiring colleagues. His situations relate to places in social networks. They encompass no fewer than five antecedents or necessary conditions for the development of radical innovation.

Informal training with feedback from a mentor constitutes the lever for radical innovation in science and the arts. Cognitive psychologist Ericsson has demonstrated the importance of an early start for a long period of informal learning: an apprenticeship, which he calls *deliberate practice*, under the guidance of a mentor who regularly provides feedback. By this path, which can take ten years, an apprentice in relative solitude can reach *perfect performance* in sport and the performing arts, most notably the violin. According to Ericsson and his colleagues, who focus on the sports and the performing arts, there are indications that years of intensive preparation under the guidance of a teacher or mentor also precede international recognition in science. Insights into the highest achievements of athletes and musicians show that "eminent" scientists immerse themselves in their vocations to such a degree that they strongly limit all other activities. The measure of their involvement has been quantified in some studies and reveals that scientists have to work eighty hours a week over a long period to have a chance of reaching an international level in their field. According to Ericsson, "eminent" achievement in science nearly always corresponds to the development of a new theory or a new idea, published together with convincing evidence.[115]

With Weisberg (1986), Ericsson is the first cognitive psychologist to abandon the concept of "talent" and other presumed inborn gifts to explain exceptional achievements – and thus avoids both psychological and biological reductionism.[116] Ericsson did not find demonstrable empirical proof for talent, and argues that what we usually call "talent" may be the consequence rather than the cause of perfect achievements, which can only be brought about by long intensive training with daily feedback from a mentor or teacher to improve execution. Even perfect pitch is an acquired skill.[117]

This well-founded and documented point of view has not been neglected in American cognitive psychology. In his later work, doyen

Robert Sternberg shows a silent, significant shift: he abandons the concept of "talent" and replaces it with the keyword "skills."[118] To elevate acquired skills above "inborn gifts," Ericsson mentions some examples from the world of sports: people who had an "anti-talent" or "negative talent," notably serious physical defects, and who through intense exercise overcame their handicap and achieved top performances. We saw how the twenty-year-old athlete Wilma Rudolph won three gold medals in athletics at the Olympic Games in Rome in 1960, even though when she was four she had lost the use of her left leg through polio. After intensive physiotherapy and training, she was able to walk without accessories at the age of eleven and to go on to devote her time to running.[119]

Accounting for exceptional or innovative achievements, Ericsson explicitly refers to the performers' positions in sets of social relationships. These concern informal settings with parents or other relatives, friends, teachers, and most notably mentors, who over a long period of apprenticeship provide feedback. Ericsson indicates the pedigree of Johann Sebastian Bach (1685–1750), often mentioned as an example of belonging to a long line of families that produced exceptional musicians and composers – to the extent that in Germany at the time music was synonymous with the name Bach, and vice versa. As he also points out, "before the advent of professional music teachers, the transmission of knowledge and skills from parent to child was natural and did not presuppose any genetic transmission of innate talent." "Similarly," notes Ericsson, "nobody would argue that bilingual children who speak a foreign language have innate abilities for speaking that particular language. Obviously they have acquired that language through social interaction with their parents or grandparents."[120]

What holds for Bach also applies to Franz Schubert (1797–1828), who had violin lessons at an early age from his father, who had recently moved with his family from the rural periphery to a district in Vienna. Franz received piano lessons from one of his older brothers, with whom he also played ensemble and for whom he later wrote his first string quartets. After lessons at home, Schubert received singing lessons from Antonio Salieri, his most important teacher, in whose famous choir he excelled. He started to compose early and Salieri taught him harmony and composition. In a strikingly short life, Schubert distinguished himself in his work through an enormous and varied output of original quality, by his need to experiment in numerous genres, his varied instrumentation, and his adventurousness in modulation. Like other pioneers he worked practically every day and explained that he wasn't able to stop composing. He wrote about 600 songs, 166 of them in the single year of 1816. Outside his circle of friends, his work met with little response during his lifetime. Only after his death did he become an ever more celebrated composer, and musicians still find new sides to his work. Schubert experienced a great deal of adversity. He was strikingly small in stature, not quite five feet tall (disguised in all his portraits), but he was also often poor and had no fixed employment – the reason he remained unmarried, he said.[121]

Because of the differences and similarities, a fruitful comparison presents itself with Felix Mendelssohn Bartholdy (1809–47), born into a well-to-do intellectual banker's family in Hamburg. His parents were assimilated Jews and could give their son and daughter the best education available. Mendelssohn was a prodigy. As a teenager he was a better composer than Beethoven or Mozart at the same age. Two of his master works – the Octet for Strings in E-flat Major, and the overture to *A Midsummer Night's Dream* – were written when he was respectively sixteen and seventeen years old. Later, the quality of his work decreased and became less original and more conservative. Yet Mendelssohn remained a celebrated composer and music performer in his own time. He took the lead in reviving the works of Bach and directed and conducted the *St. Matthew Passion* when he was just twenty-one. Why this loss of reputation before his premature death?

Art historian and leading pianist Charles Rosen argues that this decline "paradoxically enough, would require a report of the reasons of Mendelssohn's huge and easily won prestige. His weaknesses were the result of his exceptional gifts, and these gifts demand a more critical consideration."[122] Mendelssohn, writes Rosen, could execute many important parts of music easily and with grace, but his decline was located in his refusal to go beyond the area where such grace and ease were possible. Mendelssohn did not experiment much: he remained the Victorian composer held in the highest esteem in England. "Perhaps he was," argues Rosen, "a prisoner of his own genius. Life was easy for him. As the son of a banker he never had to make it himself." He got the best education and the many intellectual contacts that followed from it. Mendelssohn also spoke a number of foreign languages and he was a creditable amateur painter.

Moreover, Rosen continues, he never had to overcome his own deficiencies to reach greater heights: he did not have deficiencies. Educated in the music of Bach, Mozart, and Beethoven, who gave him the support of a ready-made tradition, he was a master of melody, harmony, and counterpoint by the time he was fifteen. He revised with great care and polished diligently. Music was easy for him. Haydn had to struggle for decades to create a new style. Beethoven, according to Rosen, could write great melodies, but it was the hard work and struggle with counterpoint over his whole life that stimulated him to create a new art in which the effort is not only visible but part of the power. Chopin and Schumann, writes Rosen, lacked Mendelssohn's instinct for great structures and that deficiency drove them to create new and idiosyncratic forms. Even Mozart had to work for years to master Haydn's stylistic innovations. "The great works of Mendelssohn that came later – The 'Italian' Symphony and the Violin Concerto in E minor – never rise above the achievements of the sixteen-year-old. With all his knowledge and mastership he remained in essence a prodigy."[123]

This account of the life and work of Mendelssohn, and the comparison with his contemporary colleagues, links up with the argument of this book on the blessings of adversity. In his conclusion, Rosen formulates a striking insight: "Most artists who survived the selection of history had to conquer a deficiency which inspired them to change the language of their art and to expand. ... Mendelssohn's early maturity was both a curse and a gift. That's why he never could match the extravagance of his contemporaries."[124]

Rosen is close to indicating the mechanism that drives radical innovation in the arts (and science). Whereas Mendelssohn, married with two children, by chance, talent, and effort found himself among the recognized greats and soon became famous, the three giants who had given him their backing had faced adversity and therefore had a greater struggle. Haydn and Schubert came from the periphery and had a background of poverty, which Schubert never completely overcame. Beethoven grew up in the Rhineland. His first teacher was a callous, alcoholic father, who gave him violin lessons but did not shrink from physical violence. His mother had died early, and after his father's death, the seventeen-year-old Beethoven had to take care of his two younger brothers. Beethoven settled unmarried in Vienna and became a sought-after piano virtuoso and successful composer. However, before he was thirty, he had to learn to cope with increasing deafness, which was later to separate him from social contact, yet give him more time for composing and experimenting. In the face of a variety of setbacks, Beethoven could more than once count his blessings. He is known as an outsider who wrote his best work at a later age and is generally considered the greatest composer in history.

Only a few pioneers came into the world and found a welcome waiting for them. Adversity marked the first years of Albert Camus

151

(1913–60) – one of the many pioneers who came "from the periphery." He was born in the northeast of French Algeria, where his father was a vineyard worker. Conscripted into military service, his father died in September 1914 from wounds suffered in the Battle of the Marne. His mother, illiterate, half deaf, and with a speech impediment, was a cleaner. After the death of her husband she took Albert and his older brother to settle with her brother in a working-class district of Algiers, where the extended family lived in a small apartment lacking the most basic facilities. Albert's mother provided for the family by working in a factory. Camus had a difficult youth, but was not always unhappy. Another maternal uncle – a butcher/intellectual – paid for his education.[125] Trips outside the city were a welcome break, as we know from Camus's first writings.

Camus did not have an easy time at school either. Stigmatized as a *pupille de la nation*, child of a victim of war, he depended on state support and was tormented by recurring health problems, but he distinguished himself as a pupil and was rewarded with a scholarship to the lycée. Situated in the kasbah, the school brought him into contact with the indigenous Muslim community and led to the early recognition of the idea of the "outsider" that would dominate his later writings. His "invisible" tuberculosis had a similar effect.

The acquisition of the scholarship would not have happened without the alertness and protection of Camus's teacher Louis Germain and his efforts to arrange a place at the lycée for a promising and diligent child from the working class. Germain had to persuade Camus's mother to let him go to the lycée and not make him do unskilled work like his elder brother. Camus's loyalty was evident thirty-four years later, when he was awarded the Nobel Prize for Literature and dedicated his acceptance speech and lecture to Germain.[126] As a university student, Camus developed a great enthusiasm for football and played as goalkeeper, but he later had to give it up because of his tuberculosis. He met another paternal teacher, Jean Grenier, who shared his interest in literature and philosophy, as well as his love of football. Grenier put him in touch with the great contemporary French writers André Gide and André Malraux. Camus's illness prevented a further university career and, after a provisional recovery in the Alps, he concentrated on writing, including for the stage. He also became politically and socially active. From 1938 onward he lived in France, where he took part in the Resistance against the German occupation. Under these circumstances, his most innovative work appeared: *The Stranger* (also translated as *The Outsider*), *The Myth of Sisyphus*, and *The Plague*. Camus admired Melville's *Billy Budd*, Dostoevsky's *Crime and Punishment*, Faulkner's *Requiem for a Nun*, and above all the stories of Kafka. He also said he was influenced by these writers. Although he was married (in 1940, to a pianist and mathematician) and had two children, he declared himself opposed to marriage and was openly promiscuous. Camus died in a car accident in January 1960 near Sens, in central France, traveling with his publisher Michel Gallimard from his house in the Vaucluse to Paris.[127]

Several antecedents or necessary conditions of radical innovation stand out in the early life of Camus and fit the scenario sketched out in this book: adversity precipitating social exclusion. He came from the periphery; in the working-class area of Algiers he suffered from bad housing, poverty, and discrimination. The shortage of basic facilities contributed to his chronic illness (tuberculosis). At school he was discriminated against because he did not have a father. Eventually he found protection and assistance from helpful teachers who took notice, encouraging his literary interests and helping him further, first at school, then at the lycée and university. A maternal uncle paid for his education. Before he was thirty, he wrote his first and groundbreaking book, *The Outsider*.

Family, teachers, mentors, and close friends also played a decisive role in the formation of other pioneers, including in the lives of those who belonged to the established bourgeoisie. Gustave Flaubert (1821–80) had the "great good fortune" to find an inspiring teacher and mentor at the gymnasium in Rouen, where his father was medical superintendent at the local hospital. Pierre-Adolphe Chéruel, a student of Jules Michelet, the greatest of the French Romantic historians, was Flaubert's history teacher during five important school years between 1834 and 1839. Loved and admired by his students, Chéruel was only ten years older than they were. Under his benignly creative influence, Flaubert acquired a taste for history that never left him."[128] Later he had his friends, with whom he discussed his work, and who provided feedback and did not hesitate, if need be, to put him right.

His family was also warmly disposed toward him. After he had failed in his law studies and his epilepsy had made itself known, his father bought a house on the Seine near Croisset, not far from Rouen, where Flaubert could retire to write and receive guests. These were three unforeseen circumstances which had a fortunate result for Flaubert, who had already begun to write as a child and wanted to become a writer. Moreover, Flaubert acknowledged yet another advantage of his illness. As biographer Wall writes:

Once he knew that he could survive the recurrent intimate disaster of the attack, he could begin to learn from it, even to experiment with it. His epilepsy, or rather what-he-did-with-what-they-called-epilepsy, confirmed in him a curious early affinity for the most extreme varieties of religious experience, the ecstatic visions and the diabolical torments of the saints. How could he make use of it, this suddenly acquired sixth sense?[129]

Flaubert possibly understood early that he was no match for his older brother Achille, who excelled at school and not only had the same name as his father but also chose the same profession as his father, medical doctor and surgeon, eventually succeeding him as director of the hospital in Rouen. Biographer Wall mentions that Flaubert disliked his brother with a "peculiar fraternal intensity," but he does not provide any evidence.[130] Achille rarely figures in the biography and is always unvaryingly helpful and friendly toward his younger brother. He appreciates and sympathizes with him because of his disease, shows admiration for his work, and believed *Trois Contes* (*Three Tales*) the best thing he had written.[131] They were too different to be close friends, but stood up for each other if need be. When it came to any rivalry between the brothers, this must have been tempered early on by the "divergence" of the youngest in the direction of art and literature. Except for the absence of sibling rivalry, Sulloway's Darwinian theory of birth order finds some confirmation at this point: as the elder brother, the firstborn and the successor to their father as medical superintendent, Achille represented the status quo, while Gustave as the younger brother resisted the established order of the bourgeoisie from the beginning and continually poked fun at it. This was shown most notably in his *Dictionnaire des idées reçues* – "dictionary" of received ideas – published after his death, although in many ways he conformed and never had any conflict with his parents, who accepted his "divergence" and probably would have been proud of him, just as his older brother Achille was.

Flaubert was known as the "hermit of Croisset." Yet this nickname only partly applies. He traveled a lot, including abroad, and was often in Paris with his mistress Louise Colet, his sole romantic love, with whom he had a tempestuous relationship for almost ten years. Later, he kept an apartment in the city for the winter and was often with the Russian émigré writer Ivan Turgenev, visiting, among other things, literary salons and public executions. In the house in Croisset, where his mother also lived, he wrote with great attention to form and *le mot juste*, which is also shown in the letters he wrote to his friends.

154

He polished and tinkered with his novels, sometimes for decades. His work on *The Temptation of Saint Anthony*, influenced by the painting by Brueghel the Younger he saw in Genoa in 1845, can serve as an example. He had read the first version to his friends Maxime Du Camp and Louis Bouilhet, who both rejected it. Flaubert finally completed the book in 1874.

The poet Bouilhet was his best friend. They knew each other from school and shared their work with each other.[132] Bouilhet edited *Madame Bovary* and Flaubert helped Bouilhet with his poems and stage plays. When, after more than twenty years of collaboration, Bouilhet died, Flaubert experienced the death of his friend as an amputation: "I say to myself, what is the use of writing now, since he's gone. It's over, the wonderful reading aloud, the shared enthusiasms, the future projects we dreamt about together." "It feels like a major amputation. A large part of me has disappeared . . . my literary conscience, my judgement, my compass."[133]

With his close friend, alter ego, and confrère in nearby Rouen, and his mother and his little niece (for whom he was a kind of father) in the house in Croisset, Flaubert's solitude as a "hermit" was relative, not to mention his love of travel and frequent presence in Paris during the winters after his thirtieth year. He was in Croisset mostly in the summer to write, including the letters to friends with whom he stayed in touch during his retreats. In his last years, when his *Trois Contes* appeared, considered by many a high point in his work, he lived there practically alone – his mother had died and his niece was unhappily married and in financial need.

When Flaubert was buried on May 11, 1880, the cortège made its way through Rouen to the cemetery located high on a hill, watched by a handful of indifferent spectators. "It was an affront," states biographer Wall, who fittingly cites a remark of Flaubert's friend Zola: "When he died four-fifths of the population of Rouen had never heard of Gustave Flaubert. The rest despised him."[134] The burial had a grotesque course. Flaubert had an unusually large frame: "Flaubert's coffin, too big to fit into the grave, had to be left stuck at an angle, head first, and only half way into the earth."[135]

The beautiful house on the river in Croisset was sold the very same month and resold in the summer of the next year. The demolition of the house and garden started in August 1881 and was completed within a month.

They cut down the apple trees that make this bit of meadow so typical of Normandy. They felled the tall 100-year-old poplars. In less than a month everything had gone: the entrance gate with its porch and its lime trees where you waited for the boat to Rouen, the tall railings where you used to see Flaubert walking, the cluster of trees where he used to sit in the summer. . .[136]

Flaubert's contemporary Herman Melville (1819–91), rediscovered and only acknowledged as the greatest American writer more than thirty years after his death, experienced frequent adversity. His father's bankruptcy, when Melville was twelve, and shortly afterwards his early death resulted in poverty and social degradation for the family and displacement to the periphery in the north of New York state. Their misery was somewhat alleviated by his mother's brother, Peter Gansevoort, who with his sister belonged to the well-to-do Dutch Protestant Hudson Valley aristocracy. Melville realized early on, after his first voyage to and from Liverpool as a cabin boy in 1839, that his adversity could also offer favorable chances. He regretted the loss of a privileged life but was also relieved to have escaped from it. Possibly, he took it amiss that his father had wasted the family's money and good name. But he also understood that the failings of a father could create freedom for a son.[137] Three years whaling in the Pacific and then time on an American warship provided an inexhaustible source for his literary work – "my Yale College and my Harvard," as Melville's Ishmael phrased it in *Moby-Dick*.[138] But after early success, he fell into oblivion as a writer before he was fifty. Melville, however, continued writing. Through his mother's family connections, he was appointed as customs inspector in the port of New York in 1866. He worked there for almost twenty years to the satisfaction of colleagues and superiors, while he continued writing stories and poems. His mother's brother Peter Gansevoort continued supporting him.[139]

Melville retired in 1886, after his wife had received an inheritance.[140] In his last years he lived alone with her in their house in New York City. They were lonely and difficult years, both because of the (violent) deaths of their two young adult sons, and also because Melville seemed totally forgotten as a writer. His work was not republished for years. At this time he worked on a story later called *Billy Budd, Sailor*, generally considered, next to *Moby-Dick*, as the high point of his oeuvre. The story concerns the fate of a popular, beautiful, naive young sailor on a British warship. Falsely accused of mutiny by a scheming elderly officer, his speech deficiency proves fatal. This novella was not to appear until 1924, thirty-three years after Melville's death. The manuscript was kept, first by his wife and afterwards by his daughter and granddaughter, until it came into the hands of Raymond Weaver, a professor at Columbia University and the first of Melville's biographers. He got in touch with Melville's granddaughter Eleanor Metcalf because of renewed interest in Melville and did his utmost to achieve the publication of the collected works.[141] *Billy Budd, Sailor* was immediately recognized as a masterwork, "as a supreme example of what the Germans call *Spätstil* – an end-of-life style of great complexity, yet filled, as has been said of the late quartets of Beethoven, with 'songful passages of extreme simplicity.'"[142] Referring to *Moby-Dick*, biographer Delbanco writes: "Ahab seems more part of us than apart from us. Like all great literary representations of evil, he is attractive as well as repulsive. And so Melville emerged in the twentieth century as the American Dostoevsky – a writer who, with terrible clairvoyance, had been waiting for the world to catch up with him."[143] As happened with Mendel, Melville's lot was to gain only posthumous honor – a necessary risk for all the outsiders who figure in this book.

In most of the cases discussed, the decisive, informal role of mentors, patrons, and friends can be singled out as a necessary condition in the achievement of radical innovation in science and the arts. However secluded the innovators, their work could not have been achieved without help from outside – the poet T. S. Eliot being an extreme case.[144] The same holds for intermediaries who facilitated the reception of their work. Illustrative of the importance of mediating roles are the "negative" cases – situations in which these brokers were absent or failed: cases of innovation in which pioneers received only posthumous recognition (Mendel, Melville), or long remained obscure and were discovered late (Cézanne, Van Gogh). Recall Planck's dark retrospective view in his *Scientific Autobiography*: "A new scientific truth does not triumph by convincing its opponents and making them see the light, but rather because its opponents eventually die, and a new generation grows up that is familiar with it."[145] This explanation testifies to the realization that radical innovation is unlikely to come from the ranks of the establishment – and in fact is improbable in those circles, if not also logically impossible.

A more recent example of late recognition is the pioneering work of Norbert Elias (1897–1990), who wrote a historical-sociological study of the civilizing process, with a focus on France. Published in German in 1939, the book was all but ignored for decades for lack of authoritative advocates, that is, intermediaries. Only in the early 1970s was Elias's masterwork rediscovered and translated into French, after it had been reprinted in Switzerland in 1969. Elias's social position may help to explain the long neglect of his book, and likewise its eventual success. Born in Breslau (now Wrocław) in the then border area between Germany and Poland, Elias was the only child of Jewish parents. As a student and teacher, he traveled a great deal, working on the fringes of academic disciplines. Unmarried, he was a political refugee and exile in the 1930s and 1940s, first in France and later in England. All these circumstances facilitated his breakthrough, but also hampered and delayed its reception. In postwar England, too, Elias led an existence bordering on isolation at a sociological institute at a provincial university in a country without a major sociological tradition and where few people read German. There was nobody with influence or authority to stand up for him. That is why his work was hardly noticed for so long – including his innovative writings in English that appeared in the 1950s and 1960s. After the Swiss reprint of his *magnum opus* had been favorably reviewed and recognized by influential historians and sociologists as an important work in the tradition of the *Annales* School, a French translation appeared in the early 1970s, published by Calmann-Lévy in Paris.[146] It became a bestseller, which also influenced Bourdieu, witness his well-known study on taste and habitus, *Distinction*, which first appeared some years later, in 1979.[147] In turn this book was translated into German with the title *Die feinen Unterschiede.*

In the field of anthropology itself, colleagues can take opposite positions and vie with each other. This happened in Paris at the beginning of the twentieth century in the circle round Émile Durkheim (1858–1917) and "his" periodical *L'Année Sociologique.* After initially friendly treatment and collaboration, the ranks closed against ethnographer and folklorist Arnold van Gennep (1873–1957). His work was first criticized and then ignored. This exclusion took place in 1913 after Van Gennep had critically reviewed Durkheim's interpretation of Australian totemism in his *Formes élémentaires de la vie réligieuse* (*The Elementary Forms of the Religious Life*) (1912). Van Gennep demonstrated that the work fell seriously short of the mark both empirically and theoretically.[148] Totemism was not a form of the earliest belief, as Durkheim argued, but according to Van Gennep, who had earlier studied the subject, it was a form of social classification, which in each culture expresses itself in its own manner. This thought, which ironically goes back to an earlier pioneering work by Durkheim and Mauss,[149] would later be elaborated by Lévi-Strauss in *Le totémisme aujourd'hui* (1962), in which he also refers to Van Gennep's work and underwrites his point of view.[150]

Durkheim's book on the elementary forms of religious life now seems almost forgotten. But this is certainly not the case with Van Gennep's *The Rites of Passage* (1909): when it was translated into English in 1960 it had an enlightening and innovative impact on the work of anthropologists and historians.[151] With his structural analysis of transition rites which mark and bring about changes in status (birth, engagement, marriage, initiation, and death), Van Gennep anticipated the structuralism of Lévi-Strauss and symbolic anthropology. With his artful discovery he brought together under a single common denominator a large quantity of ethnographic materials: transition rituals, with the threefold sequence of separation, transition, and incorporation. Each transition to a new status – which includes that of a ruler and other high officials – involves ritual separation, withdrawal, and incorporation into the new status. Van Gennep concluded that the occasion could vary, but that the "underlying arrangement" of transition rituals is always the same: "Beneath a multiplicity of forms, either consciously expressed or merely implied, a typical pattern always recurs: *the pattern of the rites of passage.*"[152] His central thesis argues that every change of status is marked and brought about at the end of the liminal stage (from *limen*, threshold), when the person is also spatially excluded from the community, and then as a person with a new status (most notably birth, marriage, and death) is incorporated into the community. In this case, too, transition and innovation are intimately connected to marginal positions.

The attention Van Gennep gives to the importance of the liminal stage is also emphasized by calling the three stages preliminal, liminal, and postliminal, respectively. This has led to further research into everything that has to do with boundaries and "liminality," and how people in different cultures deal with transition and change by means of ritualization. This has also become a field in religious studies (including of pilgrimages), and in the anthropology of the body, which has tangential parallels with the microsociology introduced by Erving Goffman in his book *Stigma* and his essay "The territories of the self," included in his *Relations in Public*.

Who was Van Gennep? Where did he come from and why could he be so innovative? His surname came from his Dutch mother after she was divorced from her French husband.[153] Van Gennep was then six years old and, with his mother, left his birthplace of Ludwigsburg in

159

Württemberg, Germany. They settled in Lyon, where his mother was later married again, to a surgeon, who became his second father.[154]

Van Gennep visited various boarding schools, first in Lyon, later in Nice and Grenoble, where he took his final examinations. He had a difference of opinion with his stepfather, rejecting medicine and surgery, and choosing foreign languages, of which he already had considerable knowledge. A breach with his parents followed his marriage to a Polish fellow student, an orphan without a dowry. Van Gennep lived with his wife for several years in Częstochowa, Poland, where he taught French at a high school. Back in France, he worked as a translator at various state institutions, and between 1904 and 1930 he wrote books and articles on ethnography, folklore, and religion.[155] After his critical review of Durkheim's views on totemism, Van Gennep remained an outsider in the academic world. He did not hold any university position, apart from a short-lived appointment between 1912 and 1915 at the University of Neuchâtel, where he occupied the first chair of ethnography in Switzerland until he was expelled from the country because of his criticism of the pro-German attitude of the Swiss government.[156]

Translations and journal articles gave Van Gennep enough income to carry out his scientific work. His breakthrough work on *The Rites of Passage*, only recognized in Anglo-American anthropology much later (after it had appeared in an English translation in 1960, three years after his death), he saw as forming the key to his lifework on the folklore of France, *Manuel de folklore français contemporain*, which appeared between 1924 and 1957 in nine volumes. Van Gennep was doubtlessly capable of this achievement, writes Zumwalt, because he did not have an academic position. He lived in isolation in Bourg-la-Reine, a small community south of Paris and now part of its southern outskirts, where as ethnographer and folklorist he laid the basis for a new discipline – folklore.[157]

Most of the scientists and artists discussed in this book show a common scenario early in life – keenly noting and seizing chances offered by parents, other relatives, friends, teachers, mentors, and sponsors. Without these encounters and relationships, we would probably never have heard of any of them. Quite a few of them were hit by adversity and social exclusion at a later age, mostly in the form of exile or detention. Their cases may not only help to explain "late production," which was still an open question in Kuhn's comments on Harvey Lehman's *Age and Achievement* (1953),[158] but may also confirm the theory advanced in this book: late production followed late adversity. Thucydides, Dante, Machiavelli, Galileo,

160

Bacon, Hobbes, Descartes, and other pioneers were exiled at a later age, while Cervantes, de Sade, and Gramsci spent years in prison. The Dutch jurist Hugo de Groot, also called Grotius (1583–1645), was condemned to life in prison in the Dutch Republic for political reasons, but he escaped after three years and left for Paris, where as an exile he obtained the favor of the king. In 1626 he completed his famous treatise *De jure belli ac paci* (*On the Law of War and Peace*) (in which he asserted the freedom of the seas), which he dedicated to his patron, Louis XIII.

To conclude these chapters on radical innovators, we look once more at the background of a pioneer to find out how early adversity and social exclusion could inspire the making of a new genre. Truman Capote (1924–84) was born in New Orleans. He is considered a major writer in North America because of his style and the creation of a new genre in literature: the nonfiction novel, of which his *In Cold Blood* (1965) – exclusively based on facts – is a prime example. Even before his parents divorced when he was five, he was a neglected child of a promiscuous and alcoholic young mother and a traveling, often absent, father. For different reasons, both had little time for him. They often sent him to family, mostly his mother's cousins who lived together in Monroeville, Alabama. When they took him with them on a trip, they would lock him in their hotel room with instructions to the staff to let him scream if he called for his parents.[159] "If . . . a child's greatest anxiety – the original fear – is that he will be deserted by his parents," writes biographer Clarke, "then he had good reason to be anxious."[160]

> "Something in my life has done a terrible hurt to me . . . and it seems to be irrevocable." That hurt – so he believed, and so was probably the case – was caused by his mother's unending rejection, and it was symbolized by the sound of a key turning in a door: the young Lillie Mae locking him in a hotel room as she left for an evening on the town . . . . "That's when my claustrophobia and fear of abandonment began . . . She was the cause of all my anxiety . . . But you don't know what you're afraid of. Except something bad is going to happen, only you don't know what it is."[161]

Much of Capote's early work harks back to this anxiety. When he was five, his mother left him behind with her family in Monroeville. The family consisted of three older sisters and an older brother, his mother's cousins, all of them unmarried and in middle life. Every now and then, his mother visited him; always a short visit. Truman remembered the moments he saw her driving away, peering at the car until it disappeared from sight.

Capote's years in Monroeville, where he mostly stayed until he was nine, also had another side. He became the darling of his mother's cousins, particularly the eldest, who pampered him, took him for walks, and read to him from Grimm's fairy tales and the Bible.[162] Truman became friends with his neighbor, the slightly older Nelle Harper Lee (later author of the bestseller *To Kill a Mockingbird*), daughter of a jurist and politician, who shared his interest in literature. Both were outsiders: Nelle because she was a tomboy and too rough for other girls, and Truman because he was small for his age, physically no match for most of the other boys, and did not like fighting, and also because of his appearance – with blond hair and blue eyes, he made a girl-like impression.

Biographer Clarke states that the best description of Truman at the time can be found in *To Kill a Mockingbird*, in which he is the model for one of the characters: Harper Lee described him as "a true curiosity."[163] When Truman was nine he left Monroeville for New York, where his mother had settled, remarried to a well-to-do Cuban American, Joe Capote, who became a good father and whose name Truman took – very much to his pleasure, because they both really liked each other. The relationship with his mother remained ambivalent, and did not improve when she had problems with his homosexuality. Truman went to private schools but did not do very well. He got on well with his female English teacher, who encouraged his writing and acted as his mentor. When he was seventeen he found office work at the *New Yorker* and started to write short stories for periodicals. Three years later he broke through with his story "Miriam." That made a great impression and earned him a literary prize. More stories followed and Truman now became the protégé of various influential literary figures, mostly women, who were not only impressed by his work but also fell for his unusual charm and wit. Others who encouraged and helped him included the much older and fatherly Newton Arvin, from whom he received further instruction in literature.[164] In 1948, *Other Voices, Other Rooms* appeared, a short novel which was received as a masterwork, and Capote, at twenty-three, instantly became famous.[165] Looking back on this "gothic" novel twenty-five years later, he said that the book was "an unconscious, altogether intuitive attempt" to drive out the demons of his youth. He had not realized, apart from some incidents and descriptions, that the book had become so strongly autobiographical.[166] His biographer Clarke remarks,

> Indeed, it was his good fortune that he was blind, at least on the conscious level, to what he was doing. Self-consciousness would have

stilled his hand helplessly above the page if he had realized that he was in fact writing not a novel but his psychological autobiography: charting, under the guise of fiction, the anguished journey that ended in his discovery of his identity as a man, as a homosexual, and as an artist.[167]

The pattern of radical innovation is clearly outlined in Capote's life: the ability to turn adversity and social exclusion into blessings by seizing chances, and using informal education and instruction to bring about a breakthrough in literature. We find here all the telltale signs, all the portents of radical innovation: origin on the periphery, early parental loss, good enough reception from surrogate parents, early literary ambition and friendship with a kindred spirit, encouragement and feedback from mentors, patronage and mediation from influential literary figures. These helping hands could also be offered thanks to Capote's unusual charm and entertaining company as a raconteur. Practically every gathering was a performance. He was also rather photogenic, and his picture by photographer Harold Halma on the back cover of *Other Voices, Other Rooms* possibly evoked more comments and made a greater impression than the novel itself.[168]

How differently his life of early anxieties and ordeals might have turned out was made plain to Capote during his research for *In Cold Blood* and his first confrontation with Perry Smith, one of the two murderers of the Clutter family in Kansas in 1959. Dick Hickock and Perry Smith were detained in prison in Garden City, Kansas, awaiting trial. Biographer Clarke shows himself a keen observer here too. He begins by mentioning that both Smith and Capote were short – they were not much taller than five feet – one of several confusing similarities.[169] Soon it became clear that the relationship between Truman and Perry was complicated:

> each looked at the other and saw, or thought he saw, the man he might have been ... They both had suffered from alcoholic [and promiscuous] mothers, absent fathers, and foster homes. At the orphanages he had been sent to, Perry had been a target of scorn because he was half-Indian and wet his bed; Truman had been ridiculed because he was effeminate.[170]

As Clarke phrased it, a psychiatrist could have been speaking about both of them when he said of Perry, "He seems to have grown up without direction, without love."[171] Lastly, both had turned to the arts as a compensation for what had been denied them. Perry was convinced he could have had some success as a painter, singer, or songwriter if he had been encouraged.[172] In Perry, continues Clarke,

[Truman] recognized his shadow, his dark side, the embodiment of his own accumulated angers and hurts. When he looked into those unhappy eyes, he was looking into a tormented region of his own unconscious, resurrecting the nightmares and fears that had found form and body in such early stories as "Miriam" and "The Headless Hawk." Reversing the coin, Perry perceived in Truman the successful artist he might have been.[173]

Perry saw Truman as someone like himself. He felt that Truman also had suffered and had guts. When Perry blamed his unhappy background for all that he had done, Truman indignantly interjected: "I had one of the worst childhoods in this world, and I'm a pretty decent, law-abiding citizen."[174]

This raises the question about differences, which (along with similarities) can explain alternative outcomes: in one case creative achievement and in the other criminality. At which point did the antecedents diverge? At issue are the circumstances after their parents' separations. For Truman, care was positive in every respect. For Perry, there was hardly anything that can be called "care." His parents were rodeo performers. The firm for which they worked did not survive the Great Depression. After his parents separated, his father left for Alaska to become a fur-trapper and prospector. After the mother's death her four children landed in foster-families and orphanages. Perry fared the worst. His habit of wetting his bed made him a target for contempt and abuse – including by the nuns, who thrashed him as a punishment. Finally he ran off and joined his father in the wilderness as a hunter. After a while, poverty drove them apart. When Perry was old enough he joined the merchant navy in the Pacific. Later he enlisted in the military and fought in the Korean War – making him familiar with the use of firearms. He mixed in bad company, committed capital crimes,[175] was arrested, tried, and after many years on death row, was hanged.

Preliminary statistical research in the United States shows that those who lost parents early are over-represented in the ranks of pioneers in science and the arts, and also among delinquents and psychiatric patients, with similarly high percentages (35 percent).[176] Yet statistical and "historiometric" research fails to single out path-breaking innovators. It also neglects their contexts of large numbers of people in the databanks and fails to explore the interconnections between biography, history, and social structure.[177] The most that can be expected is that results from large-scale statistical research will suggest "correlations" which do not explain very much but may raise questions about possible connections. Why this strong over-representation of people who lost a parent early among pioneers in science and the arts, delinquents, and the mentally ill? Only a comparative study, with special attention to the immediate settings of these people – their "place in a set of relationships, whether institutional, conjunctural, or both,"[178] as attempted in this book – can trace the circumstances in which choices to pursue specific tracks were made. This requires an analytic and systematic comparison of cases from a collective biography in which similarities and differences need to be spelled out. With the use of "negative" cases (as in the example of Capote/Smith discussed above) it is possible to find out the conditions under which both the making and the reception of pioneering work in science and the arts have been achieved – and which conditions led to other outcomes.[179]

— 6 —

CONCLUSIONS

The history of science has increasingly become the history of ideas – a *disembodied* genre in which names are mentioned but persons and their backgrounds are rarely visible. Research into the life and work of radical innovators has been assigned to biographers, who practice a descriptive, narrative, monographic genre, but seldom engage in comparative and analytical research. As a consequence, historians of science have given little attention to similarities that indicate common structural connections between the life and work of radical innovators. On the basis of a substantial collective biography, the present book tries to make up for this neglect and systematically explores the background of pioneers to pinpoint the antecedents of their radical innovations.

Within the genre of the biography itself it has been pointed out that "it is difficult for authors of a case study not to become prisoners of their subject: the stronger the lens used by the observer, the greater the possible discovery, and the greater also the danger of becoming so involved in one's case that one forgets to distance oneself from it. At that point no generalization is possible."[1] A famous example can illustrate this trend. Even in the 1990s, the size of the so-called Darwin industry could hardly be surveyed.[2] Today, twenty years later, the end is not yet in sight. Three admired scholars of Darwin's life and work (including his letters, diaries, and posthumously published writings), on which each of them has worked for decades, imperturbably observed in their summary, pocket-sized biography of 2007 that the thirty-two planned volumes of Darwin's correspondence, which should be accomplished by about 2025, will occupy biographers till far into the twenty-first century.[3]

Trying to fill the gap between description and analysis, the present book has chosen a comparative, analytical approach on the basis of a collective biography of about one hundred radical innovators in science and the arts, who worked in Europe and North America between about 1500 and 2000. Such large-scale comparative bio-graphical research pays attention to background, place, and the context of prospective pioneers and specifies what is to be explained by searching for recurring patterns in the life of pioneers in science.[4] The results are checked against those of a collective biography of innovating artists. The final outcome is, of course, hypothetical and is intended to encourage further research into this barely touched area.

Comparative research on the basis of a collective biography indi-cates that pioneers in science and the arts were probably not more gifted or intelligent than other people. Nor did they all come from privileged families. No less contrary to general expectations were their often mediocre school results and little interest in formal education. If anything, they were marked by curiosity: more interested in questions than in answers. To accomplish a breakthrough in a distinct domain, it was decisive to develop skills early with single-minded drive and feedback from a mentor. The "lonely genius" turned out be a fiction, a romantic, idealized attribution to persons who distinguished them-selves by extraordinary achievements in science or art and adopted a distinct, withdrawn lifestyle. Their accomplishments resulted from hard work, perseverance, dedication, and passion.

What propelled pioneers was early adversity that resulted in social exclusion. In the space and freedom that opened up they developed a passionate interest in a specific branch of science or the arts that did not require the presence of other people – except feedback from a mentor. Almost everything was subordinated to their work, often the only activity they felt comfortable with – as several of them explicitly testified. Thus many pioneers remained unmarried and lived in relative solitude. Yet for protection and feedback they remained dependent on friends and mentors. Moreover, the reception of their work could not take place without the mediation of sympathizers. This was most famously and spectacularly the case with the reception of Darwin's revolutionary *The Origin of Species*. His three closest friends, Lyell, Hooker, and Huxley, mediated the authoritative public presentation.

The outcome of the research for this book was further confirmed by a number of "negative" cases of pioneers whose innovative work was long ignored or recognized only posthumously, as happened to several of them, including Mendel and Wegener among the sci-entists and Rimbaud and Van Gogh in the arts. Some cases of last-minute acknowledgment underline the critical role of mediators in the reception of radical innovation. There was the timely arrival of the youthful Rheticus, professor of mathematics at the University of Wittenberg, who visited Copernicus in Frombork on the Baltic coast and took care of the publication of his *magnum opus* on heliocentrism shortly before the author's death in 1543. An example from the arts of a late and timely intervention on behalf of a neglected pioneer was the discovery of the greatness of the painter Cézanne by the young outsider and art dealer Vollard. After noticing by chance one of Cézanne's paintings in a Parisian art materials shop, he got in touch with the artist's son and in the fall of 1895 organized a successful exhibition of Cézanne's work in the French capital, so that the almost forgotten artist made a name for himself. Later, Cézanne was recognized as the founding father of modern art, most notably by one of his most famous admirers: Picasso. Outsider Ambroise Vollard catching sight of a painting by the hardly known Cézanne was a serendipitous event, fitting Merton's description, "the observation of an unanticipated, anomalous, and strategic datum . . . to produce a consequential discovery."[5]

Being unmarried, leading a somewhat withdrawn existence, and having a passionate drive are among the main characteristics of the habitus of pioneers which distinguish them from other people. Always more observer than participant, they were aware of the pressure that sooner or later emanates from any company. Many pioneers would probably have agreed with Montaigne's view, "I find that it is somewhat more tolerable to be always alone than never able to be so."[6] Inherently pleasurable activities like play, leisure, and relaxation were often anathema to them. They generally did not like sociability and small talk. That is why they were often considered shy and socially awkward. As a child, evolutionary biologist William Hamilton, who coined the concept of kin selection and found a genetic explanation for social altruism among close relatives, was taken on an excursion by his mother with his siblings. Discovering insects, he realized he would never be bored.[7]

As the collective biography clearly indicates, breakthroughs in science and the arts have been the work of people who, mostly at an early age, have had to deal with at least one form of severe misfortune. Deregulating misfortune manifested itself in a variety of forms. With the help of "conceptual assimilation," they are brought together under a common denominator.[8] This pattern of adversity encompassed illegitimate birth, early loss of parents, parental neglect and abuse, bankruptcy of the father,[9] conflict with parents, poverty, belonging to a minority, chronic illness, physical deficiencies or afflictions, neurological conditions, genetic defects, exile, and detention. Each of these untoward events and conditions resulted in social discrimination and exclusion, which estranged prospective pioneers from conventional society and led them to question established beliefs, while exceptions and anomalies in mainstream practices provoked curiosity. For all of them, exclusion turned into a blessing: an unsought, unanticipated advantage, mostly following a serendipitous encounter. Repeatedly refused a place as a graduate student at a university (following discord with his former teachers), Einstein landed at the patent office in Bern through the intervention of the father of a close friend, who put in a good word for him. Unexpectedly the office became a "secular monastery": work there dovetailed with his theoretical interests. Three years later, in 1905, he experienced his *annus mirabilis* with four revolutionary papers. He was then twenty-six years old.

Noting and seizing chances – windows of opportunity – could be demonstrated for various pioneers in science and the arts. Contrary to what is believed and prescribed in government, trade and industry, universities, and research institutions, path-breaking innovation in science cannot be planned and predicted. It remains the work of individuals who are in a position to develop an idea, to experiment, take their chances, and guess. Across the board all of them were outsiders of sorts and ready to note exceptions and anomalies in their field. Radical innovation can only be traced retrospectively and explained and understood not so much in terms of unique qualities or individual "gifts," but on the basis of the place of the innovators in "a set of relationships, whether institutional, conjunctural, or both."[10] The present book emphasizes adversity resulting in discrimination and exclusion that could be demonstrated as the preambles to the path-breaking achievements of about one hundred pioneers at work over the past five hundred years in Europe and North America.

Outsiders have little to lose and can therefore take more risks. Risk-taking is necessary for success, but also necessary for failure. This helps explain why radical innovation, also called "reconceptualization,"[11] tends to come from outsiders rather than from the established, who, by taking risks, could lose everything they have always believed in and have to start over again. Resistance to change may also explain why some outsiders had their breakthrough rejected for "insufficient evidence," as happened in the two well-known cases of posthumous recognition and rehabilitation of Mendel (genetics) and Wegener (earth sciences).

While radical innovation in the natural sciences and poetry has often been correctly associated with youth, the established are often wrongly confused with older people. This raises the still open question of "late" production from radical innovators.[12] The present book offers several examples of artists and scientists who achieved a breakthrough in their field at an advanced age following adversity. As described above, Beethoven wrote his best work after losing his hearing, which offered him more freedom and time for composing and experimentation. This also applied to Melville, who wrote a masterwork, *Billy Budd, Sailor*, at the end of his life while living in obscurity with his wife (a co-editor) in great solitude in New York City. Rembrandt likewise produced his best work at an advanced age, after the loss of dear ones and the bankruptcy that forced him to sell his large house and its valuable collections. Historian and expert in the history of the seventeenth-century Dutch Republic, Simon Schama wrote a short introduction to a recent exhibition of Rembrandt's late works. Schama is obviously impressed, but also surprised and confused, when he assumes a contradiction between Rembrandt's multiple misfortunes and the high quality of his innovative paintings, rather than noting an intimate structural connection. Writes Schama: "the reassertion of mastery so adamant that it is as if nothing troubling had befallen him."[13]

Proust (1871–1922), suffering from asthma, started writing his great, path-breaking novel, *In Search of Lost Time*, shortly after the death of his beloved mother in 1905, when he was living withdrawn in the family house in Paris.

Why and how did some radical innovators produce their best work at a later age? Pioneers in science and the arts with late achievement perfectly fit the theoretical scheme developed in this book. Age as such had little to do with their production. They had become outsiders not because of their advanced age but because they were hit by adversity, most notably bankruptcy, poverty, exile, detention, illness, and the loss of dear ones. Adversity occurred late in the lives of Thucydides, Dante, Machiavelli, Hobbes, Galileo, Cervantes, Grotius, Rembrandt, Spinoza, de Sade, Clausewitz, Beethoven, Melville, Mendel, Proust, Wegener, Buñuel, Beckett, and Polanski. Their innovation was not related to their (advanced) age but had its roots in social exclusion following untoward events.

A striking number of pioneers came from the provinces – small villages and towns in peripheral areas. Contrary to received opinion and expectations, pioneers in science and the arts coming from the periphery added luster to the radiation from the center or the metropolis.[14] The notion of the periphery as a locus of innovation links up with the critical view of historian Peter Burke about the famous center–periphery model, which met declining interest after its stormy heyday in the 1960s and 1970s.[15] Burke rightly points to the neglect of the periphery: attention to the center is out of proportion to that for the periphery, "which appears to be little more than a residual concept, the 'non-center,'" a shadow zone that serves only to show the brilliance of the center. Burke appeals for attention to be given to the creative and subversive sides of peripheral areas, of which there are several well-known examples.[16] The collective biography presented here confirms that the geographically and socially marginal positions of outsiders created space and freedom and thus provided the impulse for their breakthroughs in science and the arts, which also could not take place without serendipitous encounters: noting windows of opportunity and seizing rare chances.

In practically all the cases discussed in this book we have seen – along with a bent to solitude – the decisive role of relatives, friends, teachers, patrons, and benefactors in both the production and the reception of radical innovation in science and the arts in the period between about 1500 and 2000. Without this intervention and support from outside, the work of pioneers could not have been achieved or found its way in the relevant fields and the wider society. Sometimes a single helping hand was enough for a decisive step to be taken. Without the visit to Newton in Cambridge by the astronomer Halley in August 1684, when the guest urged the host to resume his research on orbital dynamics, Newton would probably not have completed his *Principia*. The investigation that followed this visit "transformed his life, and it transformed science."[17]

The position of pioneers in science and the arts shows family resemblances with that of anthropologists during their fieldwork. Their position and their related views form a sort of commentary on each other. Their self-exile in a peripheral area provides ethnographers with an advantage because of their position of outsider. The advantage does not lie only in "distance" in a spatial sense, far from the home country and in the immediate presence of the object of research in the periphery, but also in the social, cultural, and cognitive distance – the unfamiliarity with the culture under investigation – which after all provides the *raison d'être* of ethnographic research. The position of ethnographer is that of a relatively open-minded person eager to understand everything which the inhabitants take for granted but which is experienced as "different" by the outsider, which is what the ethnographer is and should be. "Different" means different from the culture with which the ethnographer is familiar in their country of origin. Yet the home culture remains the sounding board and also the measure by which the other culture is observed, listened to, ascertained, and finally understood. It is only through the eyes of another culture that the unfamiliar culture reveals itself more completely and deeply. Conversely, we recognize ourselves only in the confrontation with another person who holds up a mirror before us. The Ancient Greek aphorism "Know thyself" does not refer to navel-gazing or meditation but to a process that cannot take place without interaction with other people.

To recall Elizabeth Colson's remark in her review essay on anthropology in the twentieth century, and looking back at her own ethnographic fieldwork: "We live between two worlds and feel somewhat detached from both, but each gains meaning through its contrast with the other."[18] In *Apologies to Thucydides* and in a similar vein, Marshall Sahlins argues in the form of an aphorism: "It takes another culture to know another culture."[19] These two statements epitomize the epistemology adopted in the present book. Sahlins points to the strategic position of Thucydides. As a demoted Athenian general and an exiled outsider among a different party (Sparta and its allies), he could observe the Peloponnesian War over a period of twenty years from more than one side. As Thucydides put it: "It was also my fate to be an exile from my country for twenty years after my command at Amphipolis; and being present with both parties, and more especially with the Peloponnesians by reason of my exile, I had leisure to observe affairs more closely."[20]

At this point Sahlins goes further into the matter and refers to the work of the Russian literary critic and language philosopher Mikhail Bakhtin (1895–1975), who – for both the reader of a literary text and for an ethnographer – prescribes "exotopy."[21] This amounts to an external position, which makes it possible for both of these to employ their own culture for "creative understanding" of a foreign culture. A far cry from this conception comes from a colleague's valedictory lecture a few years ago, in which he referred to his fieldwork in an exotic society and emphasized that to understand this foreign culture "you have actually to forget everything that has to do with your own culture."[22]

This book has tried to show how pioneers in science and the arts came from a situation of adversity that resulted in social exclusion. Through fortunate encounters they landed in a niche that eventually made radical innovation possible. Skill, dedication, and hard work took priority over wealth and the ascription of inborn gifts. They all knew the state of the art in their field and could, because of their position as outsiders, notice exceptions and anomalies, raise

172

critical questions, and test ingrained beliefs and practices. Like the ethnographer involved in participant observation at a peripheral location, taking chances and profiting from fortunate encounters, pioneers in science and the arts were able to open new paths in their respective domains. Estranged from what was familiar, they made themselves acquainted with what was strange in order to develop a new and more encompassing point of view.[23]

APPENDICES

Table I: Antecedents of Pioneers in Science

Name	Minority status	From the periphery/provinces	Illegitimate birth	Early loss of father or mother	Early loss of both parents	Physical disability	Chronic illness	Conflict with parents	Abuse/neglect by parents	Poverty	Unmarried	Late marriage	Homosexual	Married and childless	(Self) exile	Detention
Bacon (1561–1626)											X		X		X	
Bloch (1886–1944)	X															
Boerhaave (1668–1738)				X		X	X			X		X				
Bohr (1885–1962)	X														X	
Born (1882–1970)	X														X	
Bourdieu (1930–2002)		X														
Clausewitz (1780–1831)		X									X			X		
Copernicus (1473–1543		X			X							X				
Curie (1867–1934)	X			X							X				X	
Darwin (1809–1882)		X		X				X	X							

Name	Minority status	From the periphery/provinces	Illegitimate birth	Early loss of father or mother	Early loss of both parents	Physical disability	Chronic illness	Conflict with parents	Abuse/neglect by parents	Poverty	Unmarried	Late marriage	Homosexual	Married and childless	(Self) exile	Detention
Descartes (1596–1750)		X		X					X		X				X	
Einstein (1879–1955)	X									X					X	
Elias (1897–1990)	X									X	X		X		X	
Erasmus (1466–1535)		X	X		X	X	X			X	X				X	
Faraday (1791–1867)	X			X		X				X				X		
Freud (1856–1939)	X															
Galileo (1564–1642)								X			X				X	
Goffman (1922–1982)						X										
Goodall (1934–)		X		X		X						X				
Grotius (1583–1645)															X	X
Hamilton (1936–2000)		X				X										
Harvey (1578–1657)		X				X								X		
Hertz (1857–1894)	X						X									
Hobbes (1588–1679)			X								X				X	
Huizinga (1872–1945)		X	X									X				
Humboldt (1769–1859)				X				X			X		X			

175

Name	Minority status	From the periphery/provinces	Illegitimate birth	Early loss of father or mother	Early loss of both parents	Physical disability	Chronic illness	Conflict with parents	Abuse/neglect by parents	Poverty	Unmarried	Late marriage	Homosexual	Married and childless	(Self) exile	Detention
Hume (1711–1776)				X							X					
Hutton (1726–1797)				X							X					
Huygens (1629–1695)				X							X					
Kepler (1571–1630)		X		X		X	X		X							
Keynes (1883–1946)							X					X	X	X		
Lavoisier (1743–1794)				X										X		
Leibniz (1646–1716)				X							X					
Lévi-Strauss (1908–2009)	X														X	
Lichtenberg (1742–1799)				X		X						X				
Lyell (1797–1875)		X												X		
Machiavelli (1469–1527)															X	
Malinowski (1884–1942)				X			X									
Malthus (1766–1834)		X				X						X				
Maxwell (1831–1879)		X		X		X								X		
Mendel (1822–1884)		X						X		X	X				X	
Montaigne (1533–1592)		X				X	X								X	

176

Name	Minority status	From the periphery/provinces	Illegitimate birth	Early loss of father or mother	Early loss of both parents	Physical disability	Chronic illness	Conflict with parents	Abuse/neglect by parents	Poverty	Unmarried	Late marriage	Homosexual	Married and childless	(Self) exile	Detention
Newton (1642–1727)		X		X				X	X		X				X	
Pauling (1901–1994)		X		X						X						
Perelman (1966–)	X										X				X	
Schopenhauer (1788–1860)		X		X				X			X				X	
Smith (Adam) (1723–1790)		X		X		X					X					
Spinoza (1632–1677)	X			X							X				X	
Thucydides (460–395 BC)															X	
Tillion (1907–2008)											X					
Tocqueville (1805–1859)						X	X					X		X		
Van Gennep (1873–1957)		X		X											X	
Veblen (1857–1929)		X													X	
Wallace (1823–1912)		X		X						X	X					
Watson (1928–)												X				
Weber (1864–1920)							X	X						X	X	
Wegener (1880–1930)															X	
Wittgenstein (1889–1951)	X											X	X		X	

Table II: Antecedents of Pioneers in the Arts

Name \ Features	Minority status	From the periphery/provinces	Illegitimate birth	Early loss of father or mother	Early loss of both parents	Physical disability	Chronic illness	Conflict with parents	Abuse/neglect by parents	Poverty	Unmarried	Late marriage	Homosexual	Married and childless	(Self) exile	Detention
Andersen (1805–1875)		X		X		X	X			X	X		X			
Bach (1685–1750)					X											
Balthus (1908–2001)		X		X								X			X	
Beckett (1906–1983)	X	X								X					X	
Beethoven (1770–1827)		X		X		X					X				X	
Bergman (1918–2007)								X							X	
Brâncuși (1876–1957)		X						X	X	X	X				X	
Brontë (1818–1848)		X		X			X				X				X	
Buñuel (1900–1983)		X													X	
Camus (1913–1960)		X		X			X			X					X	
Capote (1924–1984)		X		X	X				X		X		X			
Carroll (1832–1896)		X				X					X					
Cervantes (1547–1616)	X										X					X
Cézanne (1839–1906)		X	X					X			X				X	
Conrad (1856–1924)		X		X								X			X	

APPENDICES

Name	Minority status	From the periphery/provinces	Illegitimate birth	Early loss of father or mother	Early loss of both parents	Physical disability	Chronic illness	Conflict with parents	Abuse/neglect by parents	Poverty	Unmarried	Late marriage	Homosexual	Married and childless	(Self) exile	Detention
Dante (Alighieri) (1265–1321)				X											X	
Dermoût (1888–1962)	X	X		X				X							X	
Faulkner (1897–1962)		X				X		X							X	
Flaubert (1821–1880)		X					X				X				X	
Gogol (1809–1852)		X				X	X				X		X		X	
Gombrowicz (1904–1969)		X								X	X		X		X	
Hamsun (1859–1952)		X						X		X		X			X	
Hitchcock (1899–1980)	X			X		X										
Hoffmann (1776–1822)		X		X		X	X									
Ibsen (1828–1906)		X				X			X	X					X	
Kafka (1883–1924)	X						X	X			X					
Kleist (1777–1811)		X									X		X		X	
Lampedusa (1896–1957)														X	X	
Magritte (1898–1967)		X		X									X			
Melville (1819–1891)		X		X						X					X	
Poe (1809–1849)					X										X	

Name	Minority status	From the periphery/provinces	Illegitimate birth	Early loss of father or mother	Early loss of both parents	Physical disability	Chronic illness	Conflict with parents	Abuse/neglect by parents	Poverty	Unmarried	Late marriage	Homosexual	Married and childless	(Self) exile	Detention
Proust (1871–1922)	X			X			X				X		X		X	
Rilke (1875–1926)				X			X			X	X				X	
Rimbaud (1854–1891)		X		X						X	X				X	
Sade (1740–1813)		X													X	X
Schubert (1797–1828)				X		X				X	X					
Stravinsky (1882–1971)							X	X		X					X	
Strindberg (1849–1912)				X				X							X	
Van Gogh (1853–1890)		X						X		X	X				X	
Vermeer (1632–1675)	X														X	
Williams (1911–1983)		X						X			X		X			

NOTES

1 Feist (1999:284–90).
2 Weisberg (1986; 1999); Ericsson, Krampe, and Tesch-Romer (1993); Ericsson and Charness (1994).
3 To which the author adds: "Historians who have specified what is to be explained via collective biography often find themselves turning to explanations stressing the immediate setting and organization of everyday life, or relying on something vaguely called 'culture.' That moves them back towards anthropology"; Tilly (1978:209).
4 Butterfield (1959:1).
5 "[I]f both observation and conceptualization, fact and assimilation to theory, are inseparably linked in discovery, then discovery is a process and must take time. Only when all the relevant conceptual categories are prepared in advance, in which case the phenomenon would not be of a new sort, can discovering *that* and discovering *what* occur effortlessly, together, and in an instant . . . [D]iscovery involves an extended, though not necessarily long, process of conceptual assimilation"; Kuhn (1970:55–6).
6 Merton (2004:297–8 and passim).
7 Sahlins (2004:155).
8 Syme (1962:40).
9 Montias (1989:98–107).
10 Montias (1989:63–4, 98–102, 129–31).
11 Montias (1989:98–102, 129–35).
12 Montias (1989:246–62, 265–7).

1 From a letter to his son Horace, who was twenty-one and studying at Cambridge; cited in Browne (2002:334).
2 Feist (1999:286); Weisberg (1999:246–47); cf. Ericsson, Krampe, and Tesch-Romer (1993).

3 Tilly (1978:209).
4 Lehman (1953); Kuhn (1970:90, 90n). See also Klein (2004:130–1).
5 Wootton (2010:182).
6 Bruchez-Hall (1996:56).
7 Kuhn (1970:52–65).
8 For which Darwin drew on Adam Smith's concept of the "invisible hand," Lyell's notion of the slow developments of geological processes, Malthus's work on population increase, and the comparison with artificial selection among domesticated animals.
9 Einstein (1920).
10 In the social and behavioral sciences, comparison takes the place of experiment in the natural sciences. On the study of case studies and the use of "negative" cases, see Mahoney and Goertz (2004).
11 "In the field of observation chance favors only the prepared mind"; cited in Beveridge (1957:160), who adds in his chapter on chance: "Probably the majority of discoveries in biology and medicine have been come upon unexpectedly, or at least had an element of chance in them, especially the most important and revolutionary ones. It is scarcely possible to foresee a discovery that really breaks new ground, because it is often not in accord with current beliefs" (1957:31). See Merton's study of serendipity in scientific discovery, where he considers Pasteur's statement on "prepared minds" an example of "extreme psychological reductionism," in Merton and Barber (2004:258–9, 283). On Merton's view of the role of serendipity in scientific discoveries, see Merton (2004).
12 In his book *Elegance in Science: The Beauty of Simplicity*, Ian Glynn opens his Chapter 2 as follows, "Newton's laws of motion and of gravitation not only provided an elegant explanation of a vast body of astronomical observations that had been accumulated since the days of Babylon, but also proved to be fundamental steps in the development of modern physics" (2010:18).
13 Elias (1998b:97–8); cf. Blok (1974).
14 Franklin, cited in Watson (1980:124).
15 Glynn (2010:30–1).
16 Cited in Pais (1982:72).
17 See, for example, Ginzburg's recent essay on Picasso's *Guernica*, "il quadro piu documentato non solo tra quelli di Picasso, ma probabilmente nel'intera storia dell'arte occidentale [the most documented painting not only of Picasso, but probably in the whole history of western art]" (2015:159).
18 For the helpful notion of "family resemblances," see Wittgenstein (1967: 66–7); cf. Blok (1976); Zadeh (1965) on "fuzzy sets"; and Kuhn (1970: 55–6) on "conceptual assimilation."
19 "Of all forms of mental activity the most difficult to induce . . . is the art of handling the same bundle of data as before, but placing them in a new system of relations with one another by giving them a different framework"; Butterfield (1959:1), also cited by Beveridge (1957:106). Cf. Kuhn (1970:85).
20 Ginzburg in Pallares-Burke (2002:186, 190).
21 In his diary of his journey, Albrecht Dürer refers to his friend Erasmus and calls him in passing "an old manikin"; cited in Huizinga (1984:148). A letter from William Warham, Archbishop of Canterbury, his friend and benefactor, playfully refers to Erasmus's "small body"; Erasmus (2004, letter 286). For further comments on short stature, see Chapter 4.

22 Huizinga (1984:175).
23 Huizinga (1984:7).
24 Huizinga (1984:78).
25 Wilcken (2010:331).
26 Taleb (2004:xvi, 270–1).
27 *Enzyklopädie der Philosophischen Wissenschaften* #474.
28 C. Murray (2003:288).
29 C. Murray (2003:287–8).
30 Cited in Archer (1984:205–6).
31 Stoneman (1995:viii).
32 J. Barker (1994:478–85).
33 Gay (1988:14). To which Gay added: "The Freuds must have been among the very few middle-class Central European families without a piano, but that sacrifice faded in face of the glorious career they imagined for the studious, lively schoolboy in his cabinet."
34 Bourdieu (1998:76 and passim).
35 Goldsmith (2005:56, 69–70, 328–31).
36 Spoto (1983:18–22, 328–31).
37 Single philosophers can also be mentioned, including Kant, Schopenhauer, Kierkegaard, Nietzsche, Wittgenstein, and Foucault. Unmarried artists include Handel, Beethoven, Kleist, Schubert, Andersen, Poe, Gogol, Flaubert, Carroll, Rimbaud, Brâncuşi, Proust, Rilke, Kafka, Gombrowicz, Williams, and Capote, along with those already mentioned. Some of them were homosexuals, which enhanced their outsider status if it did not dominate it. Most of them figure in the Appendix to this book.
38 Cited in Gay (1988:59–61).
39 Bowlby (1990:10–11); Browne (2002:235–40).
40 Nietzsche (1966:2:749).
41 Cited in Renn and Schulmann (1992:39). On the role of Einstein's other "guardian angels" – Grossmann, Habicht, Solovine, and Besso – see Neffe (2005:121–40 and passim).
42 Pais (1982:138–9, 172–3); Renn and Schulmann (1992:xxvi–xxviii); Neffe (2005:121–22).
43 Alpers (1987:62–4); Holthusen (1958:46–56, passim). Alpers (1987) sketches the difficult life of Clara Westhoff after Rilke had moved out.
44 For an overview of his intense traveling, see Holthusen (1958:passim).
45 Holthusen (1958:69ff).
46 Holthusen (1958:46–56, 70–4, 90–1); Eijk (1988:88–9).
47 On Rilke's reservations, see Holthusen (1958:53).
48 Barlow in Darwin (1958:231–4).
49 Browne (1995:392–3); Bowlby (1990:226).
50 Beveridge (1957:143–4).
51 Watson (1980:114).
52 Fölsing (1993:202).
53 Desmond, Moore, and Browne (2007:113). This deficiency also affects biographies in encyclopedias and dictionaries.
54 The same holds for Kuhn's *Structure of Scientific Revolutions*. See, however, his critical observations on Lehman's *Age and Achievement*; Kuhn (1970:90, 90n).
55 I. B. Cohen (1985:92–4).

56 Giere (1988:227–77).
57 Monk (1990:261, 330–65).
58 Skidelsky (2010).
59 Watson (1980:115–16); Stent (1980); Merton (2004:278–84); Weisberg (2006:6–34).
60 Peterson (2006).
61 Hamilton (1996–2005:3:228); Ridley (2004); Grafen (2005).
62 Gessen (2009:viii); Szpiro (2007:95ff).
63 Szpiro (2007:viii, 205–62); Gessen (2009:148–209).
64 Szpiro (2007:111, 205–55); Gessen (2009:viii, 112ff).
65 Their boss, the lab's director Lawrence Bragg, took them off work on DNA for almost a year after a first try-out had failed, but Watson and Crick continued their work on the subject informally; Weisberg (2006:26–8).
66 Merton (2004:278–83).
67 Weisberg (2006:6–36).
68 Gay (1988:27–8, 136–41).
69 Radkau (2011:176–7), emphasis added.
70 Thucydides 5.26.5, see Strassler (1996).
71 Thucydides 1.22.4, see Strassler (1996).
72 Fölsing (1993:113ff); Neffe (2005:121–40); Isaacson (2007:62–3).
73 Poincaré summarized his view at a conference in 1900 as follows: "There is no absolute space and we only understand relative movements ..." To which biographer Neffe adds, "Einstein hätte es kaum schöner sagen können" [Einstein could have hardly phrased it more beautifully] (Neffe (2005:135); Renn and Schulmann (1992:xxvi).
74 Neffe (2005:139); Renn and Schulmann (1992:xxvi–xxviii).
75 Ericsson, Krampe, and Tesch-Romer (1993).
76 Giere (1988:229–42); Wegener (1929); Hallam (1973); Greene (1984).
77 Cited in Giere (1988:238–9).
78 Giere (1988:239).
79 Westfall (2007:49ff); Glynn (2010:48–60); I. B. Cohen (1985:38–9, 43).
80 Hallam (1973:111–140); Greene (1984:744–5); Giere (1988:240–77).
81 Greene (1984:761).
82 Greene (1984:761).
83 Neffe (2005:172–86).
84 Goodall (2000:285–6).
85 Hermans (2007:108).
86 Skidelsky (2003:217–29; 2010).
87 Skidelsky (2010:55–60).
88 Kuhn (1970:64).
89 Biographical information derived from Von Wright (1962); Malcolm (1962); Monk (1990).
90 Monk (1990:260–1).
91 Monk (1990:261); Wittgenstein (1967:#66–7).
92 Cited in Krul (1979:5).
93 For biographical data, see Locher (1958); and Krul (1979; 1990).
94 See the statement of professor of medicine Piet Borst in his column entitled "Innovative mismanagement" in NRC Handelsblad, Apr. 12–13, 2012. He criticizes optimism among industry and academia and their belief in unanimous cooperation in the planning of innovation in the following

terms: "People who are forced to establish consortia which make big and sweeping plans for innovation come to believe in these castles in the air themselves." Borst cites from their text, "In our field, industry and academia now cooperate unanimously. The noses all point in the same direction!" Comments Borst: "As if anything was ever innovated or discovered by noses that pointed in the same direction."

95 Watson (1980:189–209); Merton (2004:278–84); Weisberg (2006:16–35).
96 Koestler (1964:529).
97 Sahlins (2004:4).
98 Colson (1989:14).
99 Slotten (2004:10–12); Browne (2002:14–42).
100 Browne (2002:23ff).

2 SIBLING RIVALRY

1 Sulloway (1996:83–118).
2 "A birth order status established before an individual's seventh birthday must have remained stable until his sixteenth birthday for this information to be used as evidence"; Sulloway (1996:460 n9).
3 Sulloway (1996:12–23, 146).
4 Darwin (2009a:63ff).
5 Darwin (2009a:76).
6 On the frequency of fratricide, see Sulloway (1996:436–7), who refers to Daly and Wilson (1988).
7 Sulloway (1996:372–3).
8 In a rather critical review: Modell (1997).
9 Sulloway (1996:32–54).
10 Sulloway (1996:42). For this statement on the over-representation of later-borns, Sulloway refers to an undisclosed sample of seventy-eight individuals as initiators of scientific innovation; Sulloway (1996:464 n70).
11 Sulloway (1996:463 n58). The page references Sulloway refers to are drawn from Kuhn (1970), I. B. Cohen (1985), Hacking (1981), and the eighteen-volume *Dictionary of Scientific Biography*.
12 Sulloway (1996:36, 463 n58).
13 Modell (1997:625).
14 Townsend (1997:195–8).
15 Sulloway (1996:42, 197).
16 Sulloway (1996:38–9, 185–7). Sulloway's source, Koestler (1964:129), does not mention birth order for the two sisters; Nicolaus (1473–1543) had a brother, Andreas, four years older, and two sisters whose names and birth order are unknown, little being known about the early youth of these four children. After the loss of their parents when Nicolaus was ten, all four children came under the guardianship of their mother's brother, the future Bishop of Ermland (now Warmia) in northern Poland.
17 See his summary of "predictors" in his "family dynamics model of radical behavior," in Sulloway (1996:197, table 5).

3 Heuristic Exceptions

1 F. Darwin (1887:1:148).
2 F. Darwin (1887:1:148).
3 Kuhn (1970:52–65) points out the character of important discoveries as a process: "That awareness of anomaly opens a period in which conceptual categories are adjusted until the initially anomalous [i.e., the 'exception'] has become the anticipated" (1970:64).
4 Writes Sulloway: "In compiling this citation count for 'revolutionary' innovations, I have relied on the number of pages devoted to each theory in Kuhn (1970); I. B. Cohen (1985); Hacking (1981); and the eighteen-volume *Dictionary of Scientific Biography* (1973)"; Sulloway (1996:463 n58).
5 For his coded biographical factors (or independent variables), see Sulloway (1996:460 n9).
6 Sulloway (1996:37, 110–12). Sulloway contradicts himself in a note (1996:465 n81), where he refers to twenty-nine cases "in my [undisclosed] sample of biological laterborns [elder sons] who were raised as functional firstborns and who are statistically indistinguishable from other firstborns."
7 On Galileo, Kepler, and Newton, see Sulloway (1996:203–11, 124–33).
8 Sulloway (1996:460 n9). Sulloway discusses the "negative" case of Galileo, who did not grow up with any of his siblings, but gets sidetracked: we should regard Galileo therefore as an only child, and such children "are freer to become radicals themselves" (1996:204–5). Sulloway ignores Galileo's notoriously bad relationship with his mother and disagreement with his father about career choice. See Heilbron (2010:1–5); Wootton (2010:10–12, 93–5, 253).
9 See Sulloway (1996: 121–2, fig. 5.1) and his statement below the diagram about elder sons now coded as functional firstborns, implying their conflict with parents is like that of other firstborns: "Birth order and parental conflict interact: firstborns are particularly affected by parental conflict, as are laterborns who are the eldest of their sex." Incidentally, this statement undercuts Sulloway's main thesis about birth order: "laterborns are more likely than (functional) firstborns to initiate or support radical innovation."
10 Henig (2000:18–19).
11 Henig (2000:19–21).
12 Henig (2000:133, 166–7).
13 Dawkins (1989:106, 296–7).
14 Henig (2000: 23).
15 Sulloway (1996:110–12); Henig (2000:1–28, passim).
16 Henig (2000:152–3).
17 Kuhn (1970:65).
18 Henig (2000:1–39, 119–61; 177ff, 247ff).
19 Henig (2000:173).
20 Sulloway (1996:315).
21 Sulloway (1996:315, 526 n30), cited from Robert Palmer's collective biography (1989:4).
22 Sulloway (1996:288).
23 Townsend (1997:197).
24 See Sulloway's overview (1996:37–43,197, table 5). As noted above, this comes down to modifying ad hoc dependent and independent variables to

make them fit. The most striking example is his distinction between "techni-cal" and "radical" revolutions with the comment: "firstborns are much more likely to make breakthroughs of a technical order than they are to pioneer radical revolutions." In this way he can explain Watson and Crick's research on DNA (a revolution in molecular biology – and by implication of science itself) which is "a good example of creative puzzle solving in science, not of a radical innovation"; Sulloway (1996:329–32). This juggling with the facts (dependent and independent variables) enables him to "explain" no fewer than eleven (technical) revolutions of firstborn scientists, Harvey, Bacon, Newton, Lavoisier, Maxwell, Hertz, Lyell, Einstein, Pauling, Watson and Crick, while Sulloway wrongly codes three cases of elder sons as later-borns: Hutton, Bohr, and Mendel. This amounts to fourteen cases out of a total of eighteen firstborns (Sulloway 1996:38–43). With such poor results, why insist on birth order as the key variable in radical innovation? Are later-borns indeed more likely than firstborns to initiate radical innovation in science?

25 Sulloway (1996:124–8).
26 Koestler (1964:317–48); *Dictionary of Scientific Biography* (1973:7:289ff); Glynn (2010:27–32).
27 Koestler (1964:513); Glynn (2010:27–32).
28 Koestler (1964:239–40).
29 Koestler (1964:239).
30 Westfall (1980:1–5).
31 Westfall (1980:53–5).
32 Westfall (1980:45–73).
33 Westfall (1980:100–3).
34 Gaukroger (1995:21).
35 Sulloway (1996:142).
36 Sulloway ignores what Bowlby in his biography of Darwin has to say about Darwin's early loss of his mother and the subsequent unfriendly treatment of his father; Bowlby (1990:58–62).
37 Darwin had of course read Malthus's *Essay* before, but had not acknowl-edged its importance. The book required a second reading for the now alert Darwin. Browne (1995:385–6); S. Gould (1996).
38 Sulloway (1996:57–60).
39 Sulloway (1996:60).
40 Sulloway (1996:460 n9).
41 Sulloway seems to acknowledge this when he argues that his theory on birth order does not hold well for France because of the demographic change since the late nineteenth century, when single-child families became dominant; Sulloway (1996:36).
42 Sulloway (1996:490 n50).
43 Bowlby (1990:40, 44, 69–71, 197–8).
44 Darwin (1958:28).
45 Bowlby (1990:71).
46 Sulloway (1996:490 n50).
47 Sulloway (1996:137).
48 Sulloway (1996: 137–8, 490 n56).
49 Darwin (1958:22).
50 Sulloway (1996:140–5).

51 Sulloway (1996:83–5, 138); Geier (2009:292, 299–300).
52 Sulloway (1996:430).
53 Sulloway (1996:138–9, 490 n56).
54 Sulloway (1996: 136–40, 491 n69).
55 Kuhn (1970:52–6).
56 Adam Smith, cited in Gould (1994:149).
57 Glynn (2010:30–1).
58 Sulloway (1996:203).
59 Sulloway (1996:203).
60 Sulloway (1996:204); see also Drake (1970; 1972; 1978; 2008).
61 Townsend (1997:192).
62 Sulloway (1996:204–5).
63 Sulloway (1996:460 n9).
64 Heilbron (2010:1, 3); Wootton (2010:94). Wootton, however, adds: "Yet, if Galileo and his mother were caught up in an unending conflict, there were also times when she clutched him to her" (2010:95).
65 Drake (1978:1–2; 2008).
66 Sulloway (1996:121–3).
67 Sulloway (1996:120–3).
68 Sulloway (1996:330–1). Sulloway's use of the term "creative puzzle solving" in relation to work in science is confusing. According to Kuhn, puzzle-solving activity is normal science and "Normal science does not aim at novelties of fact or theory and, when successful, finds none" (1970:52). This point destroys Sulloway's belated distinction between "technical" and "ideological" revolutions in science.
69 Sulloway (1996:331).
70 Sulloway (1996:331, 463 n58).
71 Sulloway (1996:36–42).
72 Sulloway (1996:147).
73 Sulloway (1996:147).
74 Gruber and Wallace (1999:93–4).
75 See the overview of his "family dynamics model"; Sulloway (1996:197, table 5).
76 Sulloway (1996:112).
77 Taleb (2004:xvi).
78 Modell (1997:625).
79 On the initial enthusiastic reception of Born to Rebel in the academic community, see the critical comments of Townsend and his no less critical review of the book itself (1997:191–3). For a more positive review, see Jared Diamond in New York Review of Books (1996). The critical review by Modell (1997) has already been mentioned.
80 Sternberg and Lubart (1995a:538–9).
81 Sternberg and Lubart (1995a:538–9); cf. Sternberg and Davidson (2003: 41–92).
82 Taleb (2004:xv).
83 Peirce (1998:2:107).
84 A. I. Miller (2000:163).
85 S. Gould (1996:11).
86 Cited in Beveridge (1957:149).

4 ADVERSITY

1 Coetzee (2004:20). Coetzee neglects three other giants of American and world literature: Poe, Hawthorne, and Melville, who all had an eye for the dark side of human existence and showed the way for later generations of writers, including O'Neill, Faulkner, Tennessee Williams, and Arthur Miller – most of whom suffered adversity when growing up: early parental loss, conflict with parents, father's bankruptcy, or poverty. Few liked school or showed "early intellectual distinction."

2 This phrase appears in *Requiem for a Nun* (1951) where Faulkner experiments with narrative techniques. The novel is best known for this line.

3 Bourdieu (1992:523–33).

4 In their preface to Melville's *Billy Budd, Sailor*, its editors Harrison Hayford and Morton B. Sealts add: "As it happened, manuscripts were found in Melville's own desk at the time of his death in 1891, manuscripts which have since been judged precious . . ." (1962:v).

5 "The aspects of things that are most important for us are hidden because of their simplicity and familiarity. (One is unable to notice something – because it is always before one's eyes.)"; Wittgenstein (1967:para. 129). As shown later, this is also called "the purloined letter effect," after a famous Poe story.

6 Parini dwells on Faulkner's alcoholism and sums up his life as a quintessential outsider: "The world might have come to him at last, but he rejected that world. He didn't want the profiles in *Life* or *Time*. He did not want cheering crowds. He wanted to smoke his pipe, sail his boat, and write his books. He wanted his own vices: whiskey and women" (2004:365).

7 Israel (2002:159–60).

8 Israel (2002:160).

9 Israel (2002:161).

10 Stewart (2006:36, 141).

11 It was not by chance that all five of them were of Jewish origin and that four of them were unmarried.

12 Stewart (2006:60). Nadler mentions expert praise of Spinoza's craftsmanship and points out that "grinding and polishing lenses, in Spinoza's day, was a quiet, intense, and solitary occupation perfectly suited to Spinoza's temperament. Unfortunately, it was not as well suited to his physical constitution, and the glass dust produced by the process probably exacerbated his respiratory problems and contributed to his early death" (1999:183–4).

13 Israel (2002:165–74).

14 Koerbagh, who had studied in Leiden, was condemned for blasphemy; Nadler (1999:113, 157, 265–9); Israel (2002:175–96).

15 Nadler (1999:131).

16 Neffe (2005:357).

17 For details on excommunication from the Talmud Torah congregation and its political implications, see Israel (2002:162–74) and Nadler (1999: 116–54).

18 Israel (2002:157–96).

19 Mahoney and Goertz (2004).

20 In his new status as an apostate Jew, "Spinoza would soon test the limits of the same Dutch freedom that made his new life possible. The vituperations of the rabbis would come to seem like mild admonishments in comparison with the vitriol the Christian theologians had in store for him. Indeed, after his expulsion from the Jewish community, the philosopher entered into a kind of double exile – he was an outcast twice removed. To the Jews he was an heretic; to the Christians he was, moreover, a Jew" (Stewart 2006:36).
21 Stewart (2006:36).
22 Nadler (1999:311–14).
23 Nadler (1999:341).
24 Stewart (2006:117–19, 260–1, 277–9, 330–1).
25 S. Gould (1996:12); cf. Browne (1995:23–8).
26 Bowlby (1990:53–79).
27 Muensterberger (1994:passim).
28 Ginzburg in Pallares-Burke (2002:190); see also Chapter 1.
29 Darwin (1958:22); F. Darwin (1887:1:149); cf. Sulloway (1996:144–5, 359).
30 Cited in Browne (1995:100–1).
31 Browne (1995:20).
32 Ariès (1981).
33 Browne (2010).
34 See Bruchez-Hall (1996:56).
35 Fölsing (1993:110).
36 Darryl E. Haley (Amazon.com).
37 Time, Mar. 9, 1962, pp. 43–8.
38 Freriks (2000:329).
39 Dermoût (1958).
40 Freriks (2000:275–9); cf. Freriks (1988).
41 Freriks (2000:108–9). "Mrs Dermoût makes no concessions to her readers, imposes no hidden message or esoteric chic, but those who taste her concoction will never forget it" (Times Literary Supplement). On The Ten Thousand Things: "One of the strangest books anyone could imagine, this intensely haunting novel is an authentic evocation of life on a lush Edenic island of the Moluccas, Indonesia – but life corrupted by violence and death" (Chicago Tribune). Other important writers in Dutch literature had a similar history of exile, including Eduard Douwes Dekker (Multatuli), Louis Couperus, Jan Slauerhoff, Cola Debrot, Hella Haasse, Elisabeth Eijbers, W. F. Hermans, and Gerard Reve. Except the latter two, they all had a colonial past and led a retired life.
42 In 1926 Maria's husband was appointed President of the Council of Justice in Batavia (now Djakarta), also called Higher Court of Justice. Freriks comments: "Once Dermoût had moved to [ended up in] such a high place, the couple could no longer avoid public life and they became members of the Sociëteit [club]"; Freriks (2000:160–2).
43 Freriks (2000:108ff, 216).
44 Cited in Hall (1959).
45 Freriks (2000: 27–9).
46 Freriks (2000:36–8, 55).
47 Freriks (2000:195).

48 Aldert Brouwer was a brother of the mathematician Luitzen Brouwer (1881–1966); Freriks (2000:43ff).
49 Freriks (2000:54–61).
50 For example, the story "The Professor" in *The Ten Thousand Things*.
51 Freriks (2000:50, 58–9, 131, 188, 270).
52 Freriks (2000:50, 188, passim).
53 Freriks (2000:279).
54 Cited in Freriks (2000:275–9).
55 See Peirce (1998:106–7, 216–17).
56 See Koestler (1964:307ff); Glynn (2010:227–36).
57 Simpson (2016). See also *Dictionary of Scientific Biography*.
58 Some biographers – and also Machiavelli himself – mention San Casciano as the nearest village. According to Oppenheimer, Machiavelli's exile came down to a "self-designed exile" (2011:231–2).
59 Grafton (2003:xxix).
60 Hale (1972:5, 21).
61 Hale (1972:111–12).
62 See Strassler (1996); Syme (1962).
63 Thucydides 1.22.4, see Strassler (1996).
64 Thucydides 5.26.5, see Strassler (1996).
65 Syme (1962:40–1), emphasis added. I am most grateful to classicist Karen Bassi at the University of Santa Cruz, California, for drawing my attention to Syme's essay after I told her, several years ago now, about the theme and argument of the present book on which I was then working.
66 Syme (1962:53–5) also explains why this could happen.
67 Paret (1976:15–18).
68 Heuser (2007:vii).
69 Heuser (2007:xxiv).
70 Heuser (2007:xxiii–xxiv).
71 In the 1790s Poland was divided in three between Prussia, Russia, and Austria. The Russian regime was extraordinarily severe; it subjected the Polish population to numerous restrictions, including obligatory education in Russian and the use of that language in public offices. In a series of revolts during the nineteenth century, Poles resisted in vain. The numerous victims included the father of Marie Curie (Sklodowska) and the parents of Joseph Conrad (Korzeniowski). Curie's father lost his job at the gymnasium in Warsaw. The parents of Conrad, belonging to the Polish gentry in eastern Poland, were accused of conspiracy. With their single four-year-old child, they were banished to a camp in Russia where, after two years, the mother died from tuberculosis.
72 Heuser (2007:xv–xxxiv). To these three writers on war in exile can be added another luminary and radical innovator: the Dutch Hugo Grotius (1583–1645), author of *On the Law of War and Peace* (1625), written and published while in exile in France.
73 Stewart (2006:117–19).
74 Stewart (2006:12).
75 Stewart (2006:passim).
76 Stewart (2006:330); "Leibniz's philosophy was never one thing. It was a basket of positions, tropes, and stereotyped reactions that evolved over time".

77 Israel (2002:163, 173–4).
78 Bilaniuk (1973:320); Friederici (1973:215–16).
79 Mautner and Hatfield (1969:124); cf. Needham (1985:215–16); Friederici (1973:ix–x).
80 Cited in Needham (1985:215).
81 Friederici (1973:ix–x).
82 Bilaniuk (1973:320).
83 Dürer, cited in Huizinga (1984:148).
84 Troyat (1973:11).
85 Troyat (1973:11–20).
86 Samuel Beckett (1906–83) had to take distance from his mentor James Joyce to find his own voice, as in the famous *Waiting for Godot*: not more but less, not light but darkness, which took the form of foolishness and failing, incapacity and ignorance. "His future work would focus on poverty, failure, exile and loss – as he put it, on man as a 'non-knower' and as a 'non-can-er'"; Knowlson (1996:352–3).
87 For a summary of the duel provoked by Pushkin, see Nabokov (1975:43–50); Binyon (2003:514–41).
88 Brogan (2006:56, 395).
89 Cited in Gibian (1985:vii).
90 Gibian (1985:vii).
91 To which Pevear adds, "And indeed Gogol's art, despite its romantic ghosts and folkloric trappings, is strikingly modern in two ways: first, his works are free verbal creations, based on their own premises rather than on the conventions of nineteenth-century fiction; and second, they are highly theatrical in presentation, concentrated on figures and gestures, constructed in a way that, while admitting any amount of digression, precludes the social and psychological analysis of classical realism. His images remain ambiguous and uninterpreted, which is what makes them loom so large before us. These expressive qualities of Gogol's art influenced Dostoevsky decisively, turning him from a social romantic into a 'fantastic realist,' and they made Gogol the father of Russian modernism. His leap from the province to the capital also carried him forward in time, so that, at the beginning of the twentieth century, the symbolist Andrei Bely could say, 'We still do not know what Gogol is'" (Pevear 1998:ix–x).
92 Sahlins (2004:5).
93 Colson (1989:14).
94 Rosen (2008:304–5).
95 Rosen (2008:308); Jeanson (1958:41–2).
96 Jeanson (1958:16); cf. Kooijmans (1996).
97 Screech (1991:xiv).
98 Haynal (1989).
99 Jeanson (1958:16–17, 41–2).
100 Jeanson (1958:41–2).
101 Jeanson (1958:109–18).
102 Montaigne (1991:934; 1958:3:3).
103 Montaigne (1991:728–9; 1958:2:17).
104 Gilot and Lake (1964:224).
105 Goffman (1979:11–54).
106 Blok (2001:155–72).

107 Recall Bilaniuk's observation about Lichtenberg's physical defect, "which possibly reinforced his leaning to scientific work" (1973).
108 Solomon (1977:78).
109 Solomon (1977:42, 59–66).
110 Solomon (1977:121–5). Cf. Rosen (2012:171–9).
111 Quoted in Meyer (1967:129).
112 Quoted in Meyer (1967:148).
113 Quoted in Meyer (1967:53).
114 Fjelde (1965:xiv–xv).
115 A play he wrote in two weeks during a stay with his family on an estate in Denmark. It has the significant subtitle "A Naturalistic Tragedy" and is provided with a famous foreword that explains the new rules for writing for the stage. Meyer (1986). The play is still widely performed and has often appeared on screen.
116 Buñuel (1985:96–7, 181–3).
117 For surveys of his films, see Aranda (1985); Duncan and Krohn (2005).
118 Sadoul (1984:6).
119 Buñuel (1985: 215–18).
120 Buñuel (1985); Pérez Turrent and de La Colina (2008:5, 44–5).
121 Pérez Turrent and de La Colina (2008:5, 44–5).
122 Evans (1995:8).
123 Evans (1995:8).
124 Evans (1995:5–6).
125 Bergman (1988:15, 56–7, 76, 207–9); cf. Bergman (1994).
126 Lély (1961:18–51, 52ff).
127 Quoted in Lély (1961:462).
128 Knowles and Moore (2000:4–8).
129 Garnett cited in Watts (1989:26); Gurko (1979).
130 Gurko (1979:123).
131 Cited in Bloom (2005:73).
132 Stape (2007:271).
133 Knowles and Moore (2000:194).
134 Knowles and Moore (2000:147).
135 Watts (1989:26).
136 Schwarz (2001:16).
137 After the partitions of Poland in 1792, 1793, and 1795 between Russia, Austria, and Prussia, Poland disappeared from the map as a political unity. With the peace talks after the First World War, the Polish state was revived with new boundaries.
138 On Tadeusz Bobrowski, see Knowles and Moore (2000:45–6, 307–12).
139 Dagen (1995:passim); Vescovo (1993:passim).
140 See Dagen (1995) for six of these portraits of Madame Cézanne.
141 Dagen (1995:162–8); Athanassoglou-Kallmyer (2003:235–6).
142 For Cézanne's 1899 portrait of Vollard in the Petit Palais, Paris, see Dagen (1995:144).
143 Athanassoglou-Kallmyer (2003:235–6).
144 Cited in Hoog (1994:158).
145 Naifeh and Smith (2011:55–72, 109–28, 657, 926).
146 Kammer (2013).
147 Sulloway (1996:57–60). About the large family in which Van Gogh grew up

his biographers note: "In a family that otherwise strictly rationed displays of parental affection, Theo repaid Vincent's lavish attention with an attachment tantamount to 'worship,' according to sister Lies" (Naifeh and Smith 2011:40).

148 Sulloway (1996:57–60).

149 Robb (2000), emphasis added. As noted above, this insight is lost on Darwin's biographer Janet Browne, who categorically belittles any effect of the early death of Darwin's mother on her nine-year-old son, ignoring the point made by Bowlby (1990:57–62, 78–9). See Browne (1995:20–2).

150 Quoted in Robb (2000:12).

151 Starkie (1968:286–8, 314–19); Robb (2000:265–72).

152 For this episode, see Robb (2000:300–10).

153 Starkie (1968:382–431); Robb (2000:300ff, 452–68).

154 On the influence of Izambard as mentor, see Starkie (1968:60); on the preamble to Rimbaud's manifesto (*Lettre du Voyant*) after participation in the Paris Commune in April 1871, see Robb (2000:96–105, 122–5).

155 Starkie (1968:396).

156 See Bowlby (1990:58–62). As mentioned above, a mother's rejection had the same effect on the young Van Gogh.

157 Mortimer Herbert Morris-Goodall was a top British long-distance racing driver (for Aston Martin), not as famous as Stirling Moss, but good enough to drive with Moss in a Jaguar in the 1953 Mille Miglia. "Driving was his life's dominant passion before he was twenty." Goodall's biographer Peterson describes him as a "distant father," "a person who himself grew up without a father." "Mortimer, for all his charm, verve, and social grace, was a cool, self-contained, and a remote father." Peterson (2006:10–11, 3–4, 5–28).

158 Peterson (2006:38–52); Goodall (2000).

159 Sacks (2010:82–110).

160 Sacks (2010:88).

161 Sacks (2010:85).

162 Starkie (1968:47).

163 Darwin (1958:42–3). Enzensberger (2004:176) argues that "the genre of autobiography is inherently unreliable not so much because of what is in it but especially because of what is left out."

164 Hoogendijk (2009).

165 Simic (2006:23).

166 Ziarek (1998:9). Gombrowicz, the youngest of four children, studied law at the University of Warsaw (to please his lawyer father) and obtained a master's degree. For a while he worked as a clerk in a municipal court and learned about the wretchedness of life from both sides of the bench, closely observing "the upper spheres called upon to pass judgment on the lower ones"; Simic (2006:22).

167 Gombrowicz, *Diary*, vol. 1, cited in Ziarek (1998:9); cf. Simic (2006:23–4).

168 Ziarek (1998:10), emphasis added.

169 Simic (2006:24).

170 Simic (2006:23–4).

171 Personal communication, Magdalena Sroda, Swalk, Mazury, summer 2010.

172 Banville (2006:62).

173 Banville (2006).

174 Banville (2006:62–3).
175 Rilke (1988).
176 Holthusen (1958:145–8).
177 Holthusen (1958:141–5).
178 Banville (2006:62–3).
179 Rilke (1951).
180 About the self-willed Balthus (Balthasar Klossowski de Rola, Polish nobility) and his place in twentieth-century painting as "outsider of the modernists," see Leymarie (1979) and Spies (2001).
181 Wagenbach (1964:80–4).
182 Kakutani (1988:13).
183 Wagenbach (1964:84–6); N. Murray (2004:119).
184 Cited in Wagenbach (1964:80).
185 Cited in Wagenbach (1964:80).
186 Wagenbach (1964:80, 91–4, 99–101); see also letters to Grete Bloch in Kafka (2009:469ff).
187 Hohoff (1958:63–4, 147–54); Diamant (2003:55–7).
188 N. Murray (2004:164).
189 N. Murray (2004:180–1, 406 n5); Kafka (2009:444).
190 Quoted in Cantoni (1953:xii); Unwin (2004:166).
191 Cited in Smith (2008:17).
192 Cited in Smith (2008:17) with reference to Arendt (1968:36).
193 Adler (2001:6).
194 Wagenbach (1964:104–5).
195 For a description of this first meeting, see Wagenbach (1964:83), who cites from Kafka's diary for August 20, 1912; Kafka (2008b:2:79).
196 Wagenbach (1964:94).
197 Diary July 23 and August 14, 1913, in Kafka (2008b).
198 Wagenbach (1964:116–19); N. Murray (2004:297, 275–300).
199 Wagenbach (1964:115–20, 122–6).
200 Wagenbach (1964:81–2).
201 Diamant (2003:1–15).
202 Diamant (2003:55–7).
203 Diamant (2003:13–14, 22–3).
204 Diamant 2003:90–120); N. Murray (2004:355–84)
205 Wagenbach (1964:80–4).
206 Cited in Wagenbach (1964:116–19).
207 Wagenbach (1964:91).
208 Diary, October 21, 1921, in Kafka (2008c).
209 In his essay "Deviance as success: the double inversion of stigmatized roles," which inspired me to write this book, Jackson mentions Ira Cohen's example of the scientific researcher: "You take somebody who's compulsive and suspicious and he's a meticulous good researcher"; Jackson (1978:273).
210 Kanfer (1983).
211 Quoted in Wagenbach (1964:41).
212 Kafka broke off his second engagement with Felice in December 1917. Two years later, Felice married a well-to-do businessman and settled in Switzerland in 1931. Five years later she moved to the United States, where she died in 1960. Five years earlier she had agreed with publisher Schocken

to publish the letters from Kafka. They appeared in 1967 in a separate volume. N. Murray (2004:121).

213 J. H. Miller (2003:362, 367); J. Barker (1994).
214 Stoneman (1995:viii, xxvii–xxviii); Kermode (1975).
215 Stoneman (1995:ix–x).
216 J. H. Miller (2003:365).
217 Stoneman (1995:xi–xii), who refers to C. P. Sangers's famous essay *The Structure of Wuthering Heights* of 1926, and Lord David Cecil's essay in *Early Victorian Novelists* in 1934.
218 Stoneman (1995:xxvii–xxviii).
219 This is especially so when explanation about that disappearance is lacking. See on this point, Bowlby (1990:56–62, 457–66); Robb (2000: 28–9).
220 Cited in Poe (1974:218).
221 Lennig (1959:76); and see also pictures there.
222 Sahlins (2004:4).
223 Wittgenstein (1967:para. 129). See also Bromberger, who invokes this quotation from Wittgenstein in discussing the work of French Resistance fighter Germaine Tillion (1907–2008) on the German concentration camp Ravensbrück, where she was held and where she wrote a study about her experiences there. Bromberger comments: "The decentralization of the gaze, the comparison, the variety of experiences are the necessary conditions for that clarity and that understanding . . . Tillion provides the proof of the fertility of the *vue portée au loin* 'with the spectacles of ethnology. . .'"; Bromberger and Todorov (2002:89).
224 Allen (1938:vii).
225 Wullschlager (2000:19, 42–53).
226 Wullschlager (2000:21).
227 Wullschlager (2000:122–4).
228 Possibly Andersen suffered from Klinefelter syndrome, a genetic condition in which males have an extra X chromosome.
229 Wullschlager (2000:93).
230 Wullschlager (2000:81–3).
231 Cited in Wullschlager (2000:82).
232 Safranski (1984).
233 Wullschlager (2000:82–3).
234 Diamant (2003:57, 260).
235 Quoted in M. Cohen (1995:22).
236 On the phenomenon of the *mundus inversus* in many places and times, see Babcock's collection and her helpful introduction; Babcock (1978).
237 For Carroll's personal characteristics, see the 1899 description by Isa Bowman, one of his last friends; Bowman (1972:9–14).
238 M. Cohen (1995:xix).
239 M. Cohen (1995:xix).
240 M. Cohen (1995:279).
241 M. Cohen (1995:533).
242 M. Cohen (1995:533). Carroll paid a great deal of attention to the preparation of his lectures. Cohen emphasizes Carroll's *punctiliousness*, his obsessive *orderliness* in his work, in the care of his outward appearance (clothes), etc. With one of his little girl-friends, who stayed with him, he

went almost daily to the dentist for an inspection of her teeth. Bowman (1972:71–2).

243 M. Cohen (1995:289–90).
244 M. Cohen (1995:284).
245 On these qualities, see M. Cohen (1995:533).
246 Bowman (1972:60).
247 See reproduction in Oprea (1972).
248 See reproduction in Oprea (1972).
249 Data about Brăncuşi derived from Oprea (1972) and S. Miller (1995).
250 Bourdieu with Wacquant (1992:189–91), emphasis added.
251 Bourdieu with Wacquant (1992:136–49); Bourdieu (1984; 1998:11).

5 CHANCE AND NECESSITY

1 Huizinga (1984:1–16).
2 Huizinga (1984:16). Huizinga mentions that Erasmus was ordained on April 25, 1492 by the Bishop of Utrecht. Previously, probably in 1488, Erasmus had taken his vows at the Steyn monastery near Gouda.
3 A prebend is a stipend from the revenues of a cathedral or a collegiate church to a canon or member of the chapter.
4 Huizinga (1984:20–8).
5 Huizinga (1984:35).
6 Huizinga (1984:35).
7 W. Barker (2001:362–5); Bloch (1961:212–17); Westfall (1985).
8 This was a familiar occurrence in the prevailing patron–client system in early modern Europe. It was not uncommon for scholars to accompany their students from aristocratic families on their trips to the continent. This role fell to Hobbes and also, in another version, to Harvey. In an inverse case, in the early nineteenth century, Davy took his student Faraday as an assistant on a long scientific trip to France and Italy, during which Faraday also acted as a servant for Davy and his wife (Hamilton (2002).
9 Huizinga (1984:60).
10 Cited in Huizinga (1984:69).
11 Huizinga (1984:69).
12 Huizinga (1984:69).
13 Huizinga (1984:89–90).
14 Huizinga (1984:94).
15 Machiavelli (2003).
16 Van Delft (2008); Koestler (1964:468–78); and Galilei (2013).
17 Westfall (1985:29).
18 Biagioli (1993:1–5); Camerota (2008:99–101).
19 Pitt-Rivers (1971:140–1); Wolf (1966).
20 Westfall (1985:29); Gellner and Waterbury (1977); Eisenstadt and Roniger (1984); Wallace-Hadrill (1990).
21 Holthusen (1958:104–11).
22 On Wittgenstein's financial means to support "needy" Austrian artists, including Rilke in 1914, see Monk (1990:106–10).
23 Holthusen (1958:141–9).
24 Holthusen (1958:153–4).

25 Westfall (2007:4–6; 1980:63–73).
26 Darwin (1958:71–2); Browne (1995:145–57).
27 Weisberg (1986; 2006). See also Elias (1998b:95–106) for a clarifying deconstruction of the concept of "genius" on the basis of the life and work of Mozart – and the substantial influence of the father in the making of the composer. Elias's essay came to my attention only after revising the original Dutch version of this book.
28 Ericsson, Krampe, and Tesch-Romer (1993:398); this essay has been very influential, especially in cognitive psychology, where its nestor Robert Sternberg in his later work silently dropped the term "talent" and replaced it with the term "skills"; Sternberg and Davidson (2003:107, 225–6).
29 Gardner (1993:266–309). There are, of course, more examples of "anti-talent" inspiring perfect performance, including the top violinist Mischa Elman (1894–1946), who had to cope with short, thick fingers and is remembered for his inimitable tone. More recently, American racing cyclist Lance Armstrong, after recovering from cancer, won the Tour de France in seven consecutive years (1999–2005). Admitting to the use of drugs, he later returned his medals.
30 Keegan (1996:14–15). For more detail on this point, see Gruber (1981: 73–93).
31 Darwin (1958:42–3).
32 Darwin (1958:120).
33 Enzensberger (2004:176).
34 Sahlins (2004:4–5).
35 Darwin (1958:64).
36 Browne (1995:117ff).
37 Browne (2002:427, 430, 431).
38 Browne (2002).
39 Browne (2002:417–18).
40 Browne (1995:378–94).
41 Browne (2002:426–31).
42 Browne (2002:14–45).
43 Slotten (2004:153).
44 Slotten (2004:159).
45 Browne (2002:232ff).
46 As Hamilton phrases it himself, "People divide roughly, it seems to me, into two kinds, or rather a continuum . . .There are 'people people' and 'things people'. I undoubtedly fall on the side of the things." Furthermore he believes that "things people constitute . . . an integral and adaptively maintained part of the human pattern of variation (1996–2005:3:205, 207). Independently, Jackson makes a similar point in his essay "Deviance as success" (1978). There are also striking similarities with the private collectors of art presented in Muensterberger's *Collecting: An Unruly Passion* (1994). The author, himself a collector, registers the same syndrome and a similar background of adversity, often the impact of early loss of dear ones.
47 Rilke (1988); see Chapter 4.
48 Isaacson (2007).
49 Pais (1982:172–3); Neffe (2005:174–5).
50 Neffe (2005:357). When asked if he believed in God, he answered "I believe in the God of Spinoza" (referring to the laws of nature).

51 Cited in Browne (2002:110–22).
52 Westfall (2007:6–7, 26, 29).
53 W. Barker (2001:364).
54 W. Barker (2001:363).
55 Höweler (1949:78, 85–91); Solomon (1977:268, 316–17).
56 Koestler (1964:249–71).
57 In one of his letters Darwin acknowledged that "observation is a selective act," and added the exclamation: "How odd it is that anyone should not see that all observation must be for or against some view if it is to be of any service!" (1958:161).
58 Koestler (1964:513ff); Glynn (2010:50–7).
59 Koestler (1964:11).
60 Elias's study of the civilizing process (1969[1939]) is an early and instructive example of unplanned but structured long-term processes without a specific goal (the intertwining of state formation and the development of manners). Darwin was probably the first scientist who presented a description and model of a blind and long-term structured process, called biological evolution, and (together with Wallace) discovered its mechanism of natural selection to explain the origin of species. Gould comments: "In Darwin's scheme, we are a detail, not a purpose or embodiment of the whole – with the details, whether good or bad, left to the working out of what we may call chance" (1991:290).
61 Kuhn (1970:172–3).
62 Klein (2004:130–1).
63 See esp. Glynn (2010:1–60).
64 Quoted in I. B. Cohen (1985:442).
65 Cited in Neffe (2005:148). See also Kuhn (1970:52–65); Merton (2004:264–6). Cf. Butterfield (1959:1); Koestler (1964:528–9).
66 See discussion in Lévi-Strauss (1969:passim); Homans and Schneider (1955); Needham (1963); Evans-Pritchard (1981:200–2); Sahlins (2004:passim).
67 Dawkins (1989:88–108, 296–7), with a comment on Hamilton's rule formulated after the discovery of social altruism among insects.
68 Stape (2007:1–59).
69 Wagenbach (1964:15, 132).
70 Lottman (1979:31–2).
71 Delbanco (2005:18–31, 287).
72 Neffe (2005:28–30, 36–7, 58–9, 149).
73 Koestler (1964:121–7). The city is now called Kaliningrad and part of a Russian enclave bordering the southern Baltic.
74 Apart from working on his book, Watzenrote also acted as a personal physician for the canons, as administrator of the cathedral, and as a diplomat; Koestler (1964:143ff).
75 Koestler (1964:139, 148–9).
76 Koestler (1964:139–41).
77 "The first thing a young man should do is to provide an outstanding specimen of his work as a pledge that what is given him will not be wasted"; quoted in W. Barker (2001:364).
78 W. Barker (2001:xiii–xxi), "Montaigne's essays – which imitate the *Adages* in other fascinating ways as well – are the best-known example of the text that grows by accretion . . ."

79 Górny (2010). For a different view on Copernicus's stargazing, see Koestler (1964:125–6).
80 Neffe (2005:136 and passim).
81 Israel (2002:246ff).
82 Henig (2000:120–1, 91–2, 167–8).
83 Koestler (1964:244–8).
84 Westfall (2007:49–56); Glynn (2010:50–60).
85 Monk (1990:260–2).
86 Monk (1990:255–80).
87 Koestler (1964:151–7).
88 Koestler (1964:157ff).
89 Koestler (1964:175–8).
90 Westfall (2007:49–50); Glynn (2010:51–60).
91 Glynn (2010:57–60).
92 Pope Paul III similarly had a companion who bore him three children.
93 Gaukroger (1995:xvi–xvii).
94 Friederici (1973:xxvii–viii).
95 Fölsing (1993:28–9).
96 Neffe (2005:36, 46–7).
97 Neffe (2005:57–8).
98 Neffe (2005:28).
99 Neffe (2005:37, 149, 140–57).
100 Quoted in Neffe (2005:148). Einstein may have had Newton's break-through in mind. His statement sounds like a variation on Glynn's later summary of Newton's discovery of universal gravitation: "Newton showed that what he called *'the law of universal gravitation' could, along with his laws of motion, account for a great variety of observations*: not just the straightforward motions of planets and their satellites, but also the inter-planetary perturbation seen when the massive planets Jupiter and Saturn are in near conjunction: the perturbing action of the Sun on the motion of the Moon; the motion of comets; the phenomena of tides; the fact that the Earth is not quite spherical (bulging at the Equator and flattened at the Poles); and – a consequence of this bulging – the precession of the equi-noxes" (Glynn 2010:57).
101 Fölsing (1993:44–68); Neffe (2005:124).
102 C. Murray (2003:291–3).
103 Benveniste (1969:141).
104 C. Murray (2003:275–83).
105 Roth (1987).
106 Many of them came from eastern Europe and were students of Joseph Joachim (1831–1907) and Leopold Auer (1848–1930), the great innovators and pedagogues of violin-playing in the second half of the nineteenth century and early twentieth century.
107 Wilcken (2010:23).
108 Cited in Wilcken (2010:331). Heinrich Hertz (1857–94) was the eldest child in a well-to-do, assimilated Jewish family in Hamburg. When he went to the gymnasium his mother told him to be number one in his class. And Hertz became number one. He studied physics and chemistry under Von Helmholtz in Berlin and graduated in 1880 magnum cum laude. With the discovery of electromagnetic waves (named after him), Hertz laid the foundation of

Marconi's application of wireless (radio) communication (*Encyclopaedia Britannica* online).

109 Wilcken (2010:110–12, 331).
110 Cited in Wilcken (2010:112, 209–24).
111 Wilcken (2010:73–5, 123–9).
112 For an early and highly praised reception of this study, see the detailed review by leading Leyden anthropologist de Josselin de Jong (1952).
113 "Totemism is thus reduced to a particular fashion of formulating a general problem, viz., how to make opposition, instead of being an obstacle to integration, serve rather than produce it"; Lévi-Strauss (1969:160–1).
114 See also Kuhn's early critical remarks. Referring to Lehman's *Age and Achievement* (1953), he notes, "Almost always the men who achieve these fundamental inventions of a new paradigm have been either very young or very new to the field whose paradigm they change" (1970:90). Yet behind age lurks outsidership. Age may then be spurious.
115 Ericsson, Krampe, and Tesch-Romer (1993).
116 Merton (2004:281–3).
117 Ericsson, Krampe, and Tesch-Romer (1993:395).
118 This transition is not explained further and appears in the index in a veiled form: the keyword "talent" refers to "skills" without any comment; Sternberg and Davidson (2003:107, 225–6).
119 Ericsson, Krampe, and Tesch-Romer (1993:398).
120 Ericsson, Krampe, and Tesch-Romer (1993:398).
121 Höweler (1949:619–27); Newbould (1997).
122 Rosen (2004:3); Höweler (1949:436–42).
123 Rosen (2004:3–4).
124 Rosen (2004:4).
125 Lottmann (1979:46–7).
126 Lottmann (1979:33).
127 Lottmann (1979:617–80).
128 Wall (2001:43).
129 Wall (2001:81).
130 Wall (2001:79).
131 Wall (2001:341).
132 Wall (2001:101–2).
133 Wall (2001:300–1).
134 Wall (2001:344–5).
135 Wall (2001:345).
136 *Le Figaro*, Nov. 7, 1885, cited by Wall (2001:347).
137 Delbanco (2005:17–28). Compare the similar statement by the psychiatrist Witte Hoogendijk (2009) reflecting on the early death of his father at sea when he was seven years old, quoted in Chapter 4.
138 Delbanco (2005:30); full quotation in Chapter 4 above, from Hayford and Sealts (1962:v).
139 Delbanco (2005:18–31, 287).
140 Delbanco (2005:292).
141 Delbanco (2005:180, 290–322).
142 Delbanco (2005:290).
143 Delbanco (2005:12).
144 On Ezra Pound's share in the editing of T. S. Eliot's *The Waste Land*

(1922), Howard Gardner comments, "In his own words, Pound was the 'midwife'; in Eliot's words, Pound was *il miglior fabbro* – the better craftsman. The result is a far sharper, more compact, and telling poem. Each of the sections is more directly stated, while the actual links between the five sections of the final version are now left to the reader's construction"; Gardner (1993:243).

145 Planck (1949); cited in Kuhn (1970:151).

146 For the reception history of Elias's work, see Goudsblom (1977); Mennell and Goudsblom (1998:1–45).

147 Bourdieu (1984).

148 See summary in Lukes (1972:24–7). See also Zumwalt (1982:301–3).

149 Durkheim and Mauss (1963); Needham (1963).

150 Lévi-Strauss (1962:46–51); Zumwalt (1982:302–3).

151 In particular the British anthropologists Mary Douglas, Edmund Leach, Victor Turner, and Jean La Fontaine.

152 Van Gennep (1960:191), emphasis in the original. For initiation rites in secret societies, see La Fontaine (1985).

153 For a long time, his Dutch surname confused many colleagues: because he wrote in French they assumed he was a Belgian. Even La Fontaine, who paid a great deal of attention to Van Gennep's work in her book on initiation rituals in secret societies and acknowledges the impact of his work, writes about him as the "Belgian van Gennep" (1985:24). Nicole Belmont's (1979) biography of Van Gennep does not clarify the issue and ignores his Dutch side. We had to wait for an article in the *American Anthropologist* of 1982 in which a student, Rosemary Zumwalt, traced a publication by a daughter of Van Gennep about her father's work and got in touch with her; Zumwalt (1982:300, 309). These circumstances indicate how far Van Gennep had become an outsider in French academia after falling out with Durkheim and his entourage shortly before the start of the First World War.

154 Zumwalt (1982:299–300).

155 Zumwalt (1982:299–300).

156 Belmont (1979:11–12); Zumwalt (1982:307–8).

157 Zumwalt (1982:307–8).

158 Kuhn (1970:90, 90n).

159 Clarke (1988:11–14).

160 Clarke (1988:14–20, 400–1).

161 Clarke (1988:400–1).

162 Bruno Bettelheim underscores the beneficial effect on children of the fairy tales of Grimm precisely because of their realistic character; Bettelheim (1977).

163 Clarke (1988:21–3, 118–20).

164 Clarke (1988:104–21).

165 Clarke (1988:155–8).

166 Clarke (1988:150).

167 Clarke (1988:150).

168 Clarke (1988:158–9); picture in Clarke (1988:20–1).

169 From the very beginning, Harper Lee assisted Capote in his research in Kansas and was also present when Perry Smith was arraigned at the courthouse in Garden City, Kansas; Clarke (1988:324–6).

170 Clarke (1988:326).
171 Clarke (1988:326).
172 Clarke (1988:326).
173 Clarke (1988:326).
174 Quoted in Clarke (1988:326–7).
175 Most notably the Kansas killings; Capote (1965).
176 Eisenstadt (1978:218–22); cf. Eisenstadt et al. (1989).
177 Mills (1959:143).
178 Sahlins (2004:155).
179 Mahoney and Goertz (2004:657–60). Simonton's historiometric research of the possible effects of early parental loss on creativity among scientists and artists fails to distinguish between necessary and sufficient conditions. In the absence of detailed information about the context of individual cases (i.e. their place in sets of social relationships), Simonton cannot explain why in one case early parental loss results in creative efforts while in other cases the same form of adversity has totally different outcomes, including delinquency and psychiatric problems. Moreover, he indulges in generalizing statements about the effects of early parental loss in terms of extreme psychological reductionism: "The trauma of parental loss produces a so-called bereavement syndrome in which acts of achievement serve as emotional compensation; such adverse events nurture the development of a personality robust enough to overcome the many obstacles and frustrations standing in the path of achievement . . ."; Simonton (1999:115–16).

6 Conclusions

1 Bruchez-Hall (1996:56).
2 Keegan (1996:7–8).
3 Desmond, Moore, and Browne (2007:124).
4 "The strength of collective biography is not in supplying alternative explanations, but in specifying what is to be explained"; Tilly (1978:209).
5 Merton (2004:266, 293).
6 Montaigne (1991:934).
7 Little is known about Hamilton's early years in the Kent countryside (actually not far from where Darwin had lived). When he was a young teenager soon after the Second World War, he had a severe accident while playing with his father's munitions (his father was a military officer in the British Army) and lost two of his fingers. His mother, a medical doctor, happened to be present and saved him. The event may have prevented him from playing games with his classmates. Hence his statement on boredom from which he was freed by his passion for collecting insects.
8 For the notion of "conceptual assimilation" see Kuhn (1970:55–6).
9 In the case of Melville, then a young teenager, his father went bankrupt and died soon afterwards. It meant poverty and social degradation for the family. Delbanco (2005:17–30).
10 Sahlins (2004:155).
11 Kuhn (1970:52–65).
12 Lehman (1953); Kuhn (1970:90, 90n).
13 Schama (2015:C10).

14 Along with the numerous pioneers mentioned in this book, one should look at the classical Viennese music attached to the names of Haydn, Salieri, Mozart, Beethoven, and Schubert. What was their background? Only Schubert was born in Vienna. He was the youngest son of a family that came from Moravia. None of the other composers grew up in Vienna. Haydn came from Rohrau, a small provincial town along a tributary of the Danube. Salieri came from Legnano, Italy, not far from Verona, Mozart came from Salzburg, and Beethoven came from the Rhineland. See Newbould (1997). Another example includes the performances of Diaghilev's *Ballets Russes* in Paris between 1910 and 1920. This company provided the occasion for Stravinsky (1882–1971), in collaboration with dancer/choreographer Nijinsky and other Russian exiles, to write *The Rite of Spring* and have it performed in Paris in 1913. After a slow start this work has long since been held to be the most innovative, revolutionary, and influential composition of the twentieth century; Siohan (1965:41–7).

15 Burke (2007:82–8).

16 Burke (2007:87) mentions rebellions and heretical movements that often started in territories on the margins. He refers to the work of McNeill (1963) on frontier areas, and the studies of anthropologist Eric Wolf (1969) on the decisive role of peasants in peripheral areas during six twentieth-century revolutions: Mexico, Russia, China, Vietnam, Algeria, and Cuba. The successful popular resistance in Romania against the regime of Ceauşescu in December 1989 also developed in a border area: the Protestant and Hungarian-speaking minority in and around the city of Timişoara. Even more compelling was the Protestant resistance in the Low Countries against the Habsburg regime in the late sixteenth century, where a periphery developed into a world center within a century; Israel (1995). Finally, various contributions in Gottmann's *Centre and Periphery* (1980) offer historical examples of more varied relationships between center and periphery. For example, with the proviso of "not denying the importance of radiation from the center," Lattimore, in a short essay, outlines "the periphery as a locus of innovation" and hypothetically attributes "the origin of feudalism in both China and Europe to the impact of the periphery on the center" (1980:205, 208).

17 Westfall (2007:52–4).

18 Colson (1989:14).

19 Sahlins (2004:4).

20 Thucydides 5.26.5; see Strassler (1996).

21 Cited in Sahlins (2004:4–5).

22 Borsboom (2008).

23 In his pioneering study *Argonauts of the Western Pacific*, Malinowski (1884–1941), the founding father of modern ethnographic fieldwork, pin-points the advantage of the outsider/ethnographer in his description of the *Kula* (a form of exchange, with an extensive, intertribal character) as follows: "They have no knowledge of the *total outline* of any of their social structure. They know their own motives, know the purpose of individual actions and the rules which apply to them, but how, out of these, the whole collective institution shapes, this is beyond their mental range. Not even a partial coherent account could be obtained. For the integral picture does not exist in his mind; he is in it, and cannot see the whole from the outside" (1961:83).

BIBLIOGRAPHY

REFERENCES AND RELATED TITLES

Adler, Jeremy (2001) In the quiet corners: the vistas, cafés, offices, and brothels, which generated Kafka's art. *Times Literary Supplement*, Oct. 5, pp. 6–7.

Agus, Ayke (2005) *Heifetz As I Knew Him*. Portland, OR: Amadeus Press.

Allen, Hervey (1938) Introduction. In *The Complete Tales and Poems of Edgar Allan Poe*. New York: Modern Library.

Alpers, Else (1987) *Clara Rilke Westhoff und Rainer Maria Rilke*. Fischerhude: Galerie-Verlag.

Aranda, Francisco (1985[1969]) *Luis Buñuel: A Critical Biography*, trans. David Robinson. New York: Da Capo Press.

Archer, William (1984) *William Archer on Ibsen: The Major Essays, 1889–1919*, ed. Thomas Postlewait. London: Greenwood Press.

Arendt, Hannah (1968) Introduction. In Walter Benjamin, *Illuminations: Essays and Reflections*, ed. Hannah Arendt. New York: Schocken.

Ariès, Philippe (1981[1977]) *The Hour of Our Death*, trans. Helen Weaver. New York: Knopf.

Athanassoglou-Kallmyer, Nina (2003) *Cézanne and Provence: The Painter in His Culture*. Chicago: University of Chicago Press.

Auer, Leopold (1980[1921]) *Violin Playing As I Teach It*. New York: Dover.

Babcock, Barbara A. (1978) Introduction. In Barbara A. Babcock (ed.), *The Reversible World: Symbolic Inversion in Art and Society*. Ithaca: Cornell University Press.

Bakhtin, Mikhail (1965) *Rabelais and His World*, trans. Hélène Iswolsky. Bloomington: Indiana University Press.

Banville, John (2006) Letters from the heights. Review of *Rainer Maria Rilke and Lou Andreas-Salomé: The correspondence*, trans. Edward Snow and Michael Winkler. *New York Review of Books*, Dec. 21.

Barker, Juliet (1994) *The Brontës*. London: Weidenfeld & Nicolson.

Barker, William (ed.) (2001) *The Adages of Erasmus*. Toronto: University of Toronto Press.

Belmont, Nicole (1979) *Arnold van Gennep: The Creator of French Ethnography*, trans. Derek Coltman. Chicago: University of Chicago Press.

Benveniste, Émile (1969) Un métier sans nom. Le commerce. In *Le vocabulaire des institutions indo-européennes*, vol. 1. Paris: Minuit.

Bergman, Ingmar (1988) *The Magic Lantern: An Autobiography*, trans. Joan Tate. New York: Penguin Books.

Bergman, Ingmar (1994) *Images: My Life in Film*, trans. Marianne Ruuth. New York: Arcade.

Bettelheim, Bruno (1977) *The Uses of Enchantment: The Meaning and Importance of Fairy Tales*. New York: Vintage.

Beveridge, W. I. B. (1957) *The Art of Scientific Investigation*. New York: Norton.

Biagioli, Mario (1993) *Galileo Courtier: The Practice of Science in the Culture of Absolutism*. Chicago: University of Chicago Press.

Biagioli, Mario (2006) *Galileo's Instruments of Credit: Telescopes, Images, Secrecy*. Chicago: University of Chicago Press.

Bilaniuk, O. M. (1973) Lichtenberg. In *Dictionary of Scientific Biography*, vol. 7, pp. 320–3. New York: Scribner.

Binyon, T. J. (2003) *Pushkin: A Biography*. London: HarperCollins.

Bloch, Marc (1961[1939]) *Feudal Society*, trans. L. A. Manyon. Chicago: University of Chicago Press.

Blok, Anton (1974) De relatieve autonomie van klassieke romans en drama's. *De Gids* 137 (9/10): 701–8.

Blok, Anton (1976) *Wittgenstein en Elias. Een methodische richtlijn voor de antropologie*. Amsterdam: Athenaeum.

Blok, Anton (1995[1978]) *Anthropologische Perspektiven. Einführung, Kritik und Plädoyen*, trans. Klaus Schomburg. Stuttgart: Klett-Cotta.

Blok, Anton (2001[1998]) The narcissism of minor differences. In Anton Blok, *Honour and Violence*. Cambridge: Polity.

Blok, Anton (2005) Serendipity and the art of fieldwork. *Etnofoor* 18 (2): 105–23.

Bloom, Harold (2004) Introduction. In Miguel de Cervantes, *Don Quixote*, trans. Edith Grossman. New York: Random House.

Bloom, Harold (ed.) (2005) *Ernest Hemingway*. Philadelphia: Chelsea House.

Borsboom, Ad (2008) Tegenvoeters en medeburgers: Alternatieve vormen van leren en filosoferen in Aboriginal Australië [Antipodes and fellow citizens: alternative forms of learning and philosophizing in Aboriginal Australia]. Valedictory lecture, Radboud University, Nijmegen.

Bourdieu, Pierre (1984) *Distinction*, trans. Richard Nice. London: Routledge.

Bourdieu, Pierre (1992) *Les règles de l'art. Genèse et structure du champ littéraire*. Paris: Seuil.

Bourdieu, Pierre (1998) *La domination masculine*. Paris: Seuil.

Bourdieu, Pierre with Loïc J. D. Wacquant (1992) *Réponses. Pour une anthropologie réflexive*. Paris: Seuil.

Bowlby, J. (1990) *Darwin: A New Life*. New York: Norton.

Bowman, Isa (1972[1899]) *Lewis Carroll As I Knew Him*. New York: Dover.

Boyton, Robert S. (1996) The birth of an idea: a profile of Frank Sulloway. *New Yorker*, Oct. 7, pp. 72–81.

Brogan, Hugh (2006) *Alexis de Tocqueville: A Life*. New Haven: Yale University Press.

Bromberger, Christian and Tzvetan Todorov (2002) *Germaine Tillion. Une ethnologue dans le siècle*. Arles: Actes Sud.

Brontë, Emily (2003[1847]) *Wuthering Heights*, ed. Richard J. Dunn. Fourth Norton Critical Edition. New York: Norton.

Browne, Janet (1995) *Charles Darwin: Voyaging*. New York: Knopf.

Browne, Janet (2002) *Charles Darwin: The Power of Place*. New York: Knopf.

Browne, Janet (2010) Making Darwin. *Journal of Interdisciplinary History* 40 (3): 347–73.

Bruchez-Hall, Chantal (1996) Freud's early metaphors and network of enterprise: insight into a journey of scientific self-discovery. *Journal of Adult Development* 3 (1): 43–57.

Buñuel, Luis (1985) *My Last Breath*, trans. Abigail Israel. London: Flamingo.

Burke, Peter (2007) *History and Social Theory*. Cambridge: Polity.

Butterfield, Herbert (1959[1949]) *The Origins of Modern Science, 1300–1800*. London: Macmillan.

Camerota, Michele (2008) Galileo. In *New Dictionary of Scientific Biography*, vol. 3, pp. 96–103. New York: Scribner.

Cantoni, Remo (1953) Introduction. In Franz Kafka, *Diari, 1910–1923*. Verona: Mondadori.

Cantor, G. (1991) *Michael Faraday: Sandemanian and Scientist*. Basingstoke: Macmillan.

Capote, Truman (1948) *Other Voices, Other Rooms*. New York: Random House.

Capote, Truman (1965) *In Cold Blood*. New York: Random House.

Clarke, Gerald (1988) *Capote*. New York: Simon & Schuster.

Clifford, James (1988) On ethnographic self-fashioning: Conrad and Malinowski. In James Clifford, *The Predicament of Culture*. Cambridge, MA: Harvard University Press.

Coetzee, J. M. (2004) The making of William Faulkner. *New York Review of Books*, Apr. 7.

Cohen, I. Bernard (1985) *Revolution in Science*. Cambridge, MA: Belknap Press.

Cohen, Morton N. (1995) *Lewis Carroll: A Biography*. New York: Vintage.

Colson, Elizabeth (1989) Overview. *Annual Review of Anthropology* 18: 1–16.

Conrad, Joseph (1989[1897]) Preface. In Joseph Conrad, *The Nigger of the 'Narcissus'*. London: Penguin Books.

Conrad, Joseph (1997) *The Secret Sharer*, ed. Daniel R. Schwarz. New York: Bedford/St. Martin's.

Dagen, Philippe (1995) *Cézanne*. Paris: Flammarion.

Daly, Martin and Margo Wilson (1988) *Homicide*. New York: Aldine de Gruyter.

Darrigol, Olivier (2004) The mystery of the Einstein-Poincaré connection. *Isis* 95: 614–26.

Darwin, Charles (1958[1887]) *The Autobiography of Charles Darwin, 1809–1882*, ed. Nora Barlow. London: Collins.

Darwin, Charles (2009a[1859]) *On the Origin of Species: By Means of Natural Selection or the Preservation of Favoured Races in the Struggle for Life*, ed. and introd. William Bynum. London: Penguin Books.

Darwin, Charles (2009b[1859; 1839]) *The Origin of Species* and *The Voyage of the Beagle*. London: Vintage.

Darwin, Francis (ed.) (1887) *Life and Letters of Charles Darwin*. 3 vols. London: John Murray.

Dawkins, Richard (1989[1976]) *The Selfish Gene*. Oxford: Oxford University Press.

de Josselin de Jong, J. P. B. (1952) *Lévi-Strauss's Theory on Kinship and Marriage*. Leiden: Brill.

Delbanco, Andrew (2005) *Melville: His World and Work*. New York: Knopf.

Dennet, Daniel (1995) *Darwin's Dangerous Idea*. London: Penguin Books.

Dermoût, Maria (1974) *Verzameld werk* [Collected Works]. Amsterdam: Querido.

Dermoût, Maria (1958) *The Ten Thousand Things*, trans. Hans Koning. New York: Simon & Schuster.

de Sade, Donatien Alphonse François, Marquis de (1990) *Oeuvres*, vol. 1. Paris: Gallimard.

Desmond, Adrian, James Moore, and Janet Browne (2007) *Charles Darwin*. Oxford: Oxford University Press.

Diamant, Kathi (2003) *Kafka's Last Love: The Mystery of Dora Diamant*. New York: Basic Books.

Diamond, Jared (1996) The roots of radicalism. *New York Review of Books*, Nov. 14.

Douglas, Mary (1975) Pollution. In Mary Douglas, *Implicit Meanings*. London: Routledge & Kegan Paul.

Drake, Stillman (1970) *Galileo*. Oxford: Oxford University Press.

Drake, Stillman (1972) Galileo. In *Dictionary of Scientific Biography*, vol. 5. New York: Scribner.

Drake, Stillman (1978) *Galileo at Work*. Chicago: University of Chicago Press.

Drake, Stillman (2008) Galileo. In *New Dictionary of Scientific Biography*, vol. 5, pp. 237–50. New York: Scribner.

Duncan, Paul and Bill Krohn (eds) (2005) *Luis Buñuel: Chimera 1900–1983: The Complete Films*. Cologne: Taschen.

Durgnat, Raymond (1977) *Luis Buñuel*. New rev. and enlarged edn. Berkeley: University of California Press.

Durkheim, Émile (2001[1912]) *The Elementary Forms of Religious Life*, trans. Carol Cosman. Oxford: Oxford University Press.

Durkheim, Émile and Marcel Mauss (1963[1903]) *Primitive Classification*, trans. and introd. Rodney Needham. Chicago: University of Chicago Press.

Edmonds, David and John Eidinow (2001) *Wittgenstein's Poker: The Story of a Ten-Minute Argument between Two Great Philosophers*. London: Faber & Faber.

Eijk, Philip van der (1988) Nawoord. In Rainer Maria Rilke, *Brieven over Cézanne*, trans. Philip van der Eijk. Nijmegen: SUN.

Einstein, Albert (1920) XXII. A few inferences from the general theory of relativity. In *Relativity: The Special and General Theory*, trans. Robert W. Lawson. New York: Henry Holt.

Einstein, Albert (1991[1979]) *Autobiographical Notes: A Centennial Edition*, trans. and ed. Paul Arthur Schilpp. La Salle, IL: Open Court.

Einstein, Albert and Mileva Marić (1992) *The Love Letters*, ed. and introd. Jürgen Renn and Robert Schulmann, trans. Shawn Smith. Princeton: Princeton University Press.

Eisenstadt, Marvin (1978) Parental loss and genius. *American Psychologist* 33: 211–33.

Eisenstadt, Marvin et al. (1989) *Parental Loss and Achievement*. Madison, CT: International Universities Press.

Eisenstadt, S. N. and L. Roniger (1984) *Patrons, Clients and Friends: Interpersonal Relations and the Structure of Trust in Society*. Cambridge: Cambridge University Press.

Elias, Norbert (1969[1939]) *Über den Prozess der Zivilisation*. 2 vols. Munich: Franke.

Elias, Norbert (1994[1976]) Introduction: a theoretical essay on established and outsider relations. In Norbert Elias and John L. Scotson, *The Established and the Outsiders: A Sociological Enquiry into Community Problems*, 2nd edn., pp. xv–lii. London: Sage.

Elias, Norbert (1998a[1956]) Involvement and detachment. In Norbert Elias, *On Civilization, Power, and Knowledge*, ed. Stephen Mennell and Johan Goudsblom. Chicago: University of Chicago Press.

Elias, Norbert (1998b) Mozart: the artist in the human being. In Norbert Elias, *On Civilization, Power, and Knowledge*, ed. Stephen Mennell and Johan Goudsblom. Chicago: University of Chicago Press.

Elias, Norbert and John L. Scotson (1994[1965]) *The Established and the Outsiders: A Sociological Enquiry into Community Problems*, 2nd edn. London: Sage.

Enzensberger, Hans M. (2004) Interview. *Der Spiegel* 38: 175–9.

Erasmus, Desiderius (2003[1511]) *The Praise of Folly*, trans. and introd. Clarence H. Miller, 2nd edn. New Haven: Yale University Press.

Erasmus, Desiderius (2004) *De correspondentie van Desiderius Erasmus. 2: Brieven 142–297*, trans. M. J. Steens. Amsterdam: Donker.

Ericsson, K. Anders and Neil Charness (1994) Expert performance: its structure and acquisition. *American Psychologist* 49 (8): 725–47.

Ericsson, K. Anders, Ralf T. Krampe, and Clemens Tesch-Romer (1993) The role of deliberate practice in the acquisition of expert performance. *Psychological Review* 100 (3): 363–406.

Ernst, Cecile and Jules Angst (1983) *Birth Order: Its Influence on Personality*. New York: Springer.

Evans, Peter W. (1995) *The Films of Luis Buñuel: Subjectivity and Desire*. Oxford: Oxford University Press.

Evans-Pritchard, Edward E. (1981) *A History of Anthropological Thought*. London: Faber & Faber.

Faulkner, William (1977[1930]) A rose for Emily. In *Collected Stories of William Faulkner*. New York: Random House.

Feist, Gregory J. (1999) The influence of personality on artistic and scientific creativity. In Robert J. Sternberg (ed.), *Handbook of Creativity*. Cambridge: Cambridge University Press.

Fjelde, Rolf (1965) Foreword. In Henrik Ibsen, *Four Major Plays*, vol. 1, trans. Rolf Fjelde. New York: New American Library.

Fjelde, Rolf (1970) Foreword. In Henrik Ibsen, *Four Major Plays*, vol. 2, trans. Rolf Fjelde. New York: New American Library.

Fjelde, Rolf (1978) Introduction. In Henrik Ibsen, *The Complete Major Prose Plays*, trans. Rolf Fjelde. New York: Farrar, Straus & Giroux.

Flaubert, Gustave (1973) *Correspondence*, vol. 1. Paris: Gallimard.

Fölsing, Albrecht (1993) *Albert Einstein. Eine Biographie*. Frankfurt/Main: Suhrkamp.

209

Forrer, Matthi (1991) *The Art of Hokusai*. Catalogue. London: Royal Academy of Arts.

Frank, Katherine (1990) *Emily Brontë: A Chainless Soul*. London: Hamish Hamilton.

Freriks, Kester (1988) Bij de 100ste geboortedag van Maria Dermoût. *NRC Handelsblad*, June 10.

Freriks, Kester (2000) *Geheim Indië. Het leven van Maria Dermoút 1888–1962*. Amsterdam: Querido.

Friederici, Hans (1973) Einleitung. In *Lichtenbergs Werke*. Berlin: Aufbau.

Gablik, Suzi (1985) *Magritte*. London: Thames & Hudson.

Galilei, Galileo (2013) *Dialoog over de twee voornaamste wereldsystemen*, trans. Hans van den Berg. Amsterdam: Athenaeum.

Gardner, Howard (1993) *Creating Minds: An Anatomy of Creativity Seen through the Lives of Freud, Einstein, Picasso, Stravinsky, Eliot, Graham, and Gandhi*. New York: Basic Books.

Gaukroger, Stephen (1995) *Descartes: An Intellectual Biography*. Oxford: Clarendon Press.

Gay, Peter (1988) *Freud: A Life of Our Time*. New York: Norton.

Geertz, Clifford (1973) Thick description. In Clifford Geertz, *The Interpretation of Culture*. New York: Basic Books.

Geertz, Clifford (1983) "From the native's point of view": on the nature of anthropological understanding. In Clifford Geertz, *Local Knowledge*. New York: Basic Books.

Geertz, Clifford (1988) The anthropologist as author. In Clifford Geertz, *Works and Lives*. Stanford: Stanford University Press.

Geier, Manfred (2009) *Die Brüder Humboldt*. Hamburg: Rowohlt.

Gellner, Ernest and John Waterbury (1977) *Patrons and Clients in Mediterranean Societies*. London: Duckworth.

Gessen, Masha (2009) *Perfect Rigor: A Genius and the Mathematical Breakthrough of the Century*. Boston: Houghton, Mifflin, Harcourt.

Gibian, George (1985) Introduction. In Nikolai Gogol, *Dead Souls*. Norton Critical Edition. New York: Norton.

Giere, Ronald N. (1988) Explaining the revolution in geology. In Ronald N. Giere, *Explaining Science: A Cognitive Approach*. Chicago: University of Chicago Press.

Gilmore, David (1996) *The Last Leopard: A Life of Giuseppe Tomasi di Lampedusa*. London: Harvill.

Gilot, Françoise and Carlton Lake (1964) *Life with Picasso*. New York: McGraw-Hill.

Ginzburg, Carlo (2015) La spada e la lampadina. Per una lettura di *Guernica*. In Carlo Ginzburg, *Paura reverenza terrore. Cinque saggi di iconografia politica*. Milan: Adelphi.

Glynn, Ian (2010) *Elegance in Science: The Beauty of Simplicity*. Oxford: Oxford University Press.

Goffman, Erving (1971) *Relations in Public: Microstudies of the Social Order*. New York: Harper & Row.

Goffman, Erving (1979) *Stigma: Notes on the Management of Spoiled Identity*. Harmondsworth: Penguin Books.

Goldsmith, Barbara (2005) *Obsessive Genius: The Inner World of Marie Curie*. London: Weidenfeld & Nicolson.

Gombrowicz, Witold (1973) *A Kind of Testament*, trans. Alistair Hamilton. Philadelphia: Temple University.

Goodall, Jane (1963) *In the Shadow of Man*. Boston: Houghton Mifflin.

Goodall, Jane (1990) *Through a Window: My Thirty Years with the Chimpanzees of Gombe*. Boston: Houghton Mifflin.

Goodall, Jane (2000) *Africa in My Blood: An Autobiography in Letters: The Early Years*, ed. Dale Peterson. Boston: Houghton Mifflin.

Górny, Jan Jerzy (2010) *Mikołaj Kopernik. Kanonik Warmiński Astronom*. Olsztyn, Poland: Warminska Kapitula Katedralna.

Gottmann, Jean (ed.) (1980) *Centre and Periphery: Spatial Variation in Politics*. London: Sage.

Goudsblom, Johan (1977) Responses to Norbert Elias's work in England, Germany, the Netherlands and France. In Peter Gleichmann, Johan Goudsblom, and Hermann Korte (eds.), *Human Figurations: Essays for Norbert Elias*. Amsterdam: Sociologisch Tijdschrift.

Gould, Roger V. (2003) *Collision of Wills: How Ambiguity about Social Rank Breeds Conflict*. Chicago: University of Chicago Press.

Gould, Stephen J. (1977) Darwin's delay. In Stephen J. Gould, *Ever Since Darwin*. Harmondsworth: Penguin Books.

Gould, Stephen J. (1991) The Burgess Shale and the nature of history. In Stephen Gould, *Wonderful Life*. Harmondsworth: Penguin Books.

Gould, Stephen J. (1994) Darwin and Paley meet the invisible hand. In Stephen Gould, *Eight Little Piggies: Reflections in Natural History*. Harmondsworth: Penguin Books.

Gould, Stephen J. (1996) Why Darwin? Review of Janet Browne, *Charles Darwin: Voyaging*. *New York Review of Books*, Apr. 4, pp. 10–14.

Grafen, Alan (2005) William Donald Hamilton. In Mark Ridley (ed.), *Narrow Roads of Gene Land: The Collected Papers of W. D. Hamilton*, vol. 3, pp. 423–57. Oxford: Oxford University Press.

Grafton, Anthony (2003) Introduction. In Niccolò Machiavelli, *The Prince*, trans. George Bull. London: Penguin Books.

Greene, Mott T. (1984) Alfred Wegener. *Social Research* (special issue) 51 (3): 739–61.

Grolle, Johann (2005) Das Wunder von Bern. *Der Spiegel*, Jan. 17, pp. 130–40.

Gruber, Howard E. (1981) *Darwin on Man: A Psychological Study of Scientific Creativity*. Chicago: University of Chicago Press.

Gruber, Howard E. (1996) Starting out: the early years of four careers: Darwin, Van Gogh, Freud, and Shaw. *Journal of Adult Development* 3: 1–6.

Gruber, Howard E. and Doris B. Wallace (1999) The case study method and evolving systems approach for understanding unique creative people at work. In Robert J. Sternberg (ed.), *Handbook of Creativity*. Cambridge: Cambridge University Press.

Gurko, Leo (1979) *Joseph Conrad: Giant in Exile*. New York: Collier.

Hacking, Ian (1981) *Scientific Revolutions*. Oxford: Oxford University Press.

Hale, J. R. (1972) *Machiavelli and Renaissance Italy*. Harmondsworth: Penguin Books.

Hall, Donald (1959) The art of poetry, 1. Interview with T. S. Eliot. *Paris Review* 21 (Spring/Summer): 47–70.

Hallam, A. (1973) *A Revolution in the Earth Sciences: From Continental Drift to Plate Tectonics*. Oxford: Clarendon Press.

Hallyn, F. (ed.) (2000) *Metaphor and Analogy in the Sciences*. Dordrecht: Kluwer.

Hamilton, James (2002) *Faraday: The Life*. New York: HarperCollins.

Hamilton, William Donald (1996–2005) *Narrow Roads of Gene Land: The Collected Papers of W. D. Hamilton*. 3 vols. Oxford: Oxford University Press.

Hampshire, Stuart (2005) *Spinoza and Spinozism*. Oxford: Clarendon Press.

Hankinson, R. J. (2008) Galilei. In *New Dictionary of Scientific Biography*, vol. 3, pp. 96–103. New York: Scribner.

Harpham, Geoffrey Galt (1996) *One of Us: The Mastery of Joseph Conrad*. Chicago: University of Chicago Press.

Hayford, Harrison and Morton N. Sealts (1962) Preface. In Herman Melville, *Billy Budd, Sailor. (An Inside Narrative.)* Chicago: University of Chicago Press.

Haynal, André (1989) Psychoanalytic discourse on orphans and deprivation. In Marvin Eisenstadt et al., *Parental Loss and Achievement*. Madison, CT: International Universities Press.

Heilbron, Johan (2007) Pierre Bourdieu and the peculiarities of sociological knowledge. MS.

Heilbron, John L. (2010) *Galileo*. Oxford: Oxford University Press.

Henig, Robin Marantz (2000) *The Monk in the Garden: The Lost and Found Genius of Gregor Mendel, the Father of Genetics*. Boston: Houghton Mifflin.

Hermans, W. F. (2007[1966]) *Nooit meer slapen*. Amsterdam: De Bezige Bij.

Heuser, Beatrice (2007) Introduction. In Carl von Clausewitz, *On War*, ed. and trans. Michael Howard and Peter Paret. Oxford: Oxford University Press.

Hobsbawm, Eric and Joan Scott (1980) Political shoemakers. *Past and Present* 89: 86–114.

Hohoff, Curt (1960) *Heinrich von Kleist*. Hamburg: Rowohlt.

Hollinger, David A. (2002) Why are Jews preeminent in science and scholarship? The Veblen thesis reconsidered. *Aleph* 2: 145–63.

Holthusen, Hans Egon (1958) *Rainer Maria Rilke*. Hamburg: Rowohlt.

Homans, George C. and David M. Schneider (1955) *Marriage, Authority, and Final Causes: A Study of Unilateral Cross-Cousin Marriage*. Glencoe, IL: Free Press.

Hoog, Michel (1994) *Cézanne: The First Modern Painter*, trans. Rosemary Stonehewer. London: Thames & Hudson.

Hoogendijk, Witte (2009) Interview (Coen Verbraak). *Hollands Diep*, July/Aug., pp. 59–64.

Howe, Michael J. A. (1999) *Genius Explained*. Cambridge: Cambridge University Press.

Höweler, Casper (1949) *X-Y-Z der muziek*. Utrecht: De Haan.

Hubert, Renée Riese (1978–9) The otherworldly landscapes of E. A. Poe and René Magritte. *Substance* 6/7: 68–78.

Huizinga, Johan (1955[1938]) *Homo Ludens: A Study of the Play-Element in Culture*. Boston: Beacon Press.

Huizinga, Johan (1976[1919]) *The Waning of the Middle Ages: A Study of the Forms of Life, Thought, and Art in France and the Netherlands in the Fourteenth and Fifteenth Centuries*, trans. F. Hopman. Harmondsworth: Penguin Books.

Huizinga, Johan (1984[1924]) *Erasmus and the Age of Reformation*, trans. F. Hopman. Princeton: Princeton University Press.

Iltis, Hugo (1924) *Gregor Johann Mendel. Leben, Werk und Wirkung.* Berlin: Julius Springer.

Isaacson, Walter (2007). *Einstein: His Life and Universe.* New York: Simon & Schuster.

Israel, Jonathan (1995) *The Dutch Republic: Its Rise, Greatness, and Fall.* Oxford: Clarendon Press.

Israel, Jonathan (2002) *Radical Enlightenment: Philosophy and the Making of Modernity 1650–1750.* Oxford: Oxford University Press.

Jackson, Bruce (1978) Deviance as success: the double inversion of stigmatized roles. In Barbara Babcock (ed.), *The Reversible World: Symbolic Inversion in Art and Society,* pp. 258–75. Ithaca: Cornell University Press.

Jeanson, Francis (1958) *Montaigne,* trans. Paul Meyer. Hamburg: Rowohlt.

Kafka, Franz (1983) *The Complete Stories,* ed. Nahum N. Glazer. New York: Schocken Books.

Kafka, Franz (2004) *Briefe an Milena. Erweiterte Neuausgabe.* Frankfurt/Main: Fischer Taschenbuch.

Kafka, Franz (2008a) *Tagebücher,* vol. 1: *1909–1912.* Frankfurt/Main. Fischer Taschenbuch.

Kafka, Franz (2008b) *Tagebücher,* vol. 2: *1912–1914.* Frankfurt/Main. Fischer Taschenbuch.

Kafka, Franz (2008c) *Tagebücher,* vol. 3: *1914–1923.* Frankfurt/Main: Fischer Taschenbuch.

Kafka, Franz (2009) *Briefe an Felice und andere Korrespondenz aus der Verlobungszeit,* ed. Erich Heller and Jürgen Born. Frankfurt/Main: Fischer Taschenbuch.

Kakutani, Michiko (1988) Kafka's Kafkaesque love letters. Review of Franz Kafka, *Letters to Felice,* ed. Erich Heller and Jurgen Born. *New York Times,* Apr. 2.

Kammer, Claudia (2013) Van Goghs mythe ontrafeld. *NRC Handelsblad,* Apr. 26, pp. 1–3.

Kanfer, Stefan (1983) The malady was life itself. Review of Franz Kafka, *The Complete Stories,* ed. Nahum N. Glazer. *Time,* July 18.

Keegan, Robert T. (1996) Getting started: Charles Darwin's early steps toward a creative life in science. *Journal of Adult Development* 3 (1): 7–20.

Kermode, Frank (1975) *Wuthering Heights* as classic. In Frank Kermode (ed.), *The Classic.* London: Faber & Faber.

Klein, Stefan (2004) *Alles Zufall. Die Kraft, die unser Leben bestimmt.* Hamburg: Rowohlt.

Knowles, Owen and Gene M. Moore (2000) *The Oxford Reader's Companion to Conrad.* Oxford: Oxford University Press.

Knowlson, James (1996) *Damned to Fame: The Life of Samuel Beckett.* London: Bloomsbury.

Koestler, Arthur (1964) *The Sleepwalkers: A History of Man's Changing Vision of the Universe.* Harmondsworth: Penguin Books.

Kooijmans, Luuc (1996) *Vriendschap en de kunst van het overleven in de zeventiende en achttiende eeuw.* Amsterdam: Bert Bakker.

Kooijmans, Luuc (2011) *Het orakel. De man die de geneeskunde opnieuw uitvond: Herman Boerhaave 1668–1739.* Amsterdam: Balans.

Krul, W. E. (1979) Johan Huizinga. Nederlands beroemdste historicus. *Intermediair* 15 (43): 1–9.

Krul, W. E. (1990) *Historicus tegen de tijd. Opstellen over leven en werk van Johan Huizinga*. Groningen: Historische Uitgeverij.

Kuhn, Thomas S. (1970) *The Structure of Scientific Revolutions*. Chicago: University of Chicago Press.

La Fontaine, Jean S. (1985) *Initiation: Ritual Drama and Secret Knowledge across the World*. Harmondsworth: Penguin Books.

Lagercrantz, Olof (1979) *August Strindberg*, trans. Anselm Hollo. New York: Farrar, Straus & Giroux.

Lattimore, Owen (1967[1940]) *Inner Asian Frontiers of China*. Boston: Beacon Press.

Lattimore, Owen (1980) The periphery as a locus of innovation. In Jean Gottmann (ed.), *Centre and Periphery: Spatial Variation in Politics*. London: Sage.

Leach, Edmund (1976) *Culture and Communication*. Cambridge: Cambridge University Press.

Legrand, H. E. (1988) *Drifting Continents and Shifting Theories*. Cambridge: Cambridge University Press.

Lehman, Harvey C. (1953) *Age and Achievement*. Princeton: Princeton University Press.

Lély, Gilbert (1961) *The Marquis de Sade: A Biography*, trans. Alec Brown. New York: Grove Press.

Lennig, Walter (1959) *Edgar Allan Poe*. Hamburg: Rowohlt.

Lescourret, Marie-Anne (2008) *Bourdieu. Vers une économie du bonheur*. Paris: Flammarion.

Lévi-Strauss, Claude (1955) *Tristes tropiques*. Paris: Plon.

Lévi-Strauss, Claude (1962) *Le totémisme aujourd'hui*. Paris: Presses Universitaires de France.

Lévi-Strauss, Claude (1969[1949]) *The Elementary Structures of Kinship*, ed. Rodney Needham. Boston: Beacon Press.

Leymarie, Jean (1979) *Balthus*. New York: Rizzoli.

Locher, G. W. (1958) Huizinga en de culturele antropologie. *Bijdragen voor Taal-, Land- en Volkenkunde* 114: 170–91.

Lottmann, Herbert R. (1979) *Albert Camus: A Biography*. New York: Doubleday.

Lukes, Steven (1972) *Emile Durkheim: His Life and Work: A Historical and Critical Study*. New York: Harper & Row.

Machiavelli, Niccolò (2003) *The Prince*, trans. George Bull, rev. edn. London: Penguin Books.

Maddox, Brenda (2002) *Rosalind Franklin: The Dark Lady of DNA*. New York: HarperCollins.

Maddox, Brenda (2008) Rosalind Franklin. In *New Dictionary of Scientific Biography*. New York: Scribner.

Mahoney, James and Gary Goertz (2004) The possibility principle: choosing negative cases in comparative research. *American Political Science Review* 98 (4): 653–69.

Malcolm, Norman (1962) *Wittgenstein: A Memoir. With a Biographical Sketch by Georg Henrik von Wright*. Oxford: Oxford University Press.

Malinowski, Bronislaw (1961[1922]) *Argonauts of the Western Pacific: An Account of Native Enterprise and Adventure in the Archipelagos of Melanesian New Guinea*. New York: Dutton.

214

Marvin, Ursula (1973) *Continental Drift: The Evolution of a Concept.* Washington, DC: Smithsonian Institution Press.

Mauss, Marcel (1954[1925]) *The Gift: Forms and Functions of Exchange in Archaic Societies*, trans. Ian Cunnison. London: Cohen & West.

Mautner, Franz and Henry Hatfield (eds.) (1969) *Lichtenberg: Aphorisms and Letters.* London: Jonathan Cape.

McFarlane, James (ed.) (1994) *The Cambridge Companion to Ibsen.* Cambridge: Cambridge University Press.

McFarlane, James (1998) Introduction. In Henrik Ibsen, *Four Major Plays.* Oxford: Oxford University Press.

McNeill, William H. (1963) *The Rise of the West: A History of the Human Community.* Chicago: University of Chicago Press.

Meijknecht, J. G. (1950) *Gregor Mendel. De ontdekker van de erfelijkheidswetten.* Bussum, Netherlands: Paul Brand.

Mennell, Stephen and Johan Goudsblom (1998) Introduction. In Norbert Elias, *On Civilization, Power, and Knowledge.* Chicago: University of Chicago Press.

Merton, Robert K. (2004) Afterword. In Robert K. Merton and Elinor Barber, *The Travels and Adventures of Serendipity.* Princeton: Princeton University Press.

Merton, Robert K. and Elinor Barber (2004) *The Travels and Adventures of Serendipity.* Princeton: Princeton University Press.

Meyer, Michael (1967) *Henrik Ibsen: The Making of a Dramatist 1828–1906.* London: Rupert Hart-Davis.

Meyer, Michael (1986) *File on Strindberg.* London: Methuen.

Miller, Arthur (1994) Ibsen and the drama of today. In James McFarlane (ed.), *Cambridge Companion to Ibsen.* Cambridge: Cambridge University Press.

Miller, Arthur I. (1984) Imagery in scientific thought. *Creativity Research Journal* (special issue) 9 (2/3): 113–30.

Miller, Arthur I. (2000) Metaphor and scientific creativity. In Fernand Hallyn (ed.), *Metaphor and Analogy in the Sciences.* Dordrecht: Kluwer.

Miller, J. Hillis (1997) A deconstructive perspective: sharing secrets. In Joseph Conrad, *The Secret Sharer*, ed. Daniel R. Schwarz. New York: Bedford/St. Martin's.

Miller, J. Hillis (2003[1982]) *Wuthering Heights*: repetition and the "uncanny." Repr. in Richard J. Dunn (ed.), *Wuthering Heights* by Emily Brontë. Fourth Norton Critical Edition. New York: Norton.

Miller, Sanda (1995) *Constantin Brâncuşi: A Survey of his Work.* Oxford: Clarendon Press.

Mills, C. Wright (1959) *The Sociological Imagination.* Oxford: Oxford University Press.

Modell, J. (1997) Family niche and intellectual bent. Review of Frank Sulloway, *Born to Rebel. Science* 275: 624–5.

Monk, Ray (1990) *Ludwig Wittgenstein: The Duty of Genius.* New York: Random House.

Montaigne, Michel de (1958) *Essais.* 3 vols. Paris: Garnier.

Montaigne, Michel de (1991) *The Complete Essays*, trans. and ed. M. A. Screech. London: Allen Lane.

Montias, John Michael (1989) *Vermeer and His Milieu: A Web of Social History.* Princeton: Princeton University Press.

215

Muensterberger, Werner (1994) *Collecting: An Unruly Passion*. Princeton: Princeton University Press.

Murray, Charles (2003) *Human Accomplishment: The Pursuit of Excellence in the Arts and Sciences, 800 B.C. to 1950*. New York: HarperCollins.

Murray, Nicholas (2004) *Franz Kafka*. New Haven: Yale University Press.

Murray, Penelope (1989) *Genius: The History of an Idea*. Oxford: Oxford University Press.

Nabokov, Vladimir (1961) *Nicolai Gogol*. New York: New Directions.

Nabokov, Vladimir (1975) Commentary. In Aleksandr Pushkin, *Eugene Onegin: A Novel in Verse*, trans. Vladimir Nabokov, vol. 2. Princeton: Princeton University Press.

Nadler, Steven (1999) *Spinoza: A Life*. Cambridge: Cambridge University Press.

Naifeh, Steven and Gregory White Smith (2011) *Vincent van Gogh: The Life*. London: Profile.

Nedo, Michael and Michele Ranchetti (1983) *Wittgenstein: Sein Leben in Bildern und Texten*. Frankfurt/Main: Suhrkamp.

Needham, Rodney (1963) Introduction. In Emile Durkheim and Marcel Mauss, *Primitive Classification*, trans. Rodney Needham. Chicago: University of Chicago Press.

Needham, Rodney (1985) *Exemplars*. Berkeley: University of California Press.

Neffe, Jürgen (2005) *Einstein. Eine Biographie*. Hamburg: Rowohlt.

Newbould, Brian (1997) *Schubert: The Music and the Man*. London: Victor Gollancz.

Nietzsche, Friedrich (1966) *Jenseits von Gut und Böse*. 3 vols. Munich: Hanser.

Oppenheimer, Paul (2011) *Machiavelli: A Life beyond Ideology*. London: Continuum.

Oprea, Petre (1972) *C. Brâncuşi*. Bucharest: Muzeul de Arte al Republicii Socialiste Romania.

Orel, V. (1996) *Mendel: The First Geneticist*. Oxford: Oxford University Press.

Ortner, Sherry (1994) Theory in anthropology since the sixties. In Nicholas B. Dirks, Geoff Eley, and Sherry Ortner (eds.), *Culture/Power/History*. Princeton: Princeton University Press.

Pais, Abraham (1982) *'Subtle Is the Lord . . .': The Science and Life of Albert Einstein*. Oxford: Oxford University Press.

Pallares-Burke, Maria Lúcia G. (2002) *The New History: Confessions and Conversations*. Cambridge: Polity.

Palmer, Donald D. (1996) *Kierkegaard for Beginners*. New York: Writers & Readers.

Palmer, Robert R. (1989[1941]) *Twelve Who Ruled: The Year of Terror in the French Revolution*. Princeton: Princeton University Press.

Paret, Peter (1976) *Clausewitz and the State*. Oxford: Oxford University Press.

Parini, Jay (2004) *One Matchless Time: A Life of William Faulkner*. New York: HarperCollins.

Peirce, Charles Sanders (1998) *The Essential Peirce: Selected Philosophical Writings*. 2 vols. Bloomington: Indiana University Press.

Pérez Turrent, Tomás and José de La Colina (2008) *Conversations avec Buñuel. Il est dangereux de se pencher au-dedans*. Paris: Cahiers du Cinéma.

Peterson, Dale (2006) *Jane Goodall: The Woman Who Redefined Man*. Boston: Houghton Mifflin.

Pevear, Richard (1998) Preface. In *The Collected Tales of Nicolai Gogol*, trans. and annot. Richard Pevear and Larissa Volokhonsky. New York: Pantheon.

Pickering, George (1974) *Creative Malady: Illness in the Lives and Minds of Charles Darwin, Florence Nightingale, Mary Baker Eddy, Sigmund Freud, Marcel Proust, Elizabeth Barrett Browning*. London: George Allen & Unwin.

Pitt-Rivers, J. A. (1971[1954]) *People of the Sierra*. Chicago: University of Chicago Press.

Planck, Max (1949) *Scientific Biography and Other Papers*. New York: Philosophical Library.

Poe, Edgar Allan (1938) *The Complete Tales and Poems of Edgar Allan Poe*. New York: Modern Library.

Poe, Edgar Allan (1974[1900]) The philosophy of composition. In *The Poems of Edgar Allan Poe*. London: George Bell & Sons.

Poel, Ieme van der (2003) Leven met de Berbers. Germain Tillion was onze tijd ver vooruit. *De Academische Boekengids* 42: 9–10.

Popper, Karl (2002) *Conjectures and Refutations: The Growth of Scientific Knowledge*. London: Routledge.

Propp, V. (1968) *Morphology of the Folktale*, trans. Laurence Scott. Austin: University of Texas Press.

Radkau, Joachim (2011) *Max Weber: A Biography*, trans. Patrick Camiller. Cambridge: Polity.

Renn, Jürgen and Robert Schulmann (1992) Introduction. In Albert Einstein and Mileva Marić, *The Love Letters*, trans. Shawn Smith. Princeton: Princeton University Press.

Ridley, Mark (2004) Hamilton, William Donald (1936–2002). In *Oxford Dictionary of National Biography*. Oxford: Oxford University Press.

Rilke, Rainer Maria (1948) *Ausgewählte Gedichte. Ausgewählt von Katharina Kippenberg*. Leipzig: Insel-Verlag.

Rilke, Rainer Maria (1951) *Briefe an eine junge Frau*. Wiesbaden: Insel-Verlag.

Rilke, Rainer Maria (1955) *Rodin: Ein Vortrag. Die Briefe an Rodin*. Hamburg: Fischer Bücherei.

Rilke, Rainer Maria (1988[1952]) *Brieven over Cézanne*, trans. into Dutch by Philip van der Eijke. Nijmegen: SUN.

Rimbaud, Arthur (1972) *Oeuvres complètes*. Paris: Gallimard.

Ritvo, Lucille B. (1990) *Darwin's Influence on Freud: A Tale of Two Sciences*. New Haven: Yale University Press.

Robb, Graham (2000) *Rimbaud: A Biography*. New York: Norton.

Rosen, Charles (2004) Prodigy without peer: a composer who fell from grace by sticking to the world of ease. *Times Literary Supplement*, Mar. 19.

Rosen, Charles (2008) The genius of Montaigne. *New York Review of Books*, Feb. 14.

Rosen, Charles (2012) *Freedom and the Arts: Essays on Music and Literature*. Cambridge, MA: Harvard University Press.

Roth, H. (1987) *Master Violinists in Performance: Critical Evaluation of over 100 Twentieth Century Virtuosi*. Los Angeles: Panjandrum Books.

Ryan, Alan (2007) Tocqueville: the flaws of genius. *New York Review of Books*, Nov. 22.

Sacks, Oliver (2010) *The Mind's Eye*. London: Picador.

Sadoul, Georges (1984) Preface. In Luis Buñuel, *Viridiana. Scénario et dialogues, variantes, dossier historique et critique*. Paris: Filméditions P. L'Herminier.

Safranski, Rüdiger (1984) *E. T. H. Hoffmann. Das Leben eines skeptischen Phantasten*. Munich: Hanser.

Sahlins, Marshall (2004) *Apologies to Thucydides: Understanding History as Culture and Vice Versa*. Chicago: University of Chicago Press.

Said, Edward W. (2002[1985]) *Reflections on Exile and Other Essays*. Cambridge, MA: Harvard University Press.

Sayre, Anne (1975) *Rosalind Franklin and DNA*. New York: Norton.

Screech, M. A. (1991) Introduction. In Michel de Montaigne, *The Complete Essays*. London: Allen Lane.

Schama, Simon (2015) Rembrandt. Verbluffende late werken [Rembrandt: astounding late works]. *NRC Handelsblad*, supplement, Feb. 5, pp. C10–C11. (Published earlier as "Late Rembrandt," *Financial Times*, Oct. 17, 2014.)

Schwarz, Daniel R. (2001) *Rereading Conrad*. Columbia: University of Missouri Press.

Schwarzbach, Martin (1986) *Alfred Wegener: The Father of Continental Drift*. Madison, WI: Science Tech, Inc.

Sebeok, Thomas A. and Jean Umiker-Sebeok (1988) "You know my method": a juxtaposition of Charles S. Peirce and Sherlock Holmes. In Umberto Eco and Thomas Sebeok (eds.), *The Sign of Three: Dupin, Holmes, Peirce*. Bloomington: Indiana University Press.

Shermer, Michael (2002) *In Darwin's Shadow: The Life and Science of Alfred Russel Wallace: A Biographical Study on the Psychology of History*. Oxford: Oxford University Press.

Simic, Charles (2006) Salvation through laughter. [On Witold Gombrowicz.] *New York Review of Books*, Jan. 12, pp. 22–5.

Simonton, Dean K. (1999) *Origins of Genius: Darwinian Perspectives on Creativity*. Oxford: Oxford University Press.

Simpson, David (2016) Francis Bacon (1561–1626). In *Internet Encyclopedia of Philosophy*, at http://www.iep.utm.edu/bacon/.

Singal, Daniel G. (1997) *William Faulkner: The Making of a Modernist*. Oxford: Oxford University Press.

Siohan, Robert (1963) *Stravinsky*, trans. Eric Walter White. London: Calder & Boyars.

Skidelsky, Robert (2003) *John Maynard Keynes, 1883–1946: Economist, Philosopher, Statesman*, abridged edn. London: Macmillan.

Skidelsky, Robert (2010) *Keynes: The Return of the Master*. London: Penguin Books.

Slotten, Ross A. (2004) *The Heretic in Darwin's Court: The Life of Alfred Russel Wallace*. New York: Columbia University Press.

Smallenburg, Sandra (2015) Late Rembrandt. *NRC Handelsblad*, Feb. 7, p. 31.

Smith, Adam (1904[1776]) *An Inquiry into the Nature and Causes of the Wealth of Nations*, 5th edn. London: Methuen.

Smith, Zadie (2008) F. Kafka, everyman. Review of Louis Begley, *The Tremendous World I Have Inside My Head: Franz Kafka: A Biographical Essay. New York Review of Books*, July 17.

Sobel, Dava (2012) *A More Perfect Heaven: How Copernicus Revolutionized the Cosmos*. London: Bloomsbury.

Solomon, Maynard (1977) *Beethoven*. London: Collier Macmillan.

Spies, Werner (2001) An anomaly in Paris: the painter [Balthus] who avoided the avant-garde. *Frankfurter Allgemeine Zeitung*, Sept. 2, p. 7.

Spoto, Donald (1983) *The Dark Side of Genius: The Life of Alfred Hitchcock*. London: Collins.

Stape, John (2007) *The Several Lives of Joseph Conrad*. London: Heinemann.

Starkie, Enid (1968) *Arthur Rimbaud*. New York: New Directions.

Stent, Gunther S. (1980[1968]) Introduction. In James D. Watson, *The Double Helix: A Personal Account of the Discovery of the Structure of DNA*, ed. Gunther S. Stent. Norton Critical Edition. New York: Norton.

Sternberg, Robert (ed.) (1999) *Handbook of Creativity*. Cambridge: Cambridge University Press.

Sternberg, Robert J. and Janet E. Davidson (eds.) (1995) *The Nature of Insight*. Cambridge, MA: MIT Press.

Sternberg, Robert J. and Janet E. Davidson (2003) *Wisdom, Intelligence, and Creativity Synthesized*. Cambridge: Cambridge University Press.

Sternberg, Robert J. and Todd I. Lubart (1995a) An investment perspective on creative insight. In Robert J. Sternberg and Janet E. Davidson (eds.), *The Nature of Insight*. Cambridge, MA: MIT Press.

Sternberg, Robert J. and Todd I. Lubart (1995b) *Defying the Crowd: Cultivating Creativity in a Culture of Conformity*. New York: Free Press.

Stewart, Matthew (2006) *The Courtier and the Heretic: Leibniz, Spinoza, and the Fate of God in the Modern World*. New York: Norton.

Stoneman, Patsy (1995) Introduction. In Emily Brontë, *Wuthering Heights*, ed. Ian Jack. Oxford: Oxford University Press.

Strassler, Robert B. (ed.) (1996) *The Landmark Thucydides: A Comprehensive Guide to the Peloponnesian War*. Newly rev. edn. of the Richard Crawley translation. New York: Simon & Schuster.

Strindberg, August (1964) Author's preface. In *Miss Julie: A Naturalistic Tragedy*, trans. and introd. Michael Meyer. London: Methuen.

Sulloway, Frank (1996) *Born to Rebel: Birth Order, Family Dynamics, and Creative Lives*. New York: Random House.

Sutton, Nina (1996) *Bruno Bettelheim: A Life and a Legacy*, trans. David Sharpe. Boulder, CO: Westview.

Syme, Ronald (1962) Thucydides: lecture on a mastermind. *Proceedings of the British Academy* 48: 39–56.

Szpiro, George G. (2007) *Poincaré's Prize: The Hundred-Year Quest to Solve One of Math's Greatest Puzzles*. New York: Dutton.

Taleb, Nassim Nicholas (2004) *Fooled by Randomness*. London: Penguin Books.

Tilly, Charles (1978) Anthropology, history, and the *Annales*. *Review* 1 (3/4): 207–13.

Tocqueville, Alexis de (1969) *Democracy in America*, ed. J. P. Mayer, trans. George Lawrence. Garden City, NY: Doubleday Anchor.

Townsend, Frederic (1997) Rebelling against *Born to Rebel*. *Journal of Social and Evolutionary Systems* 20 (2): 191–204.

Troyat, Henri (1973) *Divided Soul: The Life of Gogol*, trans. Nancy Amphoux. New York: Doubleday.

Turner, Victor and Edith Turner (1978) *Image and Pilgrimage in Christian Culture: Anthropological Perspectives*. Oxford: Basil Blackwell.

Tweney, R. D. (1989) Fields of enterprise: on Michael Faraday's thought. In D. B. Wallace and H. E. Gruber (eds.), *Creative People at Work: Twelve Cognitive Case Studies*. New York: Oxford University Press.

219

Unwin, Timothy (ed.) (2004) *The Cambridge Companion to Flaubert.* Cambridge: Cambridge University Press.

Updike, John (1982) Foreword. In Franz Kafka, *The Complete Stories: Centennial Edition,* ed. Nahoun N. Glatzer. New York: Schocken.

Van Delft, Dirk et al. (2008) *De telescoop. Erfenis van een Nederlandse uitvinding* [The telescope: legacy of a Dutch invention]. Amsterdam: Bert Bakker.

Van Gennep, Arnold (1960[1909]) *The Rites of Passage,* trans. Monika B. Vizedom and Gabrielle L. Caffee. Chicago: University of Chicago Press.

Veblen, Thorstein (1919) The intellectual pre-eminence of Jews in modern Europe. *Political Science Quarterly* 34: 33–42.

Veblen, Thorstein (1960[1899]) *The Theory of the Leisure Class: An Economic Study of Institutions.* New York: New American Library.

Vescovo, Marisa (1993) *Cézanne.* Art et Dossier 75. Florence: Giunti.

Vickers, Brian (ed.) (1996) *Francis Bacon.* New York: Oxford University Press.

Von Wright, Georg Henrik (1962) A biographical sketch. In Norman Malcolm, *Ludwig Wittgenstein: A Memoir.* Oxford: Oxford University Press.

Wagenbach, Klaus (1964) *Franz Kafka.* Hamburg: Rowohlt.

Wall, Geoffrey (2001) *Flaubert: A Life.* London: Faber & Faber.

Wallace, Alfred Russel (1855) On the law which has regulated the introduction of new species. *Annals and Magazine of Natural History,* 2nd series, 16: 184–95.

Wallace, Alfred Russel (1858) On the tendency of varieties to depart indefinitely from the original type. *Proceedings of the Linnean Society* 3: 53–62.

Wallace, D. B. and H. E. Gruber (eds.) (1989) *Creative People at Work.* New York: Oxford University Press.

Wallace-Hadrill, Andrew (ed.) (1990) *Patronage in Ancient Society.* London: Routledge.

Watson, James D. (1980[1968]) *The Double Helix: A Personal Account of the Discovery of the Structure of DNA,* ed. Gunther S. Stent. Norton Critical Edition. New York: Norton.

Watts, Cedric (1989) *Joseph Conrad: A Literary Life.* London: Macmillan.

Weber, Max (1958[1904–5]) *The Protestant Ethic and the Spirit of Capitalism,* trans. Talcott Parsons. New York: Scribner.

Wegener, Alfred (1926) *The Origin of Continents and Oceans.* London: Methuen.

Wegener, Alfred (1929[1915]) *Die Enstehung der Koninenten und Ozeanen.* Brunswick: Vieweg.

Weinert, Friedel (2009) *Copernicus, Darwin and Freud: Revolutions in the History and Philosophy of Science.* Chichester: Wiley Blackwell.

Weisberg, Robert W. (1986) *Creativity: Genius and Other Myths.* New York: Freeman.

Weisberg, Robert W. (1999) Creativity and knowledge: a challenge to theories. In Robert J. Sternberg (ed.), *Handbook of Creativity.* Cambridge: Cambridge University Press.

Weisberg, Robert W. (2006) *Creativity: Understanding Innovation in Problem Solving, Science, Invention and the Arts.* Hoboken, NJ: John Wiley & Sons.

Westfall, Richard (1980) *Never at Rest: A Biography of Isaac Newton.* Cambridge: Cambridge University Press.

Westfall, Richard (1985) Science and patronage: Galileo and the telescope. *Isis* 76: 11–30.

Westfall, Richard (2007) *Isaac Newton.* Oxford: Oxford University Press.

Wilcken, Patrick (2010) *Claude Lévi-Strauss: The Poet in the Laboratory.* New York: Penguin Press.

Williams, L. Pearce (1665) *Michael Faraday: A Biography.* London: Chapman & Hall.

Wittgenstein, Ludwig (1963[1922]) *Tractatus Logico-Philosophicus.* London: Routledge.

Wittgenstein, Ludwig (1967[1953]) *Philosophical Investigations.* Oxford: Basil Blackwell.

Wittgenstein, Ludwig (1991[1967]) *Remarks on Frazer's Golden Bough*, ed. Rush Rhees. Harlestone, UK: Brynmill Press.

Wolf, Eric R. (1966) Kinship, friendship, and patron–client relations in complex societies. In Michael Banton (ed.), *The Social Anthropology of Complex Societies.* London: Tavistock.

Wolf, Eric R. (1969) *Peasant Wars of the Twentieth Century.* New York: Harper & Row.

Wootton, David (2010) *Galileo: Watcher of the Skies.* New Haven: Yale University Press.

Wuchterl, Kurt and Adolf Hübner (1979) *Wittgenstein*: Hamburg: Rowohlt.

Wullschlager, Jackie (2000) *Hans Christian Andersen: The Life of a Storyteller.* London: Penguin Press.

Zadeh, Lotti A. (1965) Fuzzy sets. *Information and Control* 8: 338–53.

Ziarek, Ewa Płonowska (1998) Introduction. In Ewa Płonowska Ziarek (ed.), *Gombrowicz's Grimaces.* Albany: State University of New York Press.

Zumwalt, Rosemary (1982) Arnold van Gennep: the hermit of Bourg-la-Reine. *American Anthropologist* 84: 299–313.

REFERENCE BOOKS

Baker's Biographical Dictionary of Music and Musicians: Centennial Edition. Farmington Hills, MI: Schirmer Reference, 2001.

The Concise Grove Dictionary of Music. Oxford: Oxford University Press, 2004.

Dictionary of Scientific Biography, 18 vols. New York: Scribner, 1970–80.

Encyclopaedia Britannica (online).

New Dictionary of Scientific Biography, 16 vols. New York: Scribner, 2008.

Oxford Dictionary of Scientific Biography. Oxford: Oxford University Press, 2004–8.

INDEX OF NAMES

Note: Names of pioneers are *italicized*

INDEX OF SUBJECTS